CHAUCER IN DENMARK

A Study of the Translation and Reception History
1782-2012

Roskilde University, The English Programme,
Department of Culture and Identity

To the memory of Jørgen Erik Nielsen

Ebbe Klitgård

CHAUCER IN DENMARK

A Study of the Translation and Reception History

1782-2012

UNIVERSITY PRESS OF SOUTHERN DENMARK

University of Southern Denmark Studies in Literature vol. 60

© The author and University Press of Southern Denmark 2013
Cover layout by Donald Jensen, Unisats ApS
Set and printed by Narayana Press, Denmark
ISBN 978-87-7674-705-3

Cover illustration: British Library, MS Harley 4866,
Hoccleve, *The Regement of Princes*. f. 88r.

Printed with support from
Landsdommer V. Gieses Legat
Roskilde Universitet
Institut for Kultur og Identitet, Roskilde Universitet

University Press of Southern Denmark
Campusvej 55
DK-5230 Odense M
Phone: +45 6615 7999
Fax: +45 6615 8126
Press@forlag.sdu.dk
www.universitypress.dk

Distribution in the United States and Canada:
International Specialized Book Services
5804 NE Hassalo Street
Portland, OR 97213-3644 USA
www.isbs.com

Distribution in the United Kingdom:
Gazelle
White Cross Mills
Hightown
Lancaster
LA1 4 XS
U.K.
www.gazellebooks.co.uk

Akademisk Råd på Roskilde Universitet har på sit møde den 7. november 2012
antaget denne afhandling til offentligt at forsvares for den filosofiske doktorgrad.

Forsvaret er fastsat til afholdelse fredag den 15. marts 2013 kl. 13 i store auditorium, bygning 00.

CONTENTS

PREFACE AND ACKNOWLEDGEMENTS   9

INTRODUCTION   13

Thesis statement and delimitations   13

An overview of the most important sources discussed and a chapter-by-chapter guide   16

A guide to reading, including referencing and documentation   21

METHODOLOGICAL AND THEORETICAL CONSIDERATIONS   25

Chaucer studies, especially in the fields of reception and translation   25

Reception studies, studies of English in Denmark, and Danish doctoral dissertations (Habilitations) in related fields   28

Textual analysis, literary theory, translation critique and translation theory   31

THE LATE 18TH AND EARLY 19TH CENTURY. WESSEL AND BRUUN   35

Johan Herman Wessel and Feen Ursel   35

Thomas Christopher Bruun and English in Denmark during his time   37

Dryden and Pope   43

Slagelse-Madamen   47

Chapter conclusion   59

WESTERGAARD AND THE PERIOD 1835-65   61

Some historical and cultural events and tendencies in Westergaard's Denmark 1835-65   61

Louise Westergaard and English in Denmark ca. 1835-1865   64

Westergaard's life and works   67

Westergaard's Chaucer booklet   71

Chapter conclusion   81

MØLLER, BIERFREUND AND JESPERSEN. THE PERIOD 1865-1900   83

Chaucer and English in Denmark ca.1865-1900   85

Theodor Bierfreund   89

Otto Jespersen and Niels Møller   93

Conclusion   108

VILHELM MØLLER, UFFE BIRKEDAL AND THE PERIOD 1900-20   109

English in Denmark ca. 1900-20   110

Adolf Hansen, an anonymous encyclopedia entry, and Otto Andersson   112

Classics translations and translation from English in Møller's and Birkedal's time   115

Vilhelm Møller's Chaucer translation   117

Uffe Birkedal's Chaucer translations   124

AAGE BRUSENDORFF, NIELS MØLLER AND MARGRETHE THUNBO. 1920-40   137

Hakon Stangerup   138

English in Denmark 1920-40   138

Aage Brusendorff   140

Niels Møller   145

Margrethe Thunbo   152

Chapter conclusion   155

BERGSØE, THORBJØRNSEN AND SONNE. THE 1940S   157

English in Denmark in the 1940s   158

English Literature in Denmark in the 1940s   162

Alkjær and Bredsdorff   164

Flemming Bergsøe   166

Lis Thorbjørnsen   176

Jørgen Sonne   184

Chapter conclusion   192

THE 1950S. BOISEN AND JOHANSEN   193

English in Denmark in the 1950s   194

Grimbergs Verdenshistorie   196

Boisen and Johansen, an introduction   198

Introduction to Mogens Boisen's translation from 1952   201

Analysis of Boisen's translation   206

Euphemism, avoidance, over-explicitness: Boisen compared to Johansen   213

Johansen's translation from 1958 and his monograph Fra Chaucers tid [From Chaucer's time] from 1965   215

Further analysis of Johansen's translation   220

Chapter conclusion   233

THE PERIOD 1960-2012   235

Danes and the English language   235

Chaucer in higher education and in general public use   238

Chaucer translations in the 1960s and 1970s   240

The Danish reception of Chaucer in the 1960s and 1970s   250

Chaucer translations 1980-2012. Jørgen Sonne   255

The Danish reception of Chaucer 1980-2012. Encyclopediae and literary histories   259

Klitgård and Johansen   262

Kaaber's dramatic adaptation Chaucers Canterbury-Fortællinger   263

Two further encyclopedia entries   264

Mittet and Børch   265

Wikipedia Chaucer   266

Some odd pieces 267

Chapter conclusion 268

GENERAL CONCLUSION 269

BIBLIOGRAPHY 275

DANISH SUMMARY/DANSK RESUMÉ 295

PREFACE AND ACKNOWLEDGEMENTS

This study was first begun in 2000, when I attended the New Chaucer Society conference at the University of London. I had arranged a meeting with series editor of the *Reception of British and Irish Authors in Europe* Elinor Shaffer, who also attended the conference. I knew the series well from my wife Ida Klitgård's contribution to the Virginia Woolf volume, which was published a couple of years later (Caws and Lockhurst, eds., 2002, Shaffer, series ed. 2002-). My plain question to Dr. Shaffer was would she be interested in a volume on Chaucer reception, and would she like me to edit it? She was encouraging, and we had a meeting, but some weeks later she informed me that Continuum Press had turned the offer down for commercial reasons. I still thank Elinor Shaffer for her encouragement and a pleasant meeting.

I started looking for alternative ways of approaching my subject, and at the New Chaucer Society conference in Boulder, Colorado in 2002 I gave my first paper on Chaucer reception and translation, outlining the main Danish publications and giving examples from the 1950s *Canterbury Tales* translations by Boisen and Johansen (Boisen 1951, Johansen 1958). The session on Chaucer in translation was chaired by Steve Ellis, whose *Chaucer at Large* (Ellis 2000) remains a major inspiration for my own work. At the same session there was also a paper given by Susan Yager on R.M. Lumiansky's American Chaucer translations from the 1940s and 50s, and this paper turned out to be even more inspiring than I had first thought, as will be revealed when it is acknowledged more specifically in chapter 9 of this study. Betsy Bowden has kindly commented on the first part of chapter 3 and let me see her forthcoming work on the afterlife of the Wife of Bath. My thanks go to these Chaucerians and to the former New Chaucer Society President David Wallace, who read my paper and suggested publication in *The Chaucer Review*, where it was published under the competent editorship of Susanna Fein and David Raybin (Klitgård 2005).

A Danish version of the article appeared the year before (Klitgård

2004), edited by Viggo Hjørnager Pedersen, who then and later came up with useful feedback, for which thanks. In 2004 I was still considering a major study in Danish for the degree of Dr. Phil. What convinced me that I wanted to write a study for this degree in English was the growing interest in the academic world in reception studies generally, but more specifically the rise of the field of *medievalism* in Chaucer studies, not least with Richard Utz's important book on the German philological tradition in Chaucer studies published in 2002 (Utz 2002). I want to acknowledge this inspiration, and specifically that Utz also expressed an encouraging attitude to my work when I contacted him in 2010.

In 2008 I turned to the present doctoral dissertation more intensively, while at the same time working on an edited volume with Dr. Gerd Bayer, Erlangen University. This was published with the title *Narrative Developments from Chaucer to Defoe* in 2011 (Bayer and Klitgård 2011). Let me express my sincere thanks to Gerd for his continuous encouragement in my work also with the dissertation.

In my many years in Chaucer studies I have had brilliant teachers who later became colleagues and friends, and let me take the opportunity here to mention specifically Graham Caie and Dorrit Einersen, who since I was first brought up with Chaucer at the University of Copenhagen from 1981 have always been my ideals of good teachers. Also in the early 1980s I studied at the University of York with Derek Pearsall, one of the grand old men in Chaucer studies. He will be acknowledged here along with another important figure in Chaucer studies who has helped me greatly over the years, A.C. Spearing. Pearsall's and Spearing's examples are daunting for anyone who aspires to get to know and understand Chaucer's universe.

Besides the pleasure I feel in being part of the New Chaucer Society's invaluable network, let me also acknowledge the Danish network in the University of Copenhagen-based *Middelalderkredsen* [The medieval circle], where I have both received feedback on my own work and heard many fine informal and formal presentations over the years. My thanks also go to Hanne Jansen and Anna Wegener of the University of Copenhagen for arranging the splendid conference "Authorial and Editorial Voices in Translation" in November 2011. Also here I received important feedback and found inspiration from several papers.

As for my former colleagues from the English Department at the

University of Copenhagen, now the Department of English, Germanic and Romance Studies, I acknowledge them best by using their work on English in Denmark, which happens frequently in this study. I will not mention their names here, except that I must single out the late Dr. Jørgen Erik Nielsen. His doctoral dissertation *Den samtidige engelske litteratur og Danmark 1800-1840* [The contemporary English Literature and Denmark 1800-1840] (Nielsen 1976-1977) is a milestone in the field of English in Denmark, and I draw on it heavily in chapters 3 and 4. Jørgen Erik gave me feedback on the first articles and drafts in this project, and until his far too early death was the most kind and competent critic one could imagine. I dedicate this study to his memory.

As with all research projects that run over several years, costs of several kinds have been involved. The expenditure involved in using libraries as frequently as I have for this project means I owe many thanks to the Royal Library of Copenhagen, Tårnby Hovedbibliotek, and a number of other Danish libraries, as well as the University Library and the Minster Library in York. I thank Peter and Gitte Rannes at Hald Hovedgaard for keeping my own financial costs down by accepting me for four funded author visits in the grand natural surroundings of Hald. I also thank Garry Keyes at Ørslev Monestary near Hald for accepting me for a further research visit. To my department of Culture and Identity at Roskilde University, thanks for travel funding, and for flexibility with my research time in a strange period of research policies in Denmark, where extra research leave and funding is reserved for groups of researchers, not for individuals, and least of all for those daring to take years to write the once so celebrated Danish Dr. Phil. *disputats*, a senior doctoral dissertation corresponding to the German *Habilitation*. I also thank the Head of my department Martin Bayer and the Rector of Roskilde University Ib Poulsen for publication support. A final contribution by Landsdommer Giese's Foundation completed the publication budget, for which many thanks. Moreover I thank everyone at the University Press of Southern Denmark for their great help in preparing the dissertation for publication.

My final thanks go to my former wife Ida and my beloved daughters Louise and Laura.

CHAPTER 1

INTRODUCTION

Thesis statement and delimitations

This study is an investigation of a subject never explored before: I investigate the translations and the reception in Denmark of the most important English poet from the Middle Ages Geoffrey Chaucer (1340?-1400) from the first appearance in 1782 of a transformation of one of his Canterbury Tales, *The Wife of Bath's Tale*, to the present day. My aim is to analyse the story of Chaucer in Denmark also as an exemplary study of the history of English education, culture, language and literature in Denmark. This means that I consider a broad context of English in Denmark for my discussion of Chaucer in Denmark.

My title *Chaucer in Denmark: A Study of the Translation and Reception History 1782-2012* can be taken quite literally in the sense that I investigate all published Chaucer translations into Danish, as well as everything substantial published about Chaucer in Danish or in a Danish context in that 230-year period. Obviously I may have overlooked something. As late as a year before finishing this study, I stumbled across several Chaucer translations in a now largely forgotten literary magazine from the late 1940s, *Cavalcade* (see chapter 8). The problem turned out to be that periodicals and magazines have not been catalogued in detail in Danish libraries, which means that a search for Chaucer did not lead me to these translations. I have tried my best with several kinds of searches, including going through a large number of Danish periodicals, very few of which have published electronic lists of content. Furthermore I have been through all accessible literary histories and encyclopediae in print, and I have used newspaper databases as well as search engines in the Royal Danish Library and in Bibliotek.dk, which covers all Danish libraries. On this background I find it unlikely that I have missed anything substantial, but this remains to be seen.[1]

There are a few delimitations with respect to sources. I have chosen not to include short newspaper reviews or any mention of Chaucer in passing, but only to consider fairly substantial sources. This means in practice that I have left out a couple of extremely brief encyclopedia entries, and that I have only occasionally included reviews of published translations or brief mentions of Chaucer's name. I have also made a decision only to consider scholarly work published in Danish or at least in a Danish context, not Danish scholars publishing in an international context, although most of these studies will also be mentioned briefly. This decision may at first glance be the most controversial of my delimitations, but I want to emphasize that my focus is on sources that have been directed at a Danish audience, whether academic or general. In this way my title's promise of studying Chaucer in Denmark is fulfilled. This does not mean that I do not acknowledge the international importance of a few scholars considered, notably the most important Danish Chaucer scholar ever, Aage Brusendorff. As his seminal study published in English in 1925 as *The Chaucer Tradition* was first published in Danish as a *disputats* (Habilitation), I can fortunately still include him within my delimitation. The same goes for some foreign, mainly German, American, British, Swedish and Norwegian treatments of Chaucer that have been published in Danish.

In a Danish context it would have made sense to compare with the Nordic reception of Chaucer, besides including sources that have been translated into Danish from the other Nordic countries. I have considered this possibility and decided against it, because it would shift my focus, and because it would be more complicated than at first thought, as there are a great number of sources. The most important Chaucer translations are the Finnish-Swede Harald Jernström's Swedish *Canterbury Tales* translation from 1956, although parts of this were published in the 1920s and 1930s, Egil Tveterås's Norwegian translation from 1953

---

[1] I thank Søren Schou for providing me with two brief articles and a more substantial treatment of Chaucer in Danish after reading the first version of this dissertation. These sources, Scherr 1876, V. Møller 1901 and Hansen 1901, which I had first overlooked, are treated in chapters 5 and 6 of this second version of my dissertation.

and Toivo Lyy's Finnish translation from 1975 (Jernström 1956, Tveterås 1953, Lyy 1975). In 1932 Jernström also published a partial translation of Chaucer's *Parliament of Fowls* as "Ur Fåglarnas Ting" (Jernström 1932). I have also looked at Cecilia Milow's Swedish prose translation for young people of parts of *The Canterbury Tales*, published in 1900 (Milow 1900). It would have been tempting to compare these and many other sources to the Danish ones, but I will leave this to my Nordic colleagues.

Denmark's other nearest neighbour, Germany, has been included in part because there is a close connection to two of the most prominent Danish Chaucerians, Otto Jespersen and Aage Brusendorff, who were both familiar with and in some ways part of the great German philological tradition, as we shall see in chapters 5-7. This tradition has been recorded most prominently by Richard Utz (Utz 2002) but the more popular side of German Chaucer reception, including analysis of Chaucer translations, has not to my knowledge been treated to any great extent. The same can be said for most countries that have Chaucer translations.

The British and American reception, including modern translations of Chaucer, has been covered by Steve Ellis in his humorously titled *Chaucer at Large*, which I refer to frequently throughout this study (Ellis 2000). Besides I have used several modern English translations for comparison with the Danish translators, notably in chapter 9 on the two main translations of *The Canterbury Tales*. It has been my deliberate choice not to use the same kind of comparative analysis throughout my study. Translations and reception are frequently compared to other Danish or English sources, but I have wanted to vary my analyses, for instance by applying only text-internal analysis at points, and furthermore it has been my general aim in this long dissertation not to tire my reader by listing yet more examples of the same kind and considered all too systematically. My methodology is discussed further in chapter 2, but let me say already here that my aim has been to ensure that the examples cover as many corners of Chaucer's work as possible. It is my simple duty as a member of the New Chaucer Society to argue why Chaucer is worth reading also in the 21st century, and I can do that in no better way than by representing and discussing his work as broadly as possible, while analysing the history of his reception and translation in Denmark.

For an exemplary study of translation and reception of an English author in Denmark I might have chosen differently, especially if for a moment we forget that my background is in Chaucer studies. *The Reception of British Authors in Europe* series shows how it is possible to find a variety of Danish sources on writers such as Austen, Byron, Woolf and Joyce (Shaffer, gen. ed. 2002-). And why not choose Shakespeare? The answer to the latter question is that ten more years would probably have been needed for a study with the delimitation I have set myself here. As for the other authors mentioned, a more thorough study than those represented in the respective volumes on the European reception would of course also have been possible. However, by choosing Chaucer, an older classic than the authors mentioned, I am able to contextualize my story with a history of English in Denmark that goes back to the late 18th century, where we see the first signs of English becoming a language that has any position at all in Denmark, to the present day where English is everywhere around us. The exemplary story of Chaucer reception throws light on this main development in the same way as the story of Shakespeare reception would have done, but better than those of Austen, Byron, Woolf and Joyce, because their reception stories are more limited in time. These authors, including Shakespeare, will in fact be part of the contextualization I use, as I consider English literature in Denmark generally. Throughout the chronologically arranged chapters I also compare English language and culture in Denmark to the other two main foreign languages in Denmark, German and French, and I include a focus in this connection on the educational system and its effects. A final context is classics translations in Denmark generally.

An overview of the most important sources discussed and a chapter-by-chapter guide

All references to sources used are of course given in the bibliography, but for the purpose of giving an overview of the most important translations and treatments of Chaucer in Denmark, here is a list arranged chronologically:

Translations:

Johan Herman Wessel, transl., J.A.P. Schulz, and Thomas Thaarup, rev., *Feen Ursel eller hvad der behager Damerne*. Copenhagen, 1792 (1782).

Thomas Christopher Bruun, transl., *Slagelse-Madamen; efter Popes Konen i Bath*, Copenhagen: P.E. Martins forlag, 1823.

Charlotte Louise Westergaard, transl., *Engelske digtere*, vol. 1.: *Chaucer*. Copenhagen: Bing & Søns forlag, 1853.

Vilhelm Møller, transl., untitled translation of *The Summoner's Tale* (extracts) in "Chaucers Canterbury-Fortællinger" in *Verdenslitteraturens Perler*, vol. 3. Aarhus: Jydsk Forlags-Forretning, 1901.

Uffe Birkedal, transl., *Prologen til Kanterborg-historierne af Gotfred Chaucer*. Copenhagen: Tillges boghandel, *Studier fra sprog- og oldtidsforskning*, 1911.

Uffe Birkedal, transl., *Af Chaucer og Langlands digtning*. Copenhagen: Tillges boghandel, *Studier fra sprog- og oldtidsforskning*, 1913.

Margrethe Thunbo, ed. and transl., *Canterbury Fortællinger af Geoffrey Chaucer*. Copenhagen: Einar Harcks forlag, 1929, *Glimt af verdenslitteraturen*, vol. 2

Flemming Bergsøe, transl., *Geoffrey Chaucer, Konen fra Bath*. Copenhagen: Thaning & Appel, 1943.

Lis Thorbjørnsen, transl., *Geoffrey Chaucer, De tre drikkebrødre*. Copenhagen: Carit Andersen, 1946.

Jørgen Sonne, transl., *Geoffrey Chaucer: Canterburyfortællinger*. Copenhagen: L. Ihrichs bogtrykkeri, 1950.

Mogens Boisen, transl., *Geoffrey Chaucer: Canterburyfortællingerne*. Copenhagen: Martins Forlag, 1951.

Børge Johansen, transl., *Geoffrey Chaucer: Canterburyfortællingerne I-II*. Copenhagen: Nyt Nordisk Forlag Arnold Busck, 1958.

Treatments of Chaucer's life and works:

Theodor Bierfreund, *Palemon and Arcite: En literaturhistorisk Undersøgelse som Bidrag til Shakespearekritiken*. Copenhagen: Lehman & Stages Forlag, 1891.

–, *Kulturbærere*. Copenhagen: Andr. Fred. Høst & Søns Forlag, 1892.

Otto Jespersen, *Chaucers liv og digtning*. Copenhagen: Klein, *Studier fra sprog- og oldtidsforskning*, 1893.

Aage Brusendorff, *The Chaucer Tradition*. London and Copenhagen: Branner, 1925.

Børge Johansen, *Chaucer og hans tid*. Copenhagen: Nyt Nordisk Forlag Arnold Busck, 1965.

These are the main translations and treatments of Chaucer in Danish, and the titles will all be translated into English in the chapters where they are discussed. I emphasize that the list is selective, and as we shall see there is a host of other sources.

A chapter-by-chapter presentation will hopefully provide my reader with a further overview. After the preface and introduction in the present chapter follows chapter 2 with methodological and theoretical considerations. Here I start by discussing my work in relation to Chaucer studies. Secondly, I discuss some Danish doctoral dissertations in related fields and I compare my own methodology to these works. The chapter's final section is about the selection of theoretical tools for my analysis.

Chapter 3 considers two translations that are transformed through several filters. Both have an original source text, *The Wife of Bath's Prologue and Tale*, and both of them do not mention Chaucer with one word, but dramatist Johann Herman Wessel's *Feen Ursel eller hvad der behager Damerne* is as different from professor Thomas Bruun's *Slagelse-Madamen; efter Popes Konen i Bath* as night and day. As Bruun's title indicates, he has translated Pope's English Chaucer translation, and for that reason I include a discussion of this translation and the tradition from Dryden and Pope, who both made an effort to make Chaucer appealing to their contemporary audience. In this chapter the main context is a consideration of the status of English in Denmark in the late 18th century and early 19th century with an emphasis on language and literature. Especially after the bombardment of Copenhagen and Køge and the loss of the navy to the English in 1807, English was not the most popular language in Danmark. Yet a number of literary works were translated.

In chapter 4 the main text is Louise Westergaard's booklet *Chaucer* from 1853 in a proposed series on English poets for educational purposes. This booklet includes both Westergaard's introduction to Chaucer's life and works, her own edited Chaucer text with commentary, some summaries and some pieces of translation. My analysis of this very noteworthy pioneer effort of introducing Chaucer to a Danish audience is contextualized by a thorough consideration of Westergaard's own life and works in a time when Danish nationalism was thriving. The chapter includes a historical and cultural view on the period 1835-65, with an emphasis on these nationalist trends in a period where Denmark turned into a democracy. In this chapter, moreover, I look at other translations from English to provide a context for the Chaucer translation.

Chapter 5 covers a period, 1865-1900, where there are only some very short bits of Chaucer translation, by poet and critic Niels Møller and by linguist Otto Jespersen. The two cooperated on most of these translations in connection with Jespersen's monograph *Chaucers liv og digtning*, which he published in 1893. This monograph is the main source studied in the chapter, which includes an analysis of two short academic treatments of Chaucer by Theodor Bierfreund, including his doctoral thesis *Palemon and Arcite* from 1891. For my contextualization I have made much use of a study from 1948 by Brian W. Downs on Anglo-Danish literary relations 1867-1900. I furthermore discuss the development of international Chaucer scholarship, both in Germany and Britain, a development Jespersen was keenly aware of. One of these German scholarly treatments, a Chaucer portrait in a literary history by Johannes Scherr, was translated and edited by Frederik Winkel Horn in 1876 and is discussed at the beginning of the chapter.

Vilhelm Møller's translation of most of *The Summoner's Tale* from 1901 and Uffe Birkedal's translations from 1911 and 1913 of *The General Prologue*, *The Nun's Priest's Tale* and an extract of *The Monk's Tale* are the focus of chapter 6, which covers the period 1920. As these are the first substantial translations of Chaucer into Danish, I have chosen to use most of the chapter on translation criticism, but I also consider the first four in a long series of Chaucer portraits in literary histories and encyclopediae in the 20th century. The specific period covered in this chapter is 1900-20, and here I consider some important developments in Anglo-Danish relations and in English education. In this chapter there is a relatively thorough consideration of other classics translations, but there is also space for mentioning other translations from English, including some rather delayed translations.

Chapter 7 covers another 20 years, 1920-40, and the prime text discussed is hardly surprisingly Aage Brusendorff's *The Chaucer Tradition* from 1925. This is a text I discuss with awe. Another interesting text, but of a somewhat different calibre, is Margrethe Thunbo's *Canterbury Fortællinger af Geoffrey Chaucer* from 1929. This is the nearest we get to a translation from this period, with its summary of some of *The Canterbury Tales* for young readers. A couple of encyclopedia entries and literary histories are considered, but only one of them, written by Niels Møller in 1928, is substantial enough to be discussed at any great length. As the period leading up to the Second World War is relatively uneventful in relation to new developments in education and cultural exchanges, including translations, I have chosen in this chapter to cover this contextualization only briefly.

The 1940s see a great increase in Chaucer publications, so much so that I have chosen the war years and their aftermath for a full chapter, chapter 8. A number of *The Canterbury Tales* are translated, *The Wife of Bath's Tale* in a poetic translation by Flemming Bergsøe in 1943, and several other tales in prose translation by respectively Lis Thorbjørnsen and Jørgen Sonne, both of them publishing mainly in the literary magazine *Cavalcade*. This is a chapter where I apply both comparative translation criticism and analysis of individual translations, here for the first time also including translator's revisions, as many of these translations were published in more than one version. In this chapter I furthermore discuss a major paradigm shift in Anglo-Danish relations, which the many Chaucer translations are part of. Besides continuing my story of English in Denmark, I have a particular focus on English in the academic world and especially at the University of Copenhagen.

The 1950s get a full chapter, and if there is a main chapter in this study, chapter 9 is it. This is because there are now two full or nearly full translations of *The Canterbury Tales*, Mogens Boisen's from 1952 and Børge Johansen's from 1958. I discuss the cultural context of the translations by considering Anglo-Danish relations in the 1950s, now increasingly marked by the USA, but the main focus is on translation criticism. By including a comparison with some British and American translations published after the war, I not only show how different translators' strategies work, I also reveal a case of very serious plagiarism. Let it be no secret that the translator guilty of this is Mogens Boisen, who has translated not Chaucer, but Lumiansky's prose translation of Chaucer. However, acknowledging that Boisen is still an innovative user of the Danish language, I perform a very thorough analysis of his text and compare him with the poetic translator Børge Johansen. Johansen, in turn, is analysed carefully and besides Boisen compared both to English translators and earlier Danish translators.

Chapter 10 covers the long period 1950-2012, and considering the great number of Chaucer publications discussed, it may seem strange not to have divided this chapter into two. However, there is hardly one single, substantial source from this period, except perhaps Johansen's book on Chaucer and the Late Middle Ages *Chaucer og hans tid* from 1965, which I include in my treatment of Johansen in chapter 9. Secondly, although I have something to say in this chapter about Chaucer in the academic world and about Danes and the English language, I quickly conclude that there is little left to say about what gets translated from English, since the answer is now almost everything. Consequently the major part of chapter 10 consists of treatments of Chaucer portraits from a number of encyclopediae, literary histories and similar sources, and let me encourage my reader by saying that a number of revelations are made in this connection. I am also able to discuss a number of short and sometimes very peculiar translations of Chaucer, and some traces of Chaucer in unexpected places.

In the general conclusion I sum up the main findings, drawing directly on my chapter conclusions. Furthermore I discuss the results in relation to earlier studies in reception and relation studies, arguing that my study has added significant new knowledge to this field, as well as to Chaucer scholarship and to the research field English in Denmark.

A guide to reading, including referencing and documentation

Although this is a scholarly treatise it has been my aim to write also for the generally interested reader, and I can even say that no prior knowledge of Chaucer is required, although it is of course an advantage. Perhaps more importantly, no prior knowledge of Danish is required. I have translated or back-translated all Danish titles and quotations in square brackets, immediately following the quotation. This of course allows for the possibility that I will receive criticism from readers competent in both English and Danish, which is only fair, considering that one of my own main tasks is to provide translation critique.

Chaucer's Middle English is difficult for many readers, but this problem should be solved at least in part by my back-translations and discussions of source text versus target text. I have quoted Chaucer mainly from two standard editions, Skeat's 1897 edition of *The Canterbury Tales*

(Skeat, ed. 1897) and occasionally his editions of other works by Chaucer, and from the modern standard edition *The Riverside Chaucer* based on F.N. Robinson's second edition of the works of Chaucer from 1957 and edited by a number of scholars with Larry D. Benson as main editor (Robinson 1957, Benson, gen. ed. 1987/2008). Whenever possible I have stated which Chaucer edition has been used or has probably been used by each translator in question, but especially in the early translations I have occasionally had to give up. In such cases I quote Benson's edition.

The availability of texts without copyright on the internet is rapidly growing, and many works have been re-published as print-on-demand texts for sale. Several texts in this study, including for example the two texts written by Theodor Bierfreund, can be bought in such versions or are available for free download. In nearly all cases I have used original, printed versions acquired in antiquarian bookshops or borrowed in libraries, or studied and copied in the reading rooms of the Royal Library of Copenhagen, The Minster Library at York or The University Library of York. However, I have included a number of webpage references as a service to my reader. In the case of one of the most quoted reference works, *Den Store Danske Encyclopædi*, an important 22 volume encyclopedia, which was published between 1994 and 2006 and written by leading Danish experts with linguist Jørn Lund as main editor, I have used the printed version, except where the later internet version has been updated.

I have as far as possible avoided abbreviations such as *SDE* for the encyclopedia just mentioned, because I personally find them annoying, but I have accepted a few standard abbreviations, especially in cases where a work has been referred to several times in succession. Apart from this choice, I follow standard procedures in documentation, including having as many in-text references as possible and as short as possible. The few notes in my study are given as footnotes in cases where I have found them unavoidable.

I would like to include a final word about my treatment of sources. In respect for translators, editors, illustrators, critics, scholars and other contributors I have in a number of cases given introductions to them, most often beyond birth- and death-years. This has been possible in most cases by using authoritative reference works such as *Den Store Danske Encyclopædi* and *Dansk Biografisk Leksikon*, but in other cases I have had to use webpage references. I have taken care to identify my sources for life information also on webpages, and in cases where none are given, I have listed them in my bibliography as "anonymous". I have restricted the use of introductions to what I have deemed to be substantial contributors, and in a few cases of living persons I have found it polite not to give birth years.

CHAPTER 2

METHODOLOGICAL AND THEORETICAL CONSIDERATIONS

In this chapter I start by placing my work in the field of Chaucer studies and reception studies. Secondly, I discuss some Danish doctoral dissertations that have inspired me, and I compare my own methodology to these works. Furthermore I establish a framework for the textual analysis and translation critique that I apply in my work with the primary sources. In this connection I briefly discuss translation theory and literary theory with a view to selecting some theoretical tools for my analysis.

I have already indicated in chapter 1 that the chapters in this study are methodologically different from each other, as some are more focused on translation than reception or vice versa, and as it has been a deliberate choice not to analyse in the same way in all chapters. For instance chapter 9 compares the two main Danish *Canterbury Tales* translations with modern English translations; chapter 5 chiefly analyses Danish academic reception; chapter 4 focuses on a single translator; and chapter 10 includes treatment of a great number of short source texts. The material available in each period affects my choice of analytical method, but I have decided to apply different approaches to similar material, both for the sake of variation itself, and because different angles reveal different insights. In this chapter I will consider the main approaches in my study and link them with research traditions, methods and theory.

Chaucer studies, especially in the fields of reception and translation

Since my background is first of all in Chaucer studies, I will start by noting that my work rests firmly on the ground of Chaucer scholarship in the last 150 years, and that one consistent feature of my study is that I continually bring in textual and critical analysis as well as biographical and historical knowledge from this field. Methodologically my work is thus influenced by Chaucer scholarship in general, and by literary Chaucer criticism in particular. If I were to single out one branch of Chaucer studies that has influenced my method more than others, I would choose research that investigates Chaucer reception in the 19th, 20th and 21st centuries. I have already in my preface mentioned Steve Ellis's seminal study *Chaucer at Large: The Poet in the Modern Imagination* (Ellis 2000), which investigates the British and American popular reception and translation from the late 19th century through the 20th century. In my review in *English Studies* I praised Ellis' study for "its insights in tracing the cultural semiotics of modern representations of Chaucer" and, comparing it to earlier reception studies by Spurgeon and Brewer, I discussed Ellis's approach as distinctly broader in scope, with a stress on non-academic representations such as the chapters "Children's Chaucer" and "Performance Chaucer" (Klitgård 2003: 474-5). Ellis's study is shorter than the present one, and it is more selective and less inclusive in its choice of material to be discussed, but it remains an important methodological inspiration, especially with its chapters on popular editions and translations, and its many analyses of transformations and adaptations, many of which are far removed from their original source, Chaucer. Being English himself, Ellis feels a different kind of ownership in relation to the Chaucer tradition than I do as a Dane, and interestingly he defines a motto for his book, in which he is first of all "concerned to document Chaucer's repeated presence in our culture as well as our fundamental neglect of him" (Ellis 2000: 140). By comparison my aim is not to show Chaucer's "repeated presence" in Danish culture, but rather to show how he has been dragged on a rugged road through the Danish reception and translation of more than 200 years, sometimes with brilliant translations and insightful reception, at other times with not only neglect, but based on pure ignorance. In one respect, however, my method and aim is the same as Ellis's, and that is in always holding up Chaucer's work itself against later representations of that work.

Some further scholarly work in Chaucer reception and translation has been directly inspiring for the present study. I will discuss this in much more detail in the study itself, but in discussing methodology let me mention that Betsy Bowden's study of both the English and European afterlife of Chaucer's Wife of Bath in *The Wife of Bath in Afterlife 1660-1810*

(Bowden, forthcoming) bears many similarities with my approach here. Bowden very carefully traces the complicated steps of transformation through various genres and across European borders, as well as across time. Her interest is especially in audio-visual representations, and she also differs from me in focusing narrowly on one character from Chaucer, but we share a methodological concern for the devil in the detail. Bowden's study, and not least my personal correspondence with her, has reminded me that it is necessary to not only compare variants in language and plot, but to trace linguistic and narrative compositional processes carefully through all translations, relay translations, transformations and adaptations.

Another fellow Chaucerian, Susan Yager, has also kindly corresponded with me about her unpublished paper "'I speke in prose': Lumiansky's translation of Chaucer" (Yager 2002). Methodologically Yager has inspired me by her thorough work on the context of this American 1948 translation, considering biographical information about Lumiansky, as well as discussing the need for a popularization of a national poet just after the Second World War. Furthermore Yager has a keen eye for the translation strategies employed, including linguistic transformation in prose translation, the omission of Chaucer's *The Prioress's Tale* about evil jews, and the general use of certain euphemisms.[2] Focusing on translation strategies and context and not simply listing linguistic choices in isolation is also a major concern in the present study.

Whereas the work of Ellis, Bowden and Yager represents a so far relatively limited field of research within Chaucer studies, an even smaller research field concerns Chaucer outside the English speaking countries. A young Finnish scholar, Mari Pakkala-Weckström, whose work so far is on various aspects of power play in *The Canterbury Tales*, has included a comparison of a Finnish and two English translations in a recent article, but the translation analysis itself is fairly short (Pakkala-Weckström 2010). Besides Pakkala-Weckström's article, I have occasionally come across brief discussions of Chaucer translations into other languages than English, but I have seen nothing very substantial. Studies of Chaucer reception in Europe are also relatively rare. The most important study

---

2   As already indicated Lumiansky's strategies have direct repercussions for the most reprinted Danish translation to date, Mogens Boisen's from 1952. See chapter 9.

is still Richard Utz's *Chaucer and the Discourse of German Philology* from 2002, which I discuss at greater length in chapter 7. Suffice it to say in a chapter on methodology and theory that Utz's focus is different from mine, more or less exclusively on the philological tradition. I have certainly been inspired by Utz's thoroughness, and the two Danes that stand out as Chaucer scholars, Jespersen and Brusendorff, have been examined also on the basis of the German philological tradition they both grew out of, but this is still a relatively small part of my study.

Also Richard Utz's theoretical contribution to the growing research field of medievalism is of interest for the present study. Among Utz's work in this field is the recent article "Coming to Terms with Medievalism", which discusses a number of the often complicated theoretical positions and outlines the research history of medievalism (Utz 2011). My study is theoretically informed by the field in general, but it is beyond the scope of my work to enter into further considerations of theoretical positions, as such positions are of marginal interest to the main line of my investigation. In order to form a general theoretical basis for my analytical work, I have chosen to define the term medievalism broadly as "representation of the medieval", as this working definition will allow me both to include all reception and translation of Chaucer in Denmark and to regard this as representation, or in other words a kind of re-construction.

Reception studies, studies of English in Denmark, and Danish doctoral dissertations (Habilitations) in related fields

The second important research tradition that this study is inscribed in is the specific branch of reception studies that looks at how authors from one country get translated, read and received in the culture of other countries. Elinor Shaffer's innovative project resulting in the series *The Reception of British and Irish Authors in Europe* has already been mentioned as a prominent example of this tradition (Shaffer 2002-). However, my study also owes a great debt to a more specific "English in Denmark" tradition, which has had a particular stronghold at the University of Copenhagen with historical, cultural, literary and linguistic studies, including translation studies. Many of them were part of a common project on English in Denmark at the English Department, e.g.

historians Jørgen Sevaldsen and Jens Rahbek Rasmussen and linguists Inge Kabell and Hanne Lauridsen, who will be quoted frequently in the contextualizing parts of this study. A couple of literary scholars from the department will receive particular mention below, because they have been more direct methodological influences.

First of all Jørgen Erik Nielsen's Habilitation defended at the University of Copenhagen in 1975 and published in two parts in 1976-77, *Den samtidige engelske litteratur og Danmark 1800-1840* [The Contemporary English Literature and Denmark 1800-1840] has been a very direct inspiration. Nielsen's perspective is both narrower than mine, in looking only at a 40-year period, and much broader, in covering all authors translated in that period. Nielsen's bibliographical register alone, published as volume II of his dissertation, is impressive, and his guide through the works of translators in the main volume is undertaken with much authority. Nielsen leaves a strong impression of having registered everything there is, and his study also serves as a thorough guide to poets and novelists from the period, mainly Romantic authors. Nielsen states that his work is part of the tradition that has been called "Rezeptionsforschung" in German and that is part of comparative literary studies (Nielsen 1976-7, vol. 1: 2). Apart from this Nielsen has little to say about his methodology, which I would characterize generally as subscribing to the healthy scholarly principle of turning every stone. Besides including innumerable sources for the primary study of translated literature, Nielsen also considers some broad contexts, including the historical and cultural background (Nielsen 1976-7, vol. 1: chapter 1), English education and spread of English (chapter 2), bookshops and libraries (chapter 5), contemporary criticism (chapter 6) and other forms of reception (chapter 7). These are more or less the categories I have used for contextualization in the present study. However, it is a significant difference between my own and Nielsen's work that he has been prevented from undertaking close reading or applying translation criticism by his choice to cover so many sources.

Because I have so much focus on close reading and translation criticism, I have taken direct inspiration from two further studies, both carried out at the University of Copenhagen and defended as doctoral dissertations at the University of Southern Denmark, Odense. Ida Klitgård's investigation of Mogens Boisen's three published translations of Joyce's *Ulysses* in *Fictions of Hybridity: Translating Style in Joyce's Ulysses* is with respect to textual analysis and translation criticism on a par with the present study (I. Klitgård 2007). Clearly the focus of her investigation is very different from mine, but we share an interest in meticulous, even pedantic textual analysis.

Viggo Hjørnager Pedersen's study of English Hans Christian Andersen translations in his Habilitation *Ugly Ducklings: Studies in the English Translations of Hans Christian Andersen's Tales and Stories* (Hjørnager Pedersen 2004) has more affinities with Nielsen than with Ida Klitgård, although Hjørnager Pedersen like her practices both translation criticism and translation theory. Hjørnager Pedersen shares with Nielsen the focus of thoroughly registering published translations, although in his introduction he quotes Danish literary critic and historian Paul Rubow for his advice that "academic discussion is about judicious selection rather than about exhausting the subject as well as the reader" (Hjørnager Pedersen 2004: 9, translating Rubow 1921: 8). This is sound advice, and I have taken it into consideration in connection with my own study. Although Hjørnager Pedersen is working with translations in the opposite direction, Danish to English, I have been inspired by his technique of comparing several translators of the same text.

A final source of methodological inspiration to be mentioned in this section is Ib Poulsen's Habilitation *Radiomontagen og dens rødder: Et studie i den danske radiomontage med vægt på dens radiofoniske genreforudsætninger* [The radio montage and its roots: A study in the Danish radio montage with an emphasis on its radiophonic genre background] (Poulsen 2006). Poulsen's study is a cultural historical narrative which has not been told before, and which in an exemplary way has wider perspectives in a Danish cultural context. One of Poulsen's chief merits in his study is precisely to throw light on Danish social and cultural relations in general through his careful analysis of a specific, now almost obsolete media genre. In the present study I have wanted to tell a very different, but still exemplary narrative, which like Poulsen's will be mirrored against the culture of the time periods covered. The assumption is in other words that the practice of translation and reception of a now more than 600-year-old English poet in Denmark has a lot to say about Danish culture.

Textual analysis, literary theory, translation critique and translation theory

Throughout this study I use textual analysis in my treatment of all the primary Danish sources, and I sometimes undertake textual analysis of Chaucer's works. However, my framework for this textual analysis is not specifically informed by any one branch of literary theory. My chief method is close reading of the kind associated with New Criticism, often combined with analytical tools from such theories as structuralism, formalism and narratology. It could well be argued that these theoretical directions have in fact delivered the main tools for the field generally known as textual or literary analysis, and in a study of the present kind with its focus on an exemplary narrative in context, I see no reason to defend my theoretical position any further than that.

As for translation critique and translation theory, my chief aim has been to select some theoretical tools for my analyses rather than to establish new theoretical insights. I have been inspired by what is often referred to as the cultural turn in translation studies around 1990, and I have taken much inspiration from particular studies of translation theory, but I want to limit theoretical discussions of translation in a study where I focus mainly on the practice of translation. A few initial theoretical considerations, however, are in place.

The notion of equivalence is central in translation theory, and in my analyses I often refer implicitly or explicitly to it. The classic theory of equivalence is by Eugene Nida, who in his article "Principle of Correspondence" from 1964 advocated a dynamic rather than a formal equivalence, so that "the relationship between receptor and message should be substantially the same as that which existed between the original receptors and message" (Nida 1964/2000: 129). One of Nida's chief merits was his legitimate protest against a formalist tendency always to "determine standards of accuracy and correctness" by comparing the translation with the source text, with no regard for functional or communicative principles (129). Nida was well aware that different genres require different strategies, sometimes formal, sometimes dynamic, and this means that it is the task of the translation critic to characterize the strategies as relatively formal or dynamic. Formal and dynamic strategies are often mixed in the same translation and should be regarded as points on a scale rather than as absolute opposites. In this way equivalence can be discussed as the complicated notion it is, and I prefer this flexible categorization to more specific categorizations offered by later translation theorists.

Another important translation theorist is Susan Bassnett, who has both played a part in the mentioned cultural turn in translation studies and written extensively about the history and principles of translation. Her *Translation Studies* is a classic in the field and addresses a number of central issues in translation practice, while also covering such practices in a historical light (Bassnett 1980/1988). More recently she has published another fine translation study, *Reflections on Translation* (Bassnett 2011). Basnett is mentioned here as one out of several translation theorists that have contributed to a now well established field of study. I have thus used theoretical terms from what is now regarded as general translation theory, including terms such as addition, explication, omission, loss and gain, and I hope that my reader is able to understand these terms through the way I use them. Besides Bassnett, educational books like Anne Scholdager et al.'s *Understanding Translation* can be recommended for readers who want to explore the field of translation studies further (Scholdager et al. 2008/2010).

The cultural turn in translation studies took a leap forward with Lawrence Venuti's seminal study *The Translator's Invisibility: A History of Translation* from 1995 (Venuti 1995/2008). On the basis of especially German romantic thinking on translation, notably Schleiermacher and Goethe, Venuti establishes the important dichotomy between domestication and foreignization in translation strategies. He argues that especially Anglophone cultures have seen too much domestication, i.e. translation that has not respected the foreignness of the source text, but domesticated or familiarized the content and language. My own example to illustrate a clear case of this is the American translation of Norwegian author Jostein Gaarder's philosophical bestseller novel for young readers *Sofies Verden* from 1991, translated by Paulette Møller in 1995 as *Sophie's World* (Gaarder 1991, Møller, transl. 1995). The translation led to understandable protests, also from the author, when it was discovered that the American editors and the translator had changed the names of Norwegian romantic writers like Wergeland to English ones like Byron and also changed various plot details, such as Sofie staying up at nights to read. The American

Sophie goes to bed early like a good girl. I shall use Venuti's dichotomy in my own analyses and discuss how far domestication or foreignization strategies have played a part in Danish Chaucer translations.

Linda Hutcheon's *A Theory of Adaptation* from 2006 deserves mention in this chapter, as it is a serious and successful attempt to theorize adaptation. Hutcheon advocates respect for adaptations, and urges critics not to assume that "proximity or fidelity to the adapted text should be the criterion of judgment or the focus of analysis" (Hutcheon 2006: 6). As I have already mentioned, some of the sources treated in this study are adaptations or transformations of Chaucer's work, e.g. for children and young readers. I have tried my best to follow Hutcheon's advice and show respect for adaptors that communicate to a specific audience different from Chaucer's own, and clearly writing a children's book involves new genre demands. However, in cases where the title signals that a poem by Chaucer has been translated into Danish for a general, adult reader, I still regard proximity and fidelity as highly relevant criteria that will serve as a main focus of analysis.

CHAPTER 3

THE LATE 18ᵀᴴ AND EARLY 19ᵀᴴ CENTURY. WESSEL AND BRUUN

Chaucer reception and translation in Denmark begins at a time where English was a very foreign language and even Shakespeare had not been translated. In the 1780s German and French were the main foreign languages spoken by among others the nobility and by army officers, and the main cultural and linguistic influence came from these two language cultures. Characteristically, the story considered here thus begins with a musical drama which is a Danish version of a German *Singspiel* translated from French, and which offers little trace of Chaucer or England for its Danish audience, although it goes back to his *Wife of Bath's Tale*. Since this play, Wessel's *Feen Ursel eller hvad der behager Damerne* from 1782, is relatively far away from what Chaucer wrote, having gone through several filters, I will not provide a very thorough analysis of it, but it is still a starting point. In the main part of this chapter I will consider the career and writings of someone who started as Wessel's fellow poet and dramatist in Copenhagen, but ended up becoming the single most important person behind the gradual breakthrough of English in Denmark. This person is the first professor of English at the University of Copenhagen, poet and translator T.C. Bruun (1750-1834), and the story of Chaucer translation and of English in Danish education starts with him. Besides providing a discussion of the development of English in Denmark in Bruun's time, I will analyse Bruun's translation of Pope's version of Chaucer's *The Wife of Bath's Prologue*. The chapter will also include a treatment of the late 17th and early 18th century revival of Chaucer through Dryden and Pope.

Johan Herman Wessel and Feen Ursel

In 1782 *Feen Ursel eller hvad der behager Damerne* was first performed in Copenhagen in a translation by Johan Herman Wessel from the German *Die Fee Urgele, oder was den Damen gefällt*. This in turn had been translated by an anonymous translator from *La Fée Urgèle*, a French musical comedy from 1765 by Charles Favart (1710-92) and Egidio Duni (1709-1775) inspired by Voltaire's narrative poem *Ce qui plait aux dames, conte* from 1764 (Voltaire 1764). Voltaire (1694-1778) had taken his main plot from Dryden's version of Chaucer's *Wife of Bath's Tale*, which was published in 1700 as *The Wife of Bath her Tale* (Kinsley, ed., 1958). Wessel's *Feen Ursel* was revised after his death by German composer J.A.P. Schulz (1747-1800) and fellow musical director at the Royal Theatre of Copenhagen Thomas Thaarup (1749-1821) for a production opening on the king's birthday on January 30th 1792 (Krogh 1923: 168).[3] It is this version of what is truly a relay translation that I now turn to for a brief consideration, since it is the final version of the *Singspiel* in Danish and published in an apparently reliable 50-page manuscript now kept in the Royal Danish Library (Wessel, transl., Schulz and Thaarup, rev. 1792).

The Norwegian-Danish playwright Johan Herman Wessel (1742-1785) is best known for his parody of the French mourning play tradition *Kærlighed uden strømper* [Love without stockings] from 1772, an eminent play that is still often performed, earning his literary fame in Denmark (Bredsdorff 2001: 327). His *Feen Ursel eller hvad der behager Damerne* [The fairy Ursel or what pleases the ladies] is not among his own original works, but the translation contains examples of the linguistic and poetic wit that made him famous. The text is marked by its musical elements, which have been reorganized by Schulz and Thaarup to emphasize the song parts, and the play manuscript is thus short, with its 50 small pages containing poetic drama that adds up to a text about the size of an average Canterbury tale. It is printed in blackletter, which I will first transcribe in a rendering of the play's main plot challenge, for a knight to find out "hvad der til alle Tider behager Fruentimmere" [what pleases women at

---

[3] I owe thanks to fellow Chaucerian Betsy Bowden, who has kindly provided me with a forthcoming book chapter (Bowden forthcoming), which carefully records the many transformations of *La Fée Urgèle* and discusses the Favart/Duni play in a cultural historical context, placing it in the post Chaucer tradition. Bowden also mentions the Habilitation that the Dane Torben Krogh defended at the university of Berlin in 1923 (Krogh 1923), which records the occasion of the king's birthday performance. Krogh seems little interested in this now almost forgotten play and dismisses it as a failure in a very brief mention.

all times] (Wessel, transl., Schulz and Thaarup, rev. 1792: 23). The challenge is given to a knight here named Robert, and it echoes the main plot of Chaucer's *Wife of Bath's Tale*, but one main difference is that Robert, unlike the anonymous knight in Chaucer's tale is not a rapist. Dryden preserves the rapist motif, but Voltaire changes it to an act of consensual sexual intercourse. In Wessel's *Feen Ursel* Robert is even less than a sinner, since he has in fact only embraced the lady, named Marton, after having been refused a hand kiss. Wessel's text more or less jokingly records that this is enough for a death sentence from the queen, a sentence that will be lifted if the knight can answer the question of women's general desires. Chaucer's solution to the question is that women want mastery in marriage, and his version of this romance known in many other medieval and later analogues also includes the transformation of an old hag into a beautiful young lady, who finally marries the knight. This main plot is used again here, but the Farvard/Duni play includes a more complicated comic plot with a number of extra characters, and not much of the medieval romance is retained. Even Dryden's *The Wife of Bath's her Tale* is difficult to recognize, except for the plot skeleton. I will consequently conclude this section by stating that Chaucer is indeed lost in translation here, although his voice is vaguely echoed in the main plot, and in the twist to the plot that he added in his version, the *denouement* that women desire the upper hand. This solution to all problems in married life is worth recording also in Wessel's language:

> Men Herskab være, alt regiere. [But to be
> in power, to rule everything]
> Er deres Lyst, hvad Aar de har. [Is their want, however old they be]
> (Wessel, transl., Schulz and Thaarup, rev. 1792: 36)

Thomas Christopher Bruun and English in Denmark during his time

Also the second publication in Denmark based on Chaucer does not mention his name. In 1823 Thomas Christopher Bruun published his translation of Pope's version of *The Wife of Bath's Prologue*, which only mentions Pope's name on the title page. Before turning to an analysis of this publication, I will draw up Bruun's career as a professor, translator and author, with a focus on matters relevant for the translation. This involves a consideration of the status of English in Denmark during the first decades of the 19th century, the first part of a story continued in all remaining chapters of this study. Secondly there will be a discussion of the Chaucer tradition from Dryden and Pope, whose adaptation practices Bruun relies heavily on, most specifically Pope's. The final part of the chapter is a translation criticism of Bruun's translation, including both a comparison with Pope's rewriting of Chaucer and a discussion of Bruun's remarkable translation strategies.

T.C. Bruun became a pioneer in the field of English studies in Denmark, teaching a language and literature that few could understand and even fewer speak and write. Both as a private teacher and from 1800 as teacher at the new teacher training college of Copenhagen, the *Seminarium Pædagogikum,* Bruun became a dominant figure in the field of English, teaching also French. In 1802 Bruun was made extraordinary professor at Copenhagen University, continuing to his death in 1834, after which the seat remained empty for 17 years (Nielsen 1976-77, I: 51). As recorded by Jørgen Erik Nielsen in his dissertation *Den samtidige engelske litteratur og Danmark 1800-1840* [Contemporary English Literature and Denmark 1800-1840], this was the first Danish professorial seat in English, although there was a seat in aesthetics that included lectures on Shakespeare, given by the great Danish romantic poet Adam Oehlenschläger (Nielsen 1976-77, I: 51). By the time of his appointment at the turn of the century Bruun had already had a long career as translator, and also one as a dramatist and poet. He now started educating students who volunteered to also do modern languages, and many of them later became translators of English literature themselves (Nielsen 1976-77, I: 52).

Inge Kabell has added substantially to our understanding of Bruun's life and work in a short monograph (Kabell 1994). One of the obscure points about him is how he acquired his expert knowledge of English and French, since neither his education at the prestigious Danish boarding school Herlufsholm, nor his baccalaureate from the University of Copenhagen involved any modern languages. However, he is known to have taught languages already as a student, and as Kabell shows in an analysis of his grammar and pronunciation publications, he grew to become an important and knowledgeable linguist in his time (Kabell 1994: 1-2 and 15-21). This is naturally relevant also for his skills as a literary translator, which I will focus on in this chapter.

English literature was to some extent being translated already. The great 18th century prose writers Defoe, Swift, Richardson, Fielding, Smollett and Sterne were all available in Danish, as was Milton and from 1807 and the following years also finally Shakespeare. Nielsen's dissertation contains very thorough records of every single translation of English literature that was published in Denmark 1800-40, and whereas I cannot do full justice to his magnificent study, I can say here that Nielsen discusses translations of famous contemporaries such as Byron, Scott and the early Dickens, who all gained immediate attention in Denmark (Nielsen 1976-77 and Nielsen 2009). However, one remarkable result of his study is his record of a very different canon of writers, many of whom are now almost forgotten also in an English context. Thus among the frequently translated English writers before and up to the period investigated we find Edward Young (1683-1765), who was translated nine times between 1758 and 1785. Also James Thomson (1700-48), whose *Seasons* were translated 1803-9 for the use in concerts with music by Händel. A somewhat better remembered writer, if not at the core of the canon today, Oliver Goldsmith, was one of the most popular writers of the time, his *The Vicar of Wakefield* being translated twice, in 1797 and 1805 (Nielsen 1976: 103).

Among later famous students taught by Bruun we find the archaeologist P.O. Brøndsted and the great linguist Rasmus Rask, who both admired Bruun and remained loyal to him also in connection with some of the public feuds of the day, which Bruun took an active part in (Kabell 1994: 8-15). That Bruun also liked both as students appears from a report written by him in 1801, where they are mentioned among good students of English. Nielsen cites letters from both Brøndsted and Rask indicating that whereas they found much inspiration in Bruun's classes, they found especially English pronunciation next to impossible. Their attitude is matched by a later striking metaphor used by hymn writer and historical novelist B.S. Ingemann in a letter recording his struggles learning English in order to enjoy Sir Walter Scott's novels more. He refers to "det engelske Kjødbollesprog" [the English meat ball language], a metaphor suggesting that like when consuming food the use of speech organs is affected when speaking such a difficult, foreign language (Nielsen 1976:

52-3 and 56). Nielsen cites another famous Danish writer, St. St. Blicher, for complaining that he is only allowed to give one single lesson a week in English in a teaching job he holds in Randers in 1811, but the general impression Nielsen gives of English in the first decades of the 19th century suggests that this is actually more than usual, since French and German dominate, and English as a compulsory subject is not taught at high school level until 1871. English teachers are so few and far between in the 1840s that Metropolitanskolen [the Metropolitan school of Copenhagen] offers English only when they have a teacher available (Nielsen 1976: 47-8). Also symptomatic of the situation is a note from 1830 that Nielsen has located in The Royal Danish Military Library:

> Ligeledes skulle alle Bøger anskaffes i de Originalsprog, hvorom man kan forudsætte Kundskab hos enhver dannet Officeer, nemlig: Dansk, Svensk, Tydsk og Fransk. Af Engelske Bøger bør kun enkelte anskaffes, forsaavidt de slet ikke, eller ej godt, ere oversatte. [Likewise all books should be acquired in the original language of which you can expect knowledge from every well educated officer, i.e.: Danish, Swedish, German and French. English books should only be acquired as far as they have not been translated, or translated very poorly].
> (Nielsen 1976: 51)

English is clearly a language of strange otherness around the time that Bruun publishes his translations of English literature. It is moreover a language very difficult to get in direct contact with, as travel is not easy. Nielsen records the notes of a journey made by one of the most prominent figures in Danish cultural life in the 19th century, N.F.S. Grundtvig, who embarks on a ship in Copenhagen on May 3rd 1829, landing in London on May 16th (Nielsen 1976: 21). And not that many Englishmen passed through the other way, although one fine exception to the rule is recorded in Mary Wollstonecraft's very entertaining *Letters Written During a Short Residence in Sweden, Norway, and Denmark* from 1796 (Wollstonecraft 1796).

There was one year that the English did go to Denmark in great numbers, however, and that year, 1807, with the English navy bombing Copenhagen and Køge, sacking Copenhagen and finally taking over the Danish navy, had very serious repercussions for the relationship between the two countries. The humiliated Danes responded with great and lasting anger to what was seen as an act of terror and a mindless power demonstration (Glenthøj and Rahbek Rasmussen, eds., 2007). Professor Bruun became an eye-witness to the events in Copenhagen and we have his account of it in an essay published at a six-year distance from the events, in 1813. The essay, "Toget til Sielland og Kiøbenhavns belejring" [The Train to Zealand and the Sacking of Copenhagen], has been treated in a feature article by Inge Kabell, commemorating the 200th anniversary in 2007 (Kabell 2007). Kabell shows how Bruun gradually gets traumatized by what he sees walking through the streets of Copenhagen, and she quotes a passage of Bruun caught in the middle of events with his own family:

> Lisen var kort. Granaternes afskyelige Zisken. Brandpilenes slangeformige Ildsprudning vare saa mange Dolkestik i det. Det ængstede Blik søgte min Kone, mine Sønner. Døden var kun et slag, et Blund; men hvor ubeskriveligt elendig kunde et eneste Øjeblik giøre os. Forsynets Haand afvendte Faren. Morgenen gryede… [The peace was short. The abominable hissing sound of the grenades,[4] the spurting of fire by the snake-shaped fire arrows were so many stabs in it. My anxious eyes sought my wife, my sons. Death was only a stroke, a sleep; but how indescribably miserable could one single moment make us. The hand of Providence turned away the danger. It was dawn…]
> (Kabell 2007)

This is a passage well worthy of the poet Bruun, but it contains such a documentary directness as well that we sense the drama taking place. Bruun is seen here driven to extreme emotions, and perhaps it is no surprise that he later in the essay remarks how his hatred towards the English becomes so extreme that he starts hallucinating about murder. As one of the most competent speakers of English in town, Bruun was called in to the official negotiations in the aftermath of the bombard-

---

4   The Danish word "Zisken" or its spelling variant "Sisken" is not recorded as a sound-painting word in *Ordbog over det Danske Sprog*, and I have made a guess here and translated it as onomatopoeic.

ment, and it is here that he thinks for a moment of drawing a rapier and cutting down an English top negotiator. Fortunately, as Kabell remarks, he controls his impulse (Kabell 2007).

The picture so far of a professor on official duty for Denmark and an engaged nationalist with control of his extreme feelings has to be matched against an image of a younger Bruun, who was involved in a public scandal. His collection of poetry *Mine Frie-Timer: Fortællinger efter Boccaccio og Fontaine* [My Free Hours: Tales from Boccaccio and Fontaine], published in 1783, contained such frivolous verse that the stern prime minister Ove Guldberg ordered the book banned and Bruun fined. Also Guldberg made the newly appointed bishop N.E. Balle arrange a public apology. The scene of the apology was depicted in a copperplate, showing Bruun kneeling in front of the bishop and other members of the clergy.[5] According to literary historian Jørgen Stigel, the scandal later turned out to the benefit of Bruun, as his book escaped the ban and was now sold at an exorbitant price in many copies. Furthermore the scandal led to a public scorn of Guldberg's government for his over-reaction (Stigel 1983: 376).

Stigel does not assess the quality of Bruun's poetry and drama very highly and claims that he earned his reputation as a literary writer mainly through his frivolity and the scandal (Stigel 1983: 375-6). As for the drama, there is clear evidence that Bruun was not regarded very highly in his own time either, since all his three plays were given the minimum run of three nights at the Royal Theatre, never to be performed again (Kabell 1994: 25-26). In my own readings of Bruun's poetry, however, I have found reason to disagree with Stigel's harsh judgment, and I think that Stigel and many earlier literary historians have overlooked the single most important influence in Bruun's literary production as well as in his educational books: Alexander Pope. Like his admirer Bruun, Pope can be both frivolous and full of neoclassical *decorum* in his poetry, which is certainly the case in his Chaucer rewritings. Bruun, like many

---

5   A printed copy of the copperplate, titled in German "Verbesserung der Sitten" [Improvement of moral conduct], artist unknown, and an account of the scandal can be found in *Dansk litteraturhistorie,* volume 4, 376, written by Jørgen Stigel. Inge Kabell discusses the scandal further in a part of her monograph entitled "Bruun as a writer of pornography?", and she agrees with Stigel's conclusion that Guldberg's reaction was ridiculous in the light of the relatively innocent poetry Bruun had composed on the basis of his medieval sources. (Kabell, 3-6)

of his Danish contemporaries, has a bad habit of publishing books with lacking author names and work titles, but I have identified a great number of Pope references in his publications before the 1823 publication discussed as the main text in this chapter along with Pope's version. Whereas *Slagelse-Madamen* in 1823 does include Pope on its title page, Bruun's *Rimerier* [Rhymings], published in 1788 contains an epigraph not ascribed to Pope, but it is from his "Epistle to Miss Blount" from 1717: "Critics in wit or life are hard to please/Few write to those, and none can live to these." (Butt, ed. 1963/68: 243-4). This statement opens a collection of poetry where Bruun writes verse quite skillfully, in clear imitation of Pope. Again in 1804 Bruun turns to Pope in his *Poetisk læsebog eller Samling af Fortrinlige Engelske Digte* [Poetry Reader or Collection of Excellent English Poems], a collection that contains not one single name of the poets, but turns out to be completely dominated by selections from Pope, with the first epistle of *Essay on Man*, substantial parts of *Essay on Criticism* and the major part of *The Rape of the Lock*. Another educational publication by Bruun from 1802, *Engelsk accentueret Læsebog* [English Reader with Stress Patterns], shows a taste for classical stories, although I have identified nothing here as written by Pope.[6] However, we know from records of his advertised university courses that Pope was his absolute favourite for teaching purposes (Kabell 1994: 11). One final indication of Bruun's life-long inspiration from Pope is seen from the fact that he chooses to include his Pope translation *Slagelse-Madamen* alongside his own poems in a major collection of his main works in six volumes, published in 1816-27 (Bruun 1816-1927).

Dryden and Pope

In 1717 Pope published "Translations and Paraphrases Done in Youth" (Butt, ed., 1963/1968, 98-110), containing "Imitations" of English poets, and including his rewritings of Chaucer's *Merchant's Tale* and the text that Bruun uses, here titled *The Wife of Bath her Prologue, from Chaucer*. Pope claims to have written both Chaucerian tales "ca. 1704" publish-

---

6   The emphasis on stress patterns also reflects the fact that Danes had difficulties in pronouncing English, as we have seen.

ing the first of them in 1709 and the second one in 1713 in two different *Miscellanies*.[7] This means that Pope was only 16 when rewriting Chaucer, in his case quite a plausible claim, since his tuberculosis in the spinal marrow had led him from the age of 12 to devote all his time to books and writing.[8] Pope of course was not alone in practising his skills as a poet by imitating classics, a well-known prior example being a poet of Pope's admiration, John Dryden, who as the first great neoclassicist in England had paraphrased and translated classics from antiquity as well as Chaucer. In the year of his death in 1700 and following his lucrative translation of Vergil from 1697, Dryden published *Fables Ancient and Modern; Translated into Verse, from Homer, Ovid, Boccace, and Chaucer, with Original Poems,* containing besides a few short "Imitations" of Chaucer versions of three Canterbury tales, *The Knight's Tale, The Nun's Priest's Tale* and *The Wife of Bath's Tale,* with a title whose genitive is constructed as Pope's, i.e. *The Wife of Bath Her Tale* (Kinsley, ed., 1958). Characteristic of the otherwise brave effort to promote the then little read "father of English literature" is the attitude that Dryden makes explicit in the preface to this edition, and that finds echoes for a long time also in the Danish Chaucer reception, as we shall see later:

> I find some People are offended that I have turn'd these Tales into modern *English*; because they think them unworthy of my Pains, and look on *Chaucer* as a dry, old-fashion'd Wit, not worth receiving. [...] Chaucer, I confess, is a rough Diamond, and must first be polish'd e'er he shines. I deny not likewise, that living in our early Days of Poetry, he writes not always of a piece; but sometimes mingles trivial Things, with those of greater Moment. Sometimes also, though not often, he runs riot, like *Ovid,* and knows not when he has said enough. But there are more Great Wits, beside *Chaucer,* whose Fault is their Excess of Conceits, and those ill sorted. An Author is not to write all he can, but only all he ought. Having observ'd this Redundancy in *Chaucer,* (as it is an easie Matter for a Man of ordinary Parts to find a Fault in one of greater) I have

---

7   Butt, 76 og 98, refers to respectively Tonson's and Steele's *Miscellanies*.
8   I have written fuller portraits of Pope and Dryden in a Danish author's encyclopedia, see Klitgård 1999.

> not ty'd my self to a Literal Translation; but have often omitted what I judg'd unnecessary, or not of Dignity enough to appear in the Company of better Thoughts. I have presum'd farther in some Places and added somewhat of my own where I thought my Author was deficient, and had not given his Thoughts their true Lustre, for want of Words in the Beginning of our Language. And to this I was the more embolden'd, because (if I may be permitted to say it of my self) I found I had a Soul congenial to his, and that I had been conservant in the same Studies."
> (Kinsley, ed.: 1457).

Dryden regards himself as a soulmate of Chaucer's and recognizes the wit of the poet, but his reservations shine through and can be summed up with reference to the expression "a rough Diamond, and must first be polish'd e'er he shines." Dryden has actually got a point in comparing Chaucer's occasional running riot with Ovid's, but it should be noted that according to Dryden's neoclassical ideals of *decorum*, such wildness in poetry should be controlled. Dryden does not like Chaucer's tendency to mix high and low styles ("trivial things with those of greater Moment"). I might add that this is somewhat contradictory to his own sublime efforts in the *mock-heroic* genre, e.g. in *MacFlecknoe* from 1682, where Dryden so brilliantly describes trivial and insincere matters in high-flown heroic poetry. Yet, as far as Chaucer is concerned, Dryden insists that some obscene words in Chaucer, and Boccaccio for that matter, would be "very undecent to be heard", concluding also that "such Tales shall be left untold by me" (1456). Chaucer's "Excess of Conceit" mentioned in the quotation is clearly for Dryden in contrast to his own ideals, and it appears that in essence Dryden has not moved much further than his contemporaries when approving of Chaucer's wit, while at the same time not accepting or understanding the way this wit is administered in Chaucer's poetry. The accusation that Chaucer does not know the art of limitation and includes redundant passages in his poetry ("An Author is not to write all he can, but only all he ought"), along with the claim that his language lacks nuances because of "want of Words in the Beginning of our Language," leaves us with the impression of a patronizing Dryden unable to understand especially the linguistic premises of Chaucer's poetic art. Dryden thus appears to be the most important founder of a myth about Chaucer and late medieval poetry that has been particularly hard to get rid of. In this study we shall follow that myth through to the modern age and see how Chaucer has been twisted and changed in reception as well as translation by well-meaning writers whose knowledge of medieval poetry and language is insufficient. Dryden, however, is at least open about his adding bits and deleting others, and moreover he has made a careful choice in what he takes from Chaucer. He has selected two noble romances and a beast fable, thus avoiding the most lubricious tales such as *The Miller's Tale* or *The Reeve's Tale*. Furthermore, to be fair to Dryden, he has only trimmed language and content in his versions and not changed decisive plot lines, e.g that the Knight in *The Wife of Bath her Tale* is a rapist. (Kinsley, 1705, lines 46-60). Dryden's translations can best be characterised as transformations and retellings, including the linguistic and poetic form, which completely transfers Chaucer to the world of neoclassical poetry.

Dryden was also quite outspoken about his ideals for translation and is generally recognized as important in the history of translation theory. In his introduction to translation theory *Introducing Translation Studies,* Jeremy Munday quotes Dryden's criticism of Ben Jonson as a "verbal copier", guilty of "metaphrase" or "word by word and line by line" translation. As opposed to this Dryden promotes either "paraphrase" or "imitation", the first of these defined as "translation with latitude, where the author is kept in view by the translator, so as never to be lost, but his words are not so strictly followed as his sense." "Imitation" in turn means forsaking both words and sense, according to Munday corresponding to free verse translation, or more or less adaptation. (Munday 2001: 25/ Dryden 1680/1697). It follows that for Dryden any attempt to find formal equivalence in translations of poetry is in vain, whereas creative solutions to recreate the sense of the original are the ideal.

Pope in his imitations of Chaucer is on a par with Dryden, but more bravely chooses as one of his texts *The Wife of Bath's Prologue*, full of references to human anatomy and sexual practices, and revealing its narrator's moral problems in a religious perspective. Also Pope's other Canterbury tale, *January and May; or, the Merchant's Tale: from Chaucer* contains some problematical passages from a puritan point of view, not least in the final episode's sexual intercourse. Pope changes the ending so that May becomes an after all virtuous romance heroine. Thus Pope makes a virtue of raising the morals of Chaucer's tales to an acceptable level, and in both cases his main strategy is simply to abbreviate and simplify. Thus *The Merchant's Tale* is reduced from approximately 1200 to 800 lines, whereas *The Wife of Bath's Prologue* has been cut from 856 to 439 lines.[9] Pope's *The Wife of Bath her Prologue* focuses on the Wife's relationship with her husbands and especially the fifth husband, whereas her humorous attempt to justify herself through twisted references to the Bible have been largely left out. Besides this, frivolous passages and expressions have been excluded or euphemised, as will appear from my comparison with Bruun's translation.

Slagelse-Madamen

Bruun's translation is published in a booklet of 24 pages in blackletter. In my quotations from the Danish text I have transcribed blackletter into modern writing, but kept the original spelling. The title page reads in full quotation:

> *Slagelse-Madamen; efter Popes, Konen i Bath.* Ved T.C. Bruun, Professor. Kjøbenhavn 1823. Trykt og forlagt af Cancellie-Assessor P. E. Martin. Øesterbroe No. 58. [*The Wife of Slagelse; after Pope's The Wife in Bath.* By T.C. Bruun, Professor, Copenhagen 1823. Printed and published by cancelling assessor P.E. Martin, Østerbro, no. 58].
> (Bruun 1823: 1)

Besides leaving out Chaucer's name, Bruun has remarkably translated the title twice, i.e. both to "Konen i Bath" and to "Slagelse-Madamen." The choice of the preposition "i" [in] rather than "fra" [of/from] is odd, but not as odd as the choice of a West Zealand town, Slagelse, as her home town. There is one more Danish place name reference in the translation, to Copenhagen, where the Wife "ved Juletiid … gjorde/en Lyst-Tour" [at Christmas … made/ a pleasant outing] according to Bruun (14). As the railway line between Slagelse and Copenhagen was not opened until

---

9   John Butt in his edition lists the exact omissions by Pope.

1856, this nearly 100 km long journey will have been a hard one, if still possible in one day (Fischer-Nielsen 1998). Bruun importantly transports the Wife not only in place, but also in time. As it will appear from my further examples, not much of the medieval wife is left after Pope's and Bruun's translations and revisions.

On the title page Bruun is referred to as professor, which is of course an authoritative reference to vouch for the quality of the translation. It turns out, however, that the title of professor and Bruun's affiliation with the University of Copenhagen plays a further role in his translation, as he leaves a translator's hidden signature. A very direct reference has been inserted in the translation, as the young student who in Chaucer is called Jankyn and in Pope's version is nameless, appears as

> En ung Student, en vis hr. Rask, [a young student, a certain Mr Rask,]
> Der havde frit Logis, samt Kost og Vask [who had free lodging, as well as board and laundry catered for]
> I huset, som den salig Mages Frænde. [In the house, as the blissful wife's relative.]
> Ja, fattig rigtig nok, som en Poet, [Well, poor enough, just like a poet,]
> Men ret en vakker Fyhr, saa høijt beleven; [But a rather handsome fellow, so very affable;]
> Og i at sige smukke Ting saa dreven, [And in saying beautiful things so skilful,]
> At havde han saa dybt i Skrivten seet, [That had he looked deep into the books,]
> Han Amtsprovst, ja Professor selv var bleven. [He would have become county dean, indeed also professor]
> (15)

This is of course the translator's private joke about his model student Rasmus Rask, who despite his poor background had taken it far and in 1818 had become Bruun's professorial colleague at the university (Winge 2000: 16-7). Rask, later to be recognized as the founding father of Nordic philology and one of the most remarkable linguists of his period, was in fact a "rather handsome fellow", as can be seen from a lithograph by Emil

Bærentzen & Co. from 1844, reprinted as cover photograph in Kirsten Rask's biography of Rask (Rask 2002).[10] As the biography also indicates, Rask did in fact look deep into the books, but his habit of communicating very indiscreetly and being a generally difficult character for his surroundings made him a professor later in life than he deserved. Bruun's joke about the missed opportunities in the last line of the quotation may thus have been a bit hard on Rask, assuming he read Bruun's translation. For the general reader it may well have provoked an extra laugh, especially since the joke is prolonged when Rask becomes the Wife of Slagelse's fifth husband, which makes her Madam Rask.

The detail with the name Rask can be seen as symptomatic of Bruun's translation in general. Chaucer's original is of course full of comedy, and as Pope has not quite succeeded in subduing all the comic elements despite his attempt to make his version acceptable for a well-educated audience, it is also possible for Bruun to adopt a strategy that promotes comedy. This strategy is successful in many ways, as witnessed by the representation of the climax of *The Wife of Bath's Prologue*, the Wife's battle with her fifth husband about his book of wicked wives. The main action of the episode is maintained (19-23), if not correct in every detail. Thus Bruun's wife tears four sheets out of her husband's book rather than the three sheets in Chaucer and Pope, and the settlement between them involves in Bruun as opposed to Pope that the husband keeps some of the mastery in marriage in being allowed to rule in his own study. This can be regarded as a modification of the male humiliation in Chaucer and part of the general attempt to avoid Chaucer's feminist perspectives, but Bruun does let the wife be handy with her fists and have a triumphant laugh in a striking, idiomatic language, whose slang-like nature can be sensed in Danish, which has long since lost the expression "en af Clauses":

> Jeg gav ham en af Clauses paa hans Kiæve,
> [I gave him one of Claus's on his jaw,]
> Og bad ham, skoggerleende, god Nat. [and
> bade him, belly laughing, goodnight]
> (22)

---

10 It should be noted that Kirsten Rask, a modern linguist, is not a descendant of Rasmus Rask.

At the end of the episode with Mr and Mrs Rask united in a pact sealed in the marriage bed, Bruun himself has apparently become so "skogger-leende" or belly laughing that he dares refer to sex unmistakably for the first time: "Natuurligvis blev pagten strax paa Stand,/Og paa det allerkraftigste beseglet". [Of course the pact was immediately and forthwith/And in the strongest possible way sealed] (23). It is otherwise one of Bruun's clearest purposes to go even further than Pope in avoiding any reference to the original's very direct sexual and other offensive terms and to avoid theologically controversial passages, often by simply leaving a lacuna. Thus Chaucer's long introductory sequence with the Wife's elegant, but theologically dubious treatment of "Experience versus Auctoritee" (*Wife of Bath's Prologue 1-162* in Benson, ed., 1987), which is already strongly abbreviated by Pope, is further cut down by Bruun. As an example Bruun mentions "Sanct Paulus" only once (5) as opposed to Pope's four times. Bruun also includes fewer direct references to the bible than Pope, who has already spoiled most of Chaucer's very funny distortions of biblical matters, put into the mouth of the manipulative and in this respect feminist Wife. The general reduction of bible references may well have been because Chaucer's Wife's rather careless attitude to Christian authority, being already strong meat for Pope, was even more of a taboo for Bruun, who takes care to keep the Wife's idiom fresh, but never offensive. In this connection it is well worth citing Bruun's brief translator's note:

> Det vil ved Sammenlignelsen befindes, at jeg har forfinet alle de Pensel-Strøg i Originalen, som den engelske Frihed tillader, men som den danske Finhed sikkert vilde have fundet for stærke. [A comparison will show that I have refined all the strokes of the pen in the original which are allowed by the English freedom, but which the Danish fineness would probably have found too strong.] (5)

Here it has to be remembered that Bruun's original is Pope and not Chaucer and that Pope, as we have seen, had already thoroughly "refined" Chaucer, who in turn may well have been "refined" by copying scribes and early printers. The remarks about the English freedom are tempting to interpret further, but suffice it to say here that we are dealing with one of the few practising Danish translators proficient in English, who may simply have wanted to point to different narrative traditions, showing that the Danish publishing tradition and censorship could not fully take in Chaucer's and even his English translators' indelicacies. Dryden and Pope, and Chaucer for that matter, are representatives of a certain frivolous tone in an English tradition not yet known to a Danish reading public, and Bruun has to respect that. For Bruun personally there is also a clear motivation for showing some restraint, since he will have remembered only too well how censorship hit him hard and led to personal humiliation in 1783, as we have seen.

In *Slagelse-Madamen* Bruun generally takes a liberal stand as a translator, and he thus sticks to the Dryden and Pope inspired ideals he expressed already in that infamous book of translations from 1783, *Mine Frie Timer*, where he says in the preface that he prefers paraphrase to word-to-word translation (Kabell 1994: 5). Some major changes go beyond paraphrase and involve additions, first of all a new introduction and a new moralizing epilogue. Importantly Bruun also chooses a new metre with variations allowing freer translation. The introduction shows that he is quite able to strike the note of a colourful female narrator, even though he is now on his own, writing his own poetry rather than translating:

> At det er rart at giøre og at lade [That it is nice to do]
> Hvad selv man vil, det tør jeg bande paa, [What you like, I swear.]
> Mig Fruer, ja Madamer vil tilstaae. [Ladies, wives will grant me]
> Jeg giør af mine kunster ei Parade; [That I
> make no show of my artistry;]
> Men hvis de vort saa kaldte svage Kiøn [But
> if it can help our so-called weak sex]
> Kan hielpe til det stærke lidt at kue [To
> subdue the strong sex somewhat]
> Saa sætter jeg nok en Fier i min hue; [I will
> put another feather in my cap;]
> Og venter mine Søstres Tak til Løn; [And expect
> the thanks of my sisters as reward;]
> Om Herrerne den end med haan beskue. [Even
> if the gentlemen look at it with disdain.]
> (3, 1-9)

This original introduction in fact introduces the main theme of the Wife's prologue very well, i.e. the battle between the two sexes seen from a female point of view. Pope opens his version with a shorter introduction, "Behold the Woes of Matrimonial Life/ And hear with Rev'rence and experienc'd Wife" (Pope, 1-2), which is only a faint echo of Chaucer's "Experience, though noon auctoritee/Were in this world, is right ynogh for me" (Benson gen. ed. 1987: III, 1-2). Bruun has apparently found Pope's opening lines somewhat abrupt, and in turn Pope may well have thought of Chaucer's opening as abrupt. Quite rightly so, since *The Wife of Bath's Prologue* is the beginning of fragment III of *The Canterbury Tales* and contains no introductory dramatic dialogue or any other introduction. In the following lines (10-15) Bruun acknowledges Pope's opening by supplying a loose paraphrase of his lines 1-6, then turns to the first piece of translation from Pope:

> Thi jeg har i Triumf, som faa kun hænder, [For
> in Thriumph, as only few are allowed to]
> Fem Mænd fra Alteret til Brudesengen ført [I have
> led five men from the altar to the marriage bed]
> (Bruun, 16-17)

> For, since Fifteen, in Triumph have I led
> Five Captive Husbands from the Church to Bed.
> (Pope, 7-8)

Already in these lines we see Bruun's refinement strategy at work, and characteristically Pope has acted as an intermediary by already refining Chaucer. In Chaucer's text the decidedly promiscuous Wife of Bath has been married five times from the age of 12 (*The Wife of Bath's Prologue*, 4), and she does not hide the fact that her pilgrimage to Canterbury might with any luck lead to a sixth marriage (45). As we can see in the quotation, Pope makes the Wife's first marriage take place at the more respectable age of 15, and it takes place "in Thriumph" and decently. Bruun avoids mentioning the Wife's first marriage age altogether and adds to make it look more positive that few are granted such happiness.

In the passages cited so far it can also be seen that Chaucer's and Pope's metre has been replaced by a different one. By and large Pope follows Chaucer's couplets, (aa, bb, cc, etc.), however occasionally inserting another rhyme line (aa, bb, ccc, etc.). Generally the five foot iambs (pentameters) are only slightly more regular than Chaucer's, although Pope's tendency as a neoclassicist towards regularity does shine through. For some reason not immediately clear Bruun chooses a somewhat more complicated rhyme scheme, abba, cddc, etc., but he also, like Pope, makes it easier for himself by occasionally adding an extra rhyme line, as in lines 1-9 above, with the rhymes abba, cddcd, a pattern that furthermore is sometimes varied with the use of cross-rhymes, abab. Bruun's iambs are also pentameters and form a rhythmical foundation in the text, with a few irregularities here and there when convenient. Even though Bruun's poetry has a fairly elegant flow, it is also clear that Bruun's skills do not match Pope and Chaucer.

As seen in the title and in the transposition to a contemporary Danish setting, including characters like Rask familiar to a Danish audience, Bruun's overall translation strategy is characterized by an urge to keep as much as possible of Chaucer's and Pope's foreign universe away from the Danish readers. Bruun's translation is thus a rather extreme example of what the translation theorist Lawrence Venuti calls *domestication* as opposed to *foreignisation,* as discussed in chapter 2 (Venuti 1995). The strategy has been so consistently followed that also names of food have been culturally transferred, e.g. rendering "fine wheat" as "Makroner" [macaroons] (Pope: 48, Bruun: 5) and "Barley Bread" as "Rugbrød" [rye bread] (Pope: 49, Bruun: 5). The contrast between luxury food and everyday food is maintained well in Bruun's translation, but he evidently finds it necessary to refer to well-known Danish food rather than referring to English foods and customs.

In the light of the custom of often leaving out author's names in title pages, it is questionable whether most of Bruun's first readers will have noticed Pope's name at all, and it seems certain that hardly any of them would know that the text goes back to Chaucer. I have looked for slips or indications of something English in Bruun's text, but he has been very careful with his strategy. In carrying out his strategy Bruun has also felt assured that he could take liberties of all kinds and not have to be loyal to an original author, whether Pope or Chaucer. Such liberties are naturally easier to get away with in a Danish culture where the English language and literature is not particularly well known. And since it is also still fairly close to the events of 1807, Bruun's domestication of his text has another good reason.

Bruun's very relaxed attitude to his source text makes it reasonable to characterise his *Slagelse-Madamen* as a *transformation* rather than a mere translation. As a further example of a shape-shifting text, let us look at one of the most quoted passages from *The Wife of Bath's Prologue*. This is one of the passages where Pope has not had a very lucky hand with Chaucer, who I quote first:[11]

> But – Lord Christ! – whan that it remembreth me
> Upon my yowthe, and on my jolitee,
> It tikleth me aboute myn herte roote.
> Unto this day it dooth myn herte boote
> That I have had my world as in my time.
> But age, allas, that al wol envenyme,
> Hath me biraft my beautee and my pith.
> Lat go. Farewel! The devel go therwith!
> The flour is goon; ther is namoore to telle;
> The bren, as I best kan, now moste I selle;
> But yet to be right myrie wol I fonde.
> Now wol I tellen of my fourthe housbonde.
> (*The Wife of Bath's Prologue*, Benson, gen. ed., 1987: III, 469-480)

Pope renders the passage (221-229) as follows:

> But oh good Gods! whene'er a Thought I cast
> On all the Joys of Youth and Beauty past,
> To find in Pleasures I have had my Part,
> Still Warms me to the Bottom of my Heart.
> This wicked World was once my dear Delight;

---

11 John Butt writes in his comments to 221-8: "A poor equivalent for Chaucer" (Butt ed., 1963: 104). I agree with him. However, it is remarkable that this is Butt's only negative comment to Pope's translation. When Butt refers to parallels in Chaucer's text, it is mainly without comments, or with notes on small linguistic misunderstandings on the part of Pope. Apart from that Pope is praised rather frequently, as when Butt says about 263-76 that they represent "a straightforward version of Chaucer 525-42." "Straightforward" is a vague term to use about Pope's free translation.

> Now all my Conquests, all my Charms good night!
> The Flour consum'd, the best that now I can
> Is e'en to make my Market of the Bran

And finally Bruun (13):

> Du Naadsens Gud! Naar end jeg mig omtænker, [Oh merciful God! Whenever I think about it,]
> Hvad Løjer jeg har havt i denne Jammerdal, [The joys I've had in this vale of woe,]
> Saa, rigtigt nok, mig Tanken krænker, [The thought, to be honest, is injuring.]
>
> Jeg passer nu ei meer i Danse-Sal. [I no longer fit into the ballroom.]
> Men naar jeg mig paa samme Tiid erindrer, [But when I also recollect how often]
> Hvor tidt jeg har, og selv er bleven kyst, [I have been jokingly scared or myself tried to scare others]
> Saa – ja, endnu det gamle Øje tindrer, [Well, the old eye still shines bright]
> Og Hjertet hopper i mit Bryst. [And the heart jumps in my breast.]
> Den fierde Mand, hvis Navn Jeg førte, [The fourth husband, whose name I carried…]

Pope's version is three lines shorter than Chaucer's, but he captures the essence of the message and renders the metaphor about flour and bran well. That the world is "wicked" is Pope's own invention, but in line with the Wife's argument. The most problematic point is Pope's omission of the line "But yet to be right myrie wol I fonde" (479), because Chaucer here makes the Wife appear as a real struggler in the game about love and marriage, despite her painful self-realization. The omission is well in line with Pope's general attempt to make the Wife appear less of a man-eater, as would be one possible modern designation of her character.

Bruun has not found an equivalent for the flour-bran metaphor, but the lines "Well, the old eye still shines bright/And the heart jumps in my breast" in fact give us back Chaucer's impression of her as a struggler, although also Bruun's wife here and elsewhere would think of her "breast" rather than her "breasts." Bruun's image of the lost entrance possibility to the ballroom is also original, and the passage renders the sense well, while at the same time transforming a medieval frame of reference to a for Bruun modern one, which includes ballrooms and débutantes. Finally, "Jammerdal" is a colourful and still used Danish expression, which replaces Pope's weaker "wicked World" in an idiomatic if not absolutely precise translation.

Among Bruun's most personal touches in his textual transformation of Pope I would select the added epilogue as the most conspicuous change. Thus *Slagelse-Madamen* ends with a very different pact from that between Pope's nameless first husband and the Wife of Bath.[12] Mr and Mrs Rask agree after their fight to settle the matter in a way where Mr Rask keeps more of his personal dignity. After the earlier quoted "en af Clauses paa hans kiæve" [one of Claus's on his jaw] and the belly-laugh, the married couple reach an agreement by being indulgent towards each other. This is especially the case on the part of Mrs Rask in the ca. 50 lines that Bruun has composed himself, adding on his own account an ending that presumably pleased him better. Mrs Rask remarks for instance, "Jeg firede lidt altsaa paa min Side,/ Og lod ham stundum have Ret" [I veered out a little bit on my part/And let his opinion prevail once in a while] (Bruun, 23). Rask on his part speaks softly to her, but on the other hand makes the demand that he wants to be "ene herre" [master] if not in his own house then at least "inden mit Studerekammers Dør" [within the door of my study]. This makes Mrs Rask shout "Top!" [Deal!], and as mentioned they seal the pact in the marriage bed. The shameful book of wicked wives is put on the shelf and never read again, and the couple live happily ever after (23). The fact that Rask does not like Jankyn hand over his sovereignty to his wife, and the fact that Bruun lets him be alive still at the end of the prologue, avoiding the image of a man-hunting widow, of course

---

12 Pope in fact uses the name Jenkyn, close to Chaucer's Jankyn, but that is early in the prologue, where he appears as a "Prentice" for one of the first three husbands (Pope in Butt, ed. 1963: 118 and 151). The fifth husband is mentioned as "of Oxford … Clerk", and the Wife meets him in the house of her gossip friend Alison, by whom he is a tenant (264-6).

makes the story more morally acceptable, or in Bruun's mind "refined", but it does not leave much of Chaucer's Wife's moral that a wife's upper hand in marriage is to be preferred. It is just as well that Bruun does not also translate Dryden's version of *The Wife of Bath's Tale*, because that would give him trouble with the tale's illustration of that particular point, a point that is of course obviously true: What women desire in marriage is to be in control and have the mastery.

Bruun does not leave it at that, but adds his own conclusion in the shape of the following epilogue:

> Saaledes har jeg da mit Liv optegnet:
> [Thus I have drawn up my life]
> Som Mynster ei, men at mit Kiøn kan see, [Not in
> order to be a model, but so that my sex can see]
> At det, en hvis Paastaaenhed fraregnet, [That,
> except for a certain obstinacy,]
> Kan af Hiint Overherredømme lee; [We
> can laugh about that mastery;]
> Og lydigt kun til huusbehov sig tee. [And behave
> obediently only as much as needed.]
> Jeg haaber alle mine Mænd at finde [I
> hope to find all my husbands]
> I Himmelen naar selv jeg salig blier, [In Heaven when I die myself]
> Hvis Taalighed der ellers Udgang gier. [If
> forbearance gives me access to go out.]
> Paa Jorden jeg dem viiste, at en Qvinde [On
> earth I showed them that a woman]
> Ei voved' blot med flere an at binde, [Dared to
> take on the challenge of several men,]
> Men gjorde dem endogsaa Veien trang. [But I also
> made the road hard for them to follow.]
> Og hermed jeg for denne Sinde [And with
> this I make an end, this time,]
> Giør Ende – dog ei paa min Svanesang.
> [But I do not sing my swan song.]
> (Bruun: 24)

Just as was the case with the added introduction, Bruun is quite able to keep up the poetic tone from the translated and transformed passages from Pope. It is also understandable here that Bruun is looking for a well resolved ending, since Pope does not provide one. Pope gives up including Chaucer's frame story with the merry reactions from the other pilgrims and ends very abruptly with four lines, in which the Wife prays for her husbands (Pope, 435-9). Bruun follows Pope's reference to the husbands in Heaven, but stresses the comic element, not least from the point of view of the female sex. Bruun finds it important to say that the Wife's example should not be followed ("Som Mynster Ei"), even though we should allow ourselves to laugh with her. The moral of her life story is somewhat suppressed by Bruun, and also by Pope. Neither Bruun, nor Pope has any wish to promote the idea of a free woman who does not care a hoot about being perfect, and who wins on the battleground of marriage. In 1823 that woman still only exists in Chaucer's original, and it takes more than a century before she gets known in Danish.

As already established, the tradition from Dryden and Pope helped to create a myth of Chaucer as a writer in the "merry England" tradition in the early European reception history as well as in English literary history itself. This tendency is recorded quite prominently in a literary work published in 1819, four years before Bruun's translation, i.e. Sir Walter Scott's *Ivanhoe*. *Ivanhoe* contains chapter epigraphs quoting *The General Prologue* in ch. 2 and *The Knight's Tale* in ch. VII, VIII and XII to support the novel's celebration of knights fighting gallantly and rescuing damsels in distress in a "district of merry England" recorded in the novel's very first line (Scott 1819: 7). This romantic image of the Late Middle Ages and Chaucer's world, where everything rude or unpleasant goes unmentioned or is euphemised, has been a hard-lived myth ever since. Let me conclude on the basis of my analysis that Bruun's Chaucer, especially because of his general domestication strategy and setting in 19th century Denmark, avoids reinforcing that myth as opposed to Dryden and Pope's Chaucer.

Chapter conclusion

We have seen in this chapter how a classic author like Chaucer may find his way to new reading cultures in forms far removed from what he actually wrote, and that both Wessel's *Feen Ursel* and Bruun's translation may be more aptly named text transformation or paraphrase, several instances of textual transfer, own composition, and several types of translation being involved. Wessel's final text has been transformed through several intermediaries and like Bruun's translation extends the humour of the Wife of Bath to domestic Danish domains. Especially Bruun produces his own new text, shape-shifted as much as the old hag in Chaucer's *Wife of Bath's Tale*. In the next chapter we shall see an even more imaginative kind of Chaucer transformation than Bruun's.

CHAPTER 4

WESTERGAARD AND THE PERIOD 1835-65

The first real Chaucer publication in Denmark appears in 1853, 30 years after Bruun's *Slagelse-Madamen*. Louise Westergaard's *Engelske Digtere. Første Hefte: Chaucer* [English poets, volume one: Chaucer] will be analysed as the main text of this chapter, but first it will be considered in a broad historical and cultural context, secondly in the context of English in Denmark in the period, and finally in the more specific context of Westergaard's life and works.

Some historical and cultural events and tendencies in Westergaard's Denmark 1835-65

Charlotte Louise Westergaard, known by the name of Louise Westergaard, lived from 1826-1880 and started her long career as a teacher at 17 in 1843, later to become an important figure in Danish English education as well as an advocate of women's rights. Before going into detail with her impressive life and career, let us consider the main political events and cultural figures of the period of her formative years and the most active part of her career, the thirty years from 1835-65 that I have chosen as the delimitation for this chapter. This is very much a transition period between the absolute monarchy and the censorship we saw practised in chapter 3 and the so-called modern breakthrough that will be the period considered in chapter 5. The single most important event in the period is the invention of parliamentary democracy in Denmark with the constitution granted by King Frederik VII on June 5th 1849, a date still celebrated annually in Denmark. One of the most important effects of this constitution, besides the actual parliament, then in two chambers, the Folketing and the Landsting, was the granting of freedom to the press and freedom of religion. This was partly a consequence of the new dominance of national liberalism in Danish politics from the 1830s (Vammen 1999: 32-3), and of course it also paved the way for new freedom in the publishing world. Westergaard writes in a very different age than Wessel and Bruun, and her works are specifically marked by both nationalist and liberal thinking, as we shall see.

Nationalism was also evoked in Denmark by the wars against Germany over the border country of Schleswig-Holstein from 1848 until the final and humiliating defeat of the Danish army in 1864. Under the headline "'Den liberale Classe' ved magten 1848-64" [the liberal class in power 1848-64] literary historians and critics Martin Zerlang and Jørgen Holmgaard have given a thorough account of this period in *Dansk litteraturhistorie* [Danish Literary History] (Zerlang and Holmgaard 1985: 27-142), offering a cultural-historical context for the literature published in these years. One noteworthy example of what was written is a song composed in 1848 by poet Peter Faber and still well remembered today. This is *Den tappre Landssoldat* [the brave national soldier], also known by its first line, "Dengang jeg drog afsted" [That time I went on my way], a simple song about the soldier fighting for his girl at home and for his country. It became the nationalist tune of the war years and almost emblematic of the nationalist spirit (Zerlang and Holmgaard 1985: 45-6).

The years 1835-65 are of course also the heyday of two of the most famous Danes ever internationally, Søren Kierkegaard (1813-55) and Hans Christian Andersen (1805-75). Both the great philosopher and literary author Kierkegaard and the renowned fairytale writer, poet and novelist Andersen have strong nationalist roots in their writings, but both combine this with international orientation, not least to Germany and southern Europe, but certainly also to the English-speaking world. Whereas this study focuses on English in Denmark, it is worth noting that we have major cultural exports the other way from this period, and that Andersen was many times translated into English already in his own life-time, as appears from Viggo Hjørnager Pedersen's Habilitation *Ugly Ducklings: Studies in the English Translations of Hans Christian Andersen's Tales and Stories.* (Hjørnager Pedersen 2004).

The new nationalism also resulted in a distinctive Danish school of art, represented by such eminent artists as the painters Christen Købke (1810-48) and C.W. Eckersberg (1783-1853), whose works included many Copenhagen motifs that will have been familiar to Copenhagener

Westergaard. Another Danish artist in this tradition was sculptor Bertel Thorvaldsen (1770-1844), who earned so much fame that a museum was erected in his name (1839-48). He was, especially after his death, regarded as a national hero (Munk 2001: 67-8). Thorvaldsen was one of Westergaard's personal favourites and very capable of evoking her nationalist feelings.

Another leading cultural figure of the period, N.F.S. Grundtvig (1783-1872), should also be mentioned. In *Den Store Danske Encyklopædi* he is introduced by Christian Thodberg through a diversity of labels indicating the broad range of his influence areas: poet, vicar, historian, politician, pedagogue and philologist (Thodberg 1997: 599, my translation). Grundtvig's work as a psalmist was arguably the most prominent reason for his status, but outside the religious field his voice was also enormously influential. In the context of this study it should be mentioned that Grundtvig's insight in philology included knowledge of Old English. I will briefly return to his work on Beowulf in chapter 5.

For medieval studies generally, Grundtvig's son Svend Grundtvig (1824-83) became even more important than his father. Beginning the publication of *Danmarks gamle folkeviser* [Denmark's old folk songs] in 1853, in a series continued even after his death, Svend Grundtvig became the founding father of folklore studies in Denmark, from 1863 as a professor at the University of Copenhagen. The new university discipline of *folkemindevidenskab* [folklore] was also part of the nationalist movement in Danish culture following the Slesvig wars. As a leading folklorist Grundtvig was concerned with collecting and transcribing as many Danish folk songs and tales as possible, and he soon established good connections to rural districts of Denmark, where there was still an oral literary tradition. One of his chief connections was Evald Tang Kristensen (1843-1929), a school teacher from Gjellerup in the middle of Jutland. Tang Kristensen's fascinating life-long effort in the service of folklore and his research collaboration with Grundtvig is the subject of Palle Ove Christiansen's recent study *De forsvundne: Hedens sidste fortællere* [Those that have disappeared: the last story-tellers of the moors] (Christiansen 2011). Christiansen follows Kristensen on a particular journey in December 1873, where he records material from 11 informants, touring his neighbouring district of the Mid-Jutland moors. Here he collected Danish folk songs and fairy tales, many of which go back to the Middle

Ages, most with European parallels, but some unique. Grundtvig was in frequent correspondence with Kristensen and helped raise donations for a substitute teacher in the winters and for expenses, although Tang Kristensen lived extremely modestly and on tours had his meals also with people living in poor-houses.

Some of the folk tales recorded by Tang Kristensen in December 1873 are popular fairy tales, such as a version of the Beauty and the Beast story, whereas others are roguish stories in the fabliaux tradition that we also know from Chaucer. One informant, Jesper Pedersen Skrædder, tells such stories, e.g. "Skabet fuldt" [the closet full], about a man called Kjeld, who keeps on fooling the king so that he can fill up his closet with money. Christiansen shows how Tang Kristensen first transcribed the story in Pedersen Skrædder's actual language, which included "røv" and "pissede" ["arse" and "pissed"], but then in the editing process with Grundtvig changed such dirty words to euphemisms before publication (Christiansen 2011: 119). In other words Kristensen and Grundtvig slightly polished the language of the Danish folktales where they found it necessary, although far from as much as what Dryden and Pope did to Chaucer (see chapter 3). The language of the common people, also known in Danish as "almuesproget", was occasionally too blunt both for the editors and for the many Danish authors who now let themselves be influenced by it, such as Holger Drachmann and Jeppe Aakjær (Christiansen: 207). Folklore became an inspiration in Danish literature, but the language was adopted only in so far as it would not cause offence.

Louise Westergaard and English in Denmark ca. 1835-1865

Having established a nationalist cultural context where also Danish popular literature became celebrated, let us now return to a consideration of English in Denmark, with a focus on literature. English was still only a third foreign language after German and French, and far from everything was available in translation. In a newspaper column about languages in Denmark in the mid-19th century, the linguist Jørn Lund indicates the status of English by the example of Shakespeare translation. As Lund says, since not all of Shakespeare's works were translated until the first complete edition by Lembcke 1861-73, many would read him in German translation (Lund 2011). Another example of the changing status of English in Denmark during the period is the vacant professorial chair at the University of Copenhagen after T.C. Bruun's death in 1834, which remained vacant for 17 years until 1851 when George Stephens became a reader (Nielsen 2003: 370).

In chapter 3 I referred to Jørgen Erik Nielsen's dissertation *Den samtidige engelske litteratur og Danmark 1800-1840* (Nielsen 1977), which gives a thorough picture of literature translated into Danish in that period. In two other studies (Nielsen 2003 and 2009) Nielsen has moved further into the 19th century, first of all registering and commenting on the many translations of Dickens that appeared from 1838 onwards. Nielsen also shows that many today less read authors like Bulwer and Marryat were translated massively into Danish, in the case of Bulwer, later Bulwer-Lytton, with no less than 69 volumes of his collected works published in Danish from 1833 to 1865 (Nielsen 2003: 367). It is noteworthy that one of the now most famous 19th century authors, Jane Austen, was not translated into Danish until 1855-56 (Mortensen 2006), but still so many translations from English had been undertaken by 1850 that Nielsen estimates English translations to be "almost as common as from German and French" (Nielsen 2003: 370).

Among poets Lord Byron is by far the most influential English poet from the first half of the 19th century, and contemporary Danish poets like Frederik Paludan-Müller (1809-76) were much inspired by Byron's style, not least in his main work *Adam Homo* (1842).[13] Furthermore, in 1845 the Icelander Grimur Thorgrimsson Thomsen (1820-96) published a Danish master thesis from Copenhagen, *Om Lord Byron* [On Lord Byron] (Nielsen 2003: 365). It is thus natural that Byron was a safe selection for a writer wanting to introduce a series of English writers to a Danish audience in 1853. This writer was Louise Westergaard, and although the series ended up never being published, except for a first volume on Chaucer, we have her plan for the proposed series in that first volume. In a general preface, given the now old-fashioned name "Fortale", the

---

13 Marianne Zibrandtsen does not mention Byron's influence in her otherwise fine portrait in *Den Store Danske Encyklopædi* (Lund, gen. ed., 1999), but actually Paludan-Müller uses Byronic *ottova rima* in *Adam Homo*.

idea of the series is introduced, illustrating a canon of English poets as Westergaard saw it:

> *I sin Heelhed vil Bogen komme til at bestaa af 2 Dele, hvoraf 1ste Deel vil indbefatte 6 Hefter*) indeholdende* [In its entirety the book will consist of two volumes, of which the first volume will include 6 parts, containing]: *Chaucer, Spenser, Shakspeare, Milton, Young, Thomson, Gray, Goldsmith, Beattie, Cowper. 2den Deel: Wordsworth, Coleridge, Byron, Shelly, Moore, Tennyson.*
> *) *Kjöberen af 1ste Hefte har ingen Forpligtelse til at tage de andre Hefter* [The buyer of the first part is under no obligation to buy the other parts] (Westergaard 1853: 4. The italics and note are Westergaard's).

As it appears from this preface Chaucer is here published in a context of an already fixed old canon alongside Spenser, Shakespeare and Milton. Then, remarkably, the great neoclassical poets Dryden, Pope and Swift are passed by, and replaced with authors almost forgotten today, such as Edward Young (1683-1765) and James Thomson (1700-48). Thomas Gray (1716-71) is of course still remembered for his "Elegy Written in a Country Churchyard", if not much else, but Oliver Goldsmith (?1730-74), James Beattie (1735-1803) and William Cowper (1731-1800), are rarely taught or read today, whereas Beattie's popularity with *The Minstrel* (1771), had reached Denmark with an imprint in 1815 by Bonnier, who according to Jørgen Erik Nielsen published it in a planned series on British Poets, abandoned after the first volume, again quite possibly because of the anti-English climate after the 1807 terror-like bombardment of Copenhagen and the capturing of the Danish navy (Nielsen 1977: 74-75). Then follow four of the six now canonised romantics, with Walter Scott and Keats missing, and the Irish poet Thomas Moore (1779-1852), who according to Nielsen (Nielsen 1977: 420-3) was one of the most popular poets in Denmark, mainly because of his association with Byron. Finally, and also hardly surprising, Tennyson is included.

The publishers and Louise Westergaard have in other words chosen to introduce a series of 15 English poets and a single Irishman, with Chaucer in the position as the first in the sequence, or as Dryden has it, the father of English literature (Dryden 1697/1700, "Preface" in Kinsley, ed., 1958). What is noteworthy in the Danish context is that this is the first publication that puts Chaucer in such a distinguished company, and considering the few contemporary Danish references to Chaucer to be located up to 1853, Westergaard's effort can be characterised as a pioneer mission, well ahead of her time. It is of course a great pity that the series was abandoned after the first volume for reasons unknown to me, but Westergaard drew on her research later in one of her educational books, *Udvalg af engelske Forfattere, en Læsebog for Skolens Højere Klasser*. [A selection of English authors, a reader for secondary school education] (Westergaard 1867). Here we find most of the authors in the planned series, although not Chaucer. However, both Swift and Pope as well as several others have been added.

Westergaard's life and works

With the mention of Westergaard's works we have already introduced the focus in this section, but more should be added. In *Dansk Kvindebiografisk Leksikon* [Danish encyclopedia of women's biographies] and also briefly in *Lærerindeuddannelse: Lokalsamfundenes kamp om seminariedriften* [Education of female teachers: the struggle in local communities about the running of teacher training colleges] Adda Hilden has portrayed Louise Westergaard (Hilden 2003, Hilden and Nørr 1993). I have drawn on these portraits but also myself undertaken further research into the life and works of this pioneer within education in modern foreign languages in Denmark. Charlotte Louise Westergaard was the daughter of district surgeon Jens Anton Westergaard (1791-1829) and Johanne Wilhelmine Louise Bentzen (1799-1856). Her father died when she was three, but she was educated well enough to become a teacher in Kalundborg at 17 and continue her education in Copenhagen at 19, in 1848. She studied with author and pedagogue Athalia Schwartz and at Annestine Beyers Højere Dannelsesanstalt for Damer [Annestine Beyer's higher education institute for ladies]. She and her later well known classmate Natalie Zahle both passed as "institutbestyrere" [school managers] in 1851. Her career involved several teaching jobs until 1858, when she took over as manager of "M. Gøtzsches højere pigeskole", a school for girls' higher education. After a couple of years this private school developed a strong profile in modern languages, history and natural sciences. Besides being very active in her teaching of Danish, English and French language and culture, Westergaard also made her mark in fighting for women's rights (Hilden 2003).

Westergaard's publications are available in The Royal Danish Library, even though a couple of them, including the booklet on Chaucer, do not have her name on the cover.[14] In 1851 she published *Veileder for de Besøgende i Thorvaldsens Museum* [A Guide to visitors to Thorvaldsen's Museum], which is a very thorough catalogue of all the works of the museum. The next year followed a book that will be given a little more attention below, i.e. the children's book *Verdensmarkedet* [The world market], which describes the industrial exhibition in London in 1851, based on Westergaard's personal visit and some unnamed sources. In 1852 she handed in a so-called "prisopgave" [prize essay, a tradition still carried on at the University of Copenhagen] with the title *Den franske Tragedies national-poetiske Charakteer, og Grunden til den ringeagtende Bedømmelse, som den til en Tid har været underkastet* [The national poetic character of the French tragedy, and the reason for the disregard it has been met with for a while]. Westergaard's short treatise was accepted, probably as the first by a woman at the university (Hilden 2003). The prize essay, which was published in 1853, is marked by its author's great engagement with her subject, and she is not afraid to be highly subjective in her estimates. Discussing mainly the work of French and German critics on modern French, Westergaard calls for "et forløsende Geni" [a redeeming genius] in contemporary French drama and holds up what she considers inferior contemporary French drama against her personal favourites Corneille, Racine, Voltaire and Molière, favourites despite Westergaard's reservations that they suffer from certain "Vildfarelser" [delusions] (Westergaard 1853b: 136-7).

Besides the educational books also mentioned, Westergaard published a grammar book and undertook several translations from English. All in all she was an energetic and competent transmitter of foreign cultures into Danish. I will now turn to one of the clearest examples of this, *Verdensmarkedet,* which I use here as a link to my main subject, her Chaucer booklet. I have elsewhere written more substantially about it

---

14 I thank research librarian Jan Rittmeyer, who first helped me identify Louise Westergaard as the author of the Chaucer booklet. Westergaard's name has been entered in hand-writing in the old Royal Library catalogue.

in Danish (Klitgård in Sejten, ed., forthcoming), but will restrict myself here to a few characteristic points of Westergaard's attitude, which can also throw light on her Chaucer booklet.

The world exhibition was the first of its kinds and took place in Hyde Park, London, in 1851, in Joseph Paxton's famous building, later known as the Crystal Palace. After the exhibition the building was moved to Sydenham, where it burned down in 1931. Among the six million visitors during the six months of the exhibition we find Louise Westergaard.[15] *Verdensmarkedet: eller Beskrivelse for Børn over den store Industriudstilling i London 1851* [The world market: or description for children about the great industrial exhibition in London 1851] is an 84 pages' illustrated presentation of Westergaard's personal impressions from the visits to the exhibitions of various participating countries, which she combines with information about these countries, edited for children and based on sources that she does not state. Westergaard has clearly used encyclopediae and other handbooks, but her personal engagement and enthusiastic rendering of her experience is striking. The illustrations are colourful and appealing, not least an idealized drawing of well-dressed Englishmen visiting the exhibition, by Andr. Hansen (Westergaard 1852: i). Westergaard views the exhibition as a sound competition between nations, and frequently challenges children's imagination by mentioning exotic features like a Swiss table "forfærdiget af 38.000 Stykker Træ af 28 forskellige Farver, der saae ud som Mosaik" [made out of 38,000 pieces of wood in 28 different colours, looking like a mosaic] (3). She also talks very directly to the young reader in addresses such as "Det vilde vist more Dig meget at see det, der var sendt fra Indien" [I'm sure you would find it funny to see what was sent from India] (4). This will probably have engaged many young readers, although some of them may well have found the tone patronising.

Westergaard's presentation of various national identities is marked by the stereotypes about other nations so characteristic of the time and found in many sources, in Denmark and elsewhere (Klitgård in Sejten, ed., forthcoming). The Turk is beautiful and gentle, unless he loses his temper, in which case he becomes furious (8), the Dutch are "vindskibelige og rene" [enterprising and clean] (27), Italy full of "Lazzaroni..., Dagdrivere, der

---

15 The information about the world exhibition is based mainly on Knud J.V. Jespersen's article in *Den Store Danske Encyklopædi* (Jespersen 2001).

aldrig bryde sig om at arbeide mere end netop nødvendigt" [loafers who do not like to work more than is just necessary] (22), whereas Spaniards apparently combine some of these traits in a negative way, since they are characterised as "hverken flittige eller reenlige" [neither industrious nor clean], although they are "stolte" and "gjæstfrie" [proud and hospitable] (17). The portrait of the Germans is actually surprisingly positive, mentioning their great poets, composers and painters, but Westergaard also says "jeg er bange for, Du holder ikke af dem" [I'm afraid you don't like them very much] (25). This is a very direct reflection of the German-Danish wars over Schleswig-Holstein already mentioned, which Westergaard refers to by the term "Uret" [injustice]. The tone is that of a mother explaining the world's conflicts to her children in a gentle way.

After a rather skeptical discussion of the USA, including a remark about the rather bad manners of even rich Americans (46), Westergaard turns to England, with 8 pages by far the longest description in the book. It is also the most interesting, since much of it is based on Westergaard's personal experience rather than stereotypes found in books.Westergaard writes with enthusiasm about a visit to the Whispering Gallery in St. Paul's cathedral and with as much engagement about the transport system in London, including the Greenwich line, which had opened in 1846 (65-6, Lemberg 1998). Interestingly she compares some of the streets in London with central Copenhagen locations like Bredgade and Østergade (65), thus making her descriptions more familiar to her young readers. Generally a very positive image of England, although she mentions the London fog and a "forfærdelig Støi" [terrible noise] that is characteristic of the Manchester factories (61).

Whereas France also gets good press, not surprisingly on the background of Westergaard's work on the French tragedy, the most praise is reserved for Denmark and its small contribution to the exhibition, such as "Randers-handsker" and "stearinlys" [gloves from Randers and candles] (73). She deeply regrets the absence of a Thorvaldsens statue, which "vilde … have været det Skjønneste på den hele Udstilling [would have been the most beautiful item in the whole exhibition]" (72). Again her own work on Thorvaldsen should be kept in mind. The Denmark portrait is apart from this very much focused on Copenhagen, to a degree which suggests that Westergaard loved the city more than the country-side.

The short book ends with an invocation of God and a rather pompous comparison of the World Exhibition to the Tower of Babel, a bridge between peoples to end all wars (80-84). We are left with the impression of a somewhat naïvely positive voice, but on the other hand, despite the use of stereotypes, Westergaard has very succesfully and pedagogically enlightened her young readers about the nations of the world. She has also expressed herself in line with the nationalist feelings of her time, although the part about Denmark is overly focused on Copenhagen. The first-hand descriptions from London stand out as a remarkable presentation of a city and a culture which was so rarely visited by Danes in the mid-19th century. It is the gentle, pedagogical voice and the enthusiasm for everything English which is also found in Westergaard's Chaucer booklet published two years after the exhibition. A qualified guess would be that she got hold of her Chaucer material, as well as books by other British authors, during her visit.

Westergaard's Chaucer booklet

When Westergaard visited London in 1851 one of the new publications on the book market was Thomas Wright's edition of the collected works of Chaucer. It appeared in the years 1847-51 as a publication from the Percy Society, a society named after the great manuscript collector and publisher Thomas Percy (1729-1811), who with his collections of English and Scottish folk ballads can well be compared with the later Danish folklorists Tang Kristensen and Svend Grundtvig considered above. Wright's base text was a manuscript from the British Museum, Harley 7334, a text which would today not be selected as base text, but importantly it was edited according to the so-called "best text" principle, which has been the principle behind later editions. It means that the base text is supplemented with the most important variants from other manuscripts, which according to the editor's qualified judgement replace variants of the base text. Wright's edition is the first great, modern Chaucer edition, and whereas in 1851 it may not have been seen as a sensation, it was at least the first new edition since the 4th edition of Thomas Tyrwhitt's Chaucer from 1830, which only comprised *The Canterbury Tales,* and C.C. Clarke's popularised text edition *The Riches of Chaucer* from 1835 (Wright, ed., 1851, Tyrwhitt, ed., 1830, Clarke, ed., 1835).

Westergaard's booklet on Chaucer contains 52 pages, and the front page has "Engelske Digtere" [English Poets] as its main title, adding in subheadings that this is the "første Hefte" [first part] on "Chaucer". Approximately 18 of the 52 pages contain text by Chaucer in Middle English in modern English spelling and with Danish glosses and explanatory notes. The two main exctracts are from *The Clerk's Tale* and *The Knight's Tale*. I have compared Westergaard's Chaucer text with Wright's, Tyrwhitt's and Clarke's editions, and my conclusion is that Westergaard has edited her own Chaucer text and not copied any of the most likely sources from her own time directly. She appears to have used Clarke as her main source, but there are variants and readings which are borrowed from elsewhere, and generally Westergaard has been careful to modernize the spelling and come up with a reader-friendly text. Her work has been done so efficiently that it would be very difficult to distinguish between her textual sources, although she has most probably used the three editions mentioned.

Whereas Westergaard does not refer to any of the editions she has copied and transformed into her own text, she does include footnotes to two of the secondary sources she has used for the introductory part on Chaucer's life and works. The first of these is Thomas Warton's *History of English Poetry* (Warton 1774-81), whereas the second note only states the title *Introductory Discourse to [the] Canterbury Tales*. I have identified this as Tyrwhitt's introduction to his edition from 1775-8, probably the imprint from 1830. In her preface Westergaard mentions that she has used "de bedste Kilder" [the best of sources], but apart from Warton and Tyrwhitt she does not mention which. Westergaard states further in her preface that the volume is not "en videnskabelig-critisk Undersøgelse" [a scholarly-critical investigation] and goes on to say about her principles and method:

> Det Sprog, hvori Chaucer skrev, vilde blive for trættende, om ikke alt for vanskeligt for derigjennem ret at opfatte Digteren for de Læsere, dette Arbeide nærmest er bestemt for, hvilket vil ses af den ene Pröve, jeg i Slutningen af dette Hefte har givet derpaa i "Den gode Landsbypræst." Jeg har heller ikke anset det rigtigt at give Pröver i den moderne poetiske Omskrivning, som man har anvendt for at gjöre denne store Digter populair; thi derved

er en Deel af Chaucers originale Skrivemaade naturligviis gaaet tabt. Men jeg har foretrukket at beholde den oprindelige Form med en mere moderne Stavemaade, hvor Udtalen, der ikke er den nuværende, er angivet med Accenter. På grund af Sprogets Vanskelighed, har jeg paa Dansk kortelig angivet Indholdet af de Fortællinger, jeg har udvalgt, og kun ladet Digteren selv tale saameget, som er nødvendigt for at give Læseren et klart Billede af ham [The language that Chaucer wrote would be too tiring, if not too difficult, to make it possible to understand the poet for the readers that this work is intended for, which can be seen from the single example I have included at the end of the booklet from "The Good Parson." I have also not found it right to give examples of the modern poetic rewriting that has been used for making this great poet popular; because through this part of Chaucer's original way of writing has been lost. But I have preferred to retain the original form with a more modern spelling, where the pronunciation, which is not the present one, has been indicated with accents. Because of the difficulty of the language I have briefly indicated the content of the tales I have chosen and only let the poet speak as much as it is necessary to give the reader a clear picture of him]. (Westergaard 1853: 4)

Westergaard earns respect by not choosing to represent and translate rewritten popularised versions such as Dryden's and Pope's, as did her predecessor as Chaucer translator in Denmark T.C. Bruun, who as we saw in chapter 3 chose Pope's, not Chaucer's own *Wife of Bath's Prologue*. Westergaard clearly expresses a wish for the real thing. At the same time it is understandable that she makes some communicative choices in presenting Chaucer in a booklet format for a broad audience. The ambition is as she states to present her subject to the common reader in a form that does not make Chaucer unnecessarily difficult, while making sure not to violate the work of the great poet. It is, however, remarkable that Westergaard stresses the importance of "Indholdet af de Fortællinger, jeg har udvalgt" [the content of the tales I have chosen], which means the importance of her own summaries of Chaucer, whereas she only wants Chaucer to speak himself "saameget, som er nödvendigt for at give Læseren et klart billede af ham" [as much as it is necessary to give the reader a clear picture of him]. In other words the main purpose appears to be that the reader is made familiar with the content of the tales, whereas the poet's own voice falls in the background. As it will appear in the analysis below, this is fortunately not quite the result of Westergaard's editing process.

From a modern academic point of view the booklet's 10 pages about Chaucer's life and works are poorly documented, and Westergaard is certainly right in stating that this is not a scholarly-critical investigation. It is more like a condensed and further popularised version of Warton's and Tyrwhitt's introductions. In this connection it is unfortunate that her main source, Warton, is very unreliable and has not read Chaucer properly or in full. Thus in one of her few direct references to Warton, Westergaard cites him for the grossly mistaken belief that Chaucer's *Troilus & Criseyde* "oprindelig var bestemt til at synges til Harpen" [was originally intended to be sung to the accompaniment of the harp] (Westergaard 1853: 8), and the poem is further said to be a youthful composition full of errors. As anyone who has actually read Chaucer's now fully recognised masterpiece will know, it would be quite impossible to let this complicated composition be accompanied by a musical instrument, and the comment about errors in the poet's youth are far-fetched.

There are quite a number of further mistakes in this part, such as the information that Chaucer was born in 1328, that he met Petrarca in Genua in 1372, and that at the end of the 1380s he was imprisoned in the Tower. We know now that Chaucer was born in 1340 or 1343, that he most likely never met Petrarca, nor his more immediate inspiration Boccaccio, and that he made a settlement to pay 10 pounds in a court case about abducting a woman. With patrons such as John of Gaunt he was rarely in financial trouble, as indicated by Westergaard. The false images about Chaucer and his works will be the topic of several other parts of this study, so at this point I will only remark that also Westergaard has fallen into a well-known trap when uncritically taking over undocumented and erroneous points from her sources. These myths about Chaucer live on well into the 20th and even 21st centuries.[16]

---

16 The points quoted here are now common knowledge among Chaucerians, and can be found in several Chaucer biographies. The best life biography is still to my mind Derek Pearsall's *The Life of Geoffrey Chaucer* (Pearsall 1992).

Westergaard's remarks in the preface about "det Sprog, hvori Chaucer skrev, vilde blive for trættende," [The language that Chaucer wrote would be too tiring] is followed by a more general estimate in the introduction, where she claims that "Tidsalderens Sprog var temmelig plumpt i enkelte Udtryk" [the language of the age was rather coarse in certain expressions], which means that also in Chaucer's writing we can "træffe Steder, der paa Grund af deres ligefremhed ikke tiltale de mere Forfinede" [find places that because of their plainness do not appeal to more sophisticated people] (12). This last point is certainly true, also from a modern point of view, but the general estimate of Middle English and of Chaucer in particular is marked by a lack of knowledge about the linguistic premises of medieval poetry. The misleading adjective "plump" [coarse] is in fact the exact same that Mogens Boisen uses in the introduction to his Chaucer translation 100 years later, and as we shall see in many other examples this myth about primitive and coarse medieval poetry is generally a hard-lived one in the Danish Chaucer reception. Unfortunately the myth is just as predominant in the modern English Chaucer reception.[17]

On page 15 Westergaard finishes her introduction and begins her textual treatment of *The Canterbury Tales*, which as already indicated is a mixture of plot summaries, descriptive passages and some passages with Westergaard's own edited Chaucer text, glossed mainly in footnotes. The *General Prologue* is mainly covered by summary, but in several places these come very close to the character descriptions in the original text. One example is the description of the Knight, who is described by Westergaard as follows:

> Den fornemste var en værdig Ridder (Knight), der fra sin Ungdom af havde helliget sig til al ridderlig Daad, og elskede Sandhed og Ære, Oprigtighed og Frihed. Han havde med Hæder tjent i sin Konges Krige mod Hedninger, Russer og Tyrker... [The noblest of them was a worthy Knight, who from his youth had devoted himself to chivalry and loved truth and

---

17 Boisen will be further discussed in chapter 9. Some good examples of outrageous treatment of Chaucer's works in an English context are gathered in Steve Ellis's study *Chaucer at Large* (Ellis 2000).

honour, candour and freedom. He had with honour served in his king's wars against heathens, Russians and Turks...] (15)

In Chaucer's text the first lines of the portrait go like this:

A Knyght ther was, and that a worthy man, /That fro the tyme that he first bigan/To riden out, he loved chivalrie,/Trouthe and honour, fredom and curtesie.
(Benson, gen. ed., 1987/2008: 43-6)[18]

Here Westergaard starts with a somewhat free prose translation, where "fra sin Ungdom" [from his youth] covers the longer and more specific "fro the tyme that he first bigan/To riden out" quite well. She then moves into summary, as "Hedninger, Russer og Tyrker" [heathens, Russians and Turks] are mentioned in Chaucer's portrait, but not in that sequence and mixed with a lot more details about the places the Knight has visited in his military career. Also the remainder of the description of the Knight, and of several other pilgrims is a slightly changed translation of Chaucer's original text with a few markers of summary. Occasionally the idea of a summary is spoiled for the reader as Westergaard all of a sudden mixes the narrative voice of the prologue with her own voice. This is the case when it says about the Monk, "Jeg lagde mærke til at hans Ærmer vare kantede med det fineste graae Peltsværk" [I noticed that his sleeves were edged with the finest fur] (18). A simple explanation would be that Westergaard has been working too fast, but she may also have made a rather awkward attempt to communicate with her reader more directly, as we saw in examples from her children's book on the world exhibition.

The Knight and the Clerk, whose tales as mentioned are the two selected focal points in Westergaard's booklet, are also selected for thorough treatment in the portraits from *The General Prologue*, whereas she treats

---

18 In this chapter, where Westergaard has clearly consulted several editions, it has not been possible to make a sensible decision about which old edition to quote from, and I consequently use the modern standard edition, *The Riverside Chaucer* (Benson, gen. ed.: 1987/2008).

most other pilgrim portraits fairly quickly. Many portraits are strongly abbreviated, and at the end of her six pages of summary as translation Westergaard simply decides to mention eight pilgrims that she has not dealt with, saying that they and other pilgrims were present too. This is the point where she chooses to offer her first bit of commentary on what turns out to be her favourite tale, *The Clerk's Tale*.

With its 17 pages *The Clerk's Tale* makes up about a third of the booklet. The tale is well known in European literature and can be found in versions both by Boccaccio and Petrarca, but even though Chaucer has been inspired mostly by the latter of the two poets, his narrative voice is distinctly more engaged and directly involved in this gruesome tale than either of the Italian versions. Westergaard starts by outlining the starting point of the tale, that an "adelig Herre (Marquis)" [noble gentleman (Marquis)] in Lombardy, whom she later in the tale refers to as "Greven" [the count], wants to marry according to the wishes of his people, and ends up marrying the virtuous Griselda, even though she is from a poor background (20-22). After two pages of plot summary Westergaard prints Chaucer's own text in extracts of one to eleven stanzas, each consisting of seven lines. These are connected with further summaries and especially towards the end with Westergaard's own commentary. The extracts have been selected with a preference for the scenes of high pathos, where Walther the Marquis tests his wife's patience over a period of several years. First he humiliates her by taking away her fine clothes and letting her wear her poor clothes again. Then he lets a man abduct first her (and his own) daughter, then her son, and finally he lets her be a servant at his wedding with a new wife. This is the point where he reveals that he has wanted to test her all this time, and she is reunited with her husband and children in great celebration.

It goes without saying that a fighter for women's rights like Westergaard will have been strongly provoked by this tale, which was also in the Middle Ages under debate, even though it is possible to read it as an allegorical reminder about the humility of human beings in relation to the ways of the Lord, past our understanding. This puritan Christian interpretation of the tale is, however, not the one promoted by Chaucer's sensitive narrative voice, which invites understanding and compassion with Griselda and skepticism towards Walther. It is this compassion which clearly also takes hold of Westergaard, who starts questioning

Walther's "besynderlig[e] Attraa efter at friste sin Hustru og sætte hendes Lydighed på Prøve. Gud ved hvorfor?" [strange desire to tempt his wife and put her obedience to the test. God knows why?] (26). Towards the end of the tale Westergaard extracts the moral for the reader, first by loyally explaining the allegorical point, but then by launching a remarkable attack on the representation of love and marriage in the tale:

> Chaucer siger selv, at denne Historie er ikke bleven fortalt for at enhver Hustru skulde efterfölge Griseldis i Ydmyghed, men for at Hver i sin Stilling "Shoulde be constant in adversity/ As was Grisilde." Griseldis er fremstillet som et Sindbillede på Kjærligheden, der taaler Alt og fordrager Alt, og jo flere Fornærmelser, der bydes hende, jo mere Ondt hun maa taale, desmere faaer hun Lejlighed til at udfolde sit Væsen, der er lutter Kjærlighed. Digteren mener at have motiveret hendes ydmyge Underkastelse ved at sætte hende i det Forhold til sin Ægtefælle, at han fornemmelig er hendes Herre, hvem hun har lovet Lydighed frem for Alt. Vi mene dog, at Griseldis Historie er en misforstaaet Opfattelse af Kjærligheden; thi hendes Lydighed mod ham bringer alle andre menneskelige Fölelser til at forstumme, ja endogsaa Kjærligheden til hendes Börn. [Chaucer himself says that this story has not been told so that every Wife should follow Griseldis in humility, but that everyone in his or her own position "Should be constant in adversity/as was Grisilde". Griseldis is portrayed as an emblem of love, which endureth all and beareth all, and the more insults that are shown her, the more evil she must endure, the more she is enabled to unfold her nature, which is pure love. The poet believes to have motivated her humble submission by putting her in a relation to her spouse where he is mainly her master, to whom she has promised obedience. We believe, however, that Griseldis's Story is a misunderstood perception of love; for her obedience towards him brings all other human emotions to silence, even the love of her children.]
> (37-8)

This, I believe, is a wonderful, engaged comment, even though Westergaard apparently has not entirely understood the narrator position that

Chaucer adapts in *The Clerk's Tale*.[19] It is as if she gets so angry with the tale that also Chaucer's motives are challenged. Westergaard is not the only reader to have responded like this, but she might well be the first Danish reader to voice an indignant protest on behalf of the female sex about Griselda's cruel suppression.

Westergaard's representation of *The Knight's Tale* is shorter, but with eight pages still substantial. We get an indication of Westergaard's personal preferences when she introduces it by calling the tale "meget interessant og rig på ophøjede og pathetiske Steder" [very interesting and full of solemn and pathetic passages] (38). Most likely her other main choice, *The Clerk's Tale*, was made for the same reason. The focus on solemn and pathetic elements also marks Westergaard's summary and especially her choice of a passage for quotation, the only long one included. This is the *visio* of Arcite when he goes to visit the temple of Mars to pray for victory, and Westergaard includes most of the passage, more specifically lines 1970-2016 and 2041-2048 (Benson, gen. ed.: I 1970-2016 and 2041-2048 and Westergaard: 42-4). This passage will be further considered in chapter 9, where I analyse Børge Johansen's translation of it, but let me say here that it is understandable that it has also appealed to Westergaard. It is so much of a timeless horror vision that I know of no other poetic text as frightening as this.

After a short quotation of Theseus pronouncing that "Arcite of Thebes shall have Emily,/That by his fortune hath her fair ywon" (Westergaard: 45, cp. Benson, gen. ed.: I 2659-60), Westergaard inserts a personal comment, like in *The Clerk's Tale*. Here she says that "Der hæver sig et Jubelskrig fra Folket, der altid smigrer de Lykkelige" [An outburst of joy is heard from the people, who always flatter the fortunate ones] (45). Besides involvement this again shows the school teacher Westergaard not missing a chance to voice a general didactic point indicating her experience in life, much as the voice telling children what people are really like in her book on the world exhibition. The comments in the Chaucer

---

19 In my book *Chaucer's Narrative Voice in the Knight's Tale* (Klitgård 1995) and in a series of articles including the recent "The Encoding of Subjectivity in Chaucer's *The Wife of Bath's Tale* and *The Pardoner's Tale*" (Klitgård 2011), I have analysed narrative voice, performativity and subjectivity in Chaucer's narrative poetry. It is on purpose that I talk about Chaucer's rather than the Clerk's narrative voice.

booklet are fewer, but for that reason the more noteworthy when they occur.

The remaining six pages of the booklet include a variety of tale summaries with quotations, the only substantial ones from *The Merchant's Tale*, which Westergaard notes has also been "moderniseret ved en elegant omskrivning af Pope" [modernised in an elegant rewriting by Pope]. She mentions May's unfaithfulness, and she calls the tale humorous and one of the comic tales, but she only quotes from the opening section on January's marriage considerations, and she does not as much as mention any of the fabliaux. For someone who prefers something solemn and pathetic this is probably a wise decision, but nevertheless it is a remarkable avoidance strategy. Despite the recent legal gains in book censorship, fabliaux like *The Summoner's Tale, The Friar's Tale, The Reeve's Tale* and *The Miller's Tale* will probably have been too coarse for both Westergaard and her readers, but not to mention that they are part of *The Canterbury Tales* at all is to take the matter very far.

One tale that perhaps surprisingly is treated over nearly two pages is *The Squire's Tale* (46-7), which is incomplete and a fairly conventional romance that is relatively rarely praised or treated in Chaucer criticism. Westergaard has clearly been captured by the dramatic entry of the Knight in the King of Tartarye's hall, which she quotes from (Benson, gen. ed., V 80-88). She then proceeds with a short and fairly neutral summary, leaving a good impression of the tale's Eastern enchantment.

The Prioress' Tale is mentioned only in passing, as are Chaucer's own tales in the pilgrim contest, *Sir Thopas* and *Melibee*. The last textual extract in the booklet is contrary to this quite long, although Westergaard does not herself comment on it. This is the portrait of the Parson from *The General Prologue*, 477-528. Westergaard misses out a few lines, but apart from that the lines are reprinted without modernisations or changes from her source, or so she claims in her preface (Westergaard 1853; 50-1 and 4). I cannot with any certainty establish whether her claim is true, because I have not been able to locate an edition with exactly the spellings she uses. I have a strong feeling that changes have been made also here, and the fact that some lines are missing means that *some* changes have been made. Whether or not the text should be seen as Westergaard's attempt to reproduce the "real" Chaucer, it is still important that she chooses the Parson to end her presentation of *The Canterbury Tales*, just as Chaucer chose *The Parson's Tale* to be the last of his tales. For both Westergaard and Chaucer such a devoutly Christian ending to match all the escapades of many other tales will have been a worthy conclusion.

Chapter conclusion

As we have seen in this chapter, Westergaard's publications appear in a strongly national liberal age, where the new nationalism also includes interest in the Danish roots back to the Middle Ages, such as the popular ballads. Westergaard is very much part of the general feeling in the country after the introduction of parliamentary democracy and the wars over Schleswig-Holstein, but she is also attracted by other new developments, such as the first waves of a women's rights movement. Much of her pedagogical writing appears to have been directly intended for the teaching she undertook and the school she was running, all mainly for girls. Whether writing for children, young people or adults, she enters into an engaged educational position, showing great communicative skills. In my analysis of both *Verdensmarkedet* and *Engelske digtere: Chaucer* I have detected numerous errors, some of them serious, and proper documentation as well as stringency leave much to be desired. However, Westergaard's enthusiasm, her after all fine publications, and her pioneer work generally in the field of English studies should be applauded as a very important effort in Danish educational and cultural history.

Compared to Bruun, Westergaard's Chaucer gets a somewhat fairer deal in that much is loyally reprinted or fairly accurately represented, and because a genuine effort is made to awaken the reader's appetite for an English author hardly known to a Danish audience. However, also Westergaard allows herself the liberty both to be extremely selective in her use of Chaucer's text and to mix up summary and translation without telling her reader, producing a final blend with her own commentary.

Westergaard's and Bruun's publications are both interesting as examples of culturally and historically bound translation. Both are as translators principally concerned with their readers rather than the texts they translate, and ornament as well as a personal touch is obviously permitted. In different ways they both represent text transformation more than translation in a modern sense.

CHAPTER 5

MØLLER, BIERFREUND AND JESPERSEN. THE PERIOD 1865-1900

Wessel's drama translation *Feen Ursel*, Bruun's translation of Pope's *The Wife of Bath Her Prologue* and Louise Westergaard's booklet *Chaucer* remain the only versions of Chaucer in print in Denmark throughout the 19th century, except for a few pieces by Niels Møller in his poetry collection *Efterår* [Autumn] from 1888 and a few further translations by Møller in Otto Jespersen's study of Chaucer from 1893, *Chaucers liv og digtning* [Chaucer's life and poetry], (Møller 1988, Jespersen 1893). Jespersen's study is substantial with its 63 pages, but it is not the first academic study of Chaucer in Denmark. The year before Jespersen Theodor Bierfreund includes a chapter of 27 pages on Chaucer's life and times in his *Kulturbærere* [Carriers of culture] alongside portraits of Dante, Petrarch and Boccaccio, with also a consideration of the French troubadour tradition and Chaucer's English contemporaries (Bierfreund 1892: 171-207). Bierfreund also includes a short chapter on Chaucer's *Knight's Tale* in his doctoral thesis *Palemon and Arcite* from 1891, which is mainly on Shakespeare's play (Bierfreund 1891: 17-25).

There is one earlier general presentation of Chaucer made known to a Danish audience in the period, first written around the time of Westergaard's booklet, but translated more than 20 years later. This is a portrait of Chaucer that appears in a literary history by the German professor of History and Literature in Zürich Johannes Scherr (1817-86) and first published as *Geschichte der englischen Literatur* in 1854. The Danish translation, including some revisions, was undertaken by author and literary historian Frederik Winkel Horn (1845-98) and published in 1876 as *Almindelig Literaturhistorie: En Haandbog* [General literary history: A Handbook] (Kaalund in *Dansk Biografisk Leksikon*, Scherr, transl. Horn 1854/1876 and anonymous at http://en.wikipedia.org/wiki/Johannes_Scherr). With four pages on Chaucer and his time this is not as substantial as Westergaard's booklet, and I will discuss it here only in passing, in Horn's translation. It is of course interesting that Scherr's literary history is made available for a Danish audience, and Horn's translation suggests that the market was now ready for literary histories of the kind that became popular throughout the 20th century. However, the quality of Scherr's work leaves much room for improvement and his Chaucer portrait should be read *cum grano salis*, i.e. with the same pinch of salt that Scherr advocates for comparing Chaucer with Homer as Craik did (Scherr 1854/76: 13). Scherr's position is drawn up most clearly when he says that "Chaucer er ikke saa meget original som eftlignende Digter, og hans Fortjeneste beror mere paa et teknisk end paa et skabende Element" [Chaucer is not as much an original as an imitating poet, and his merits are based more on a technical than on a creative element] (13). Scherr goes on to debunk Chaucer's *Roman de la Rose* as a mere translation "ligefrem kun en oversættelse" [really only a translation] (14), which of course leaves little space for recognition of Chaucer's artistic recreation of Lorris' and de Meun's fine poem. Worse is Scherr's assessment of *Troilus and Cressida* (which we now more correctly refer to as *Troilus and Criseyde*) and also of *The House of Fame* and *The Legend of Good Women* as "mer eller mindre Efterligninger af de Gamle og Italienerne" [more or less imitations of the Old ones and the Italians] (14). Scherr has probably not read these works at all. His information about Chaucer's life is of a slightly higher quality than Westergaard's, using mainly German philologists as sources, but details such as Chaucer being a Wycliff follower are of course dubious guesswork characteristic also of some of the sources (13).[20]

Scherr's only really laudable contribution to the promotion of Chaucer in Denmark becomes his engaged presentation of *The Canterbury Tales*, which also in Horn's translation bears witness to personal reading. There is a page or so introducing the pilgrims and the frame story, with a special emphasis on the Prioress, the Monk and somewhat unusually the Yeoman, whose portraits are partly quoted in original Middle English in footnotes. In effect Scherr merely sums up characteristic details from the

---

20 Scherr acknowledges Müller and Fiedler as sources from the 1840s, but since the second edition of his literary history did not appear until 1883, it must be the translator and editor Horn who has added later sources by Pauli, Hertzberg and Ten Brink (13, note).

portraits in *The General Prologue*, but these details can certainly be used as appetizers for an audience considering reading the *Tales* themselves. Details include the strength and warm blood of the Wife of Bath, the forked beard of the Merchant, and the Pardoner trying to sell a part of the Holy Virgin's veil (16). Finally it is refreshing that Scherr openly admits to preferring the humorous and "plumpt Burleske" [bluntly burlesque] elements in several of the tales. Remarkably he criticizes the "flove Nyromantikere" [insipid New Romanticists] for spoiling all the fun by making the bawdy characters into a kind of "Marcipandukker" [Marzipan dolls] (16). As the present study will show, Scherr is certainly right in claiming that a certain kind of prudishness and New Romanticism has been a characteristic part of Chaucer reception, and I will end my discussion of his short Chaucer text by praising him for insight and wisdom that is more characteristic of a far later time than his own.

In this chapter I will now turn to the context of the Danish translations and critical reception of Chaucer by considering his status compared to the general reception of English literature in Denmark in the 1890s and the period leading up to this decade. Secondly I will turn to Bierfreund's and Jespersen's works on Chaucer, discussing also Møller's translations. It should be noted that Møller's later work on Chaucer will be explored more substantially in chapter 7 (Møller 1928), whereas this chapter closes my discussion of Chaucer in Denmark in the 19th century.

Chaucer and English in Denmark ca.1865-1900

One of our best sources for the reception and translation of English literature in Denmark in this period is a long article by Brian W. Downs in *The Modern Language Review* from 1948, "Anglo-Danish Literary Relations 1867-1900: The Fortunes of English Literature in Denmark" (Downs 1948). This is one of two works originally written by Downs in the late 1940s on Anglo-Scandinavian relations in the period, the other being on Norwegian reception of English literature, later expanded and published as *Modern Norwegian Literature, 1860-1918* (Downs 1966). Downs specialised in Scandinavian studies at Cambridge University, and he writes on the basis of thorough knowledge of the Scandinavian languages as well as competence in late Victorian English literature. His article on

Denmark includes lists of a range of translations, while also discussing many individual works and cultural figures from the period. He also includes a short appendix about George Stephens (1813-1895), associate professor of English from 1855-93 and in our connection particularly interesting because he filled the chair that had been left empty since T.C. Bruun's days. Downs mentions his English and Danish editions of *Macbeth* from 1876 and that Stephens also covered Anglo-Saxon, but unlike in the case of Bruun there seems to be no connection to Chaucer at all (Downs 1948: 174).[21]

One of Downs's general conclusions about Denmark in the period is this: "German was a language much better known in Denmark than English" (Downs: 145). This is undoubtedly true, although Downs draws up a picture of increased awareness of both English literature and the English language in Danish cultural life.[22] Leading figures in Downs's portrait of this period, later known in Denmark as *det moderne gennembrud* [the modern breakthrough], include the three main figures discussed in this chapter, Møller, Bierfreund and Jespersen, as well as a host of others, such as the leading figure behind the modern breakthrough, Georg Brandes (1842-1927). Brandes's main work, based on a series of lectures at the University of Copenhagen, was *Hovedstrømninger i det 19. Aarhundredes Litteratur,* translated as *Main Currents in Nineteenth Century Literature* and published in six volumes. This became one of the most influential works of literary criticism ever published in the country (Brandes 1872-5, English translation 1901-5). One of Brandes's most remarkable accom-

---

21 Stephens can be studied further in an article by Inge Kabell, "Et portræt af George Stephens – professor i engelsk ved Københavns Universitet og fremtrædende medlem af den engelske menighed i Danmark i en menneskealder" [A portrait of George Stephens – professor of English at the University of Copenhagen and a prominent member of the English church community in Denmark for a lifetime]. Kabell has also published an article in English that includes a portrait of Stephens, "Three University Teachers of Anglo-Saxon Extraction Teaching English Language and Literature at the University of Copenhagen in the Period app. 1850-1940." See Kabell 1996 and 1999. Stephens, however, never actually became a full professor, as noted by Jespersen (Jespersen 1938: 46-8).

22 The progress of English in the Danish educational system and a comparison with the dominant status of German in this period can be found in Rahbek Rasmussen 2005, which will be further discussed in chapter 6.

plishments as a young man was his translations of John Stuart Mill's *On the Subjection of Women* and *Utilitarianism* into Danish as respectively *Kvinders Underkuelse*, 1869 and *Moral Grundet paa Lykke- eller Nytteprincipet* [Morality Founded on the Happiness or Utilitarian Principle], 1870, both available in his *Samlede skrifter* [Collected Works] (Brandes 1919). According to Downs Brandes met Mill in London's Paris Hotel in 1870, and besides the translations he wrote a short study, "John Stuart Mill" (Brandes 1919, Downs 1948: 148).

From an English studies point of view the more mature Brandes is best known for his influential work on Shakespeare, but Downs also notes his interest in contemporary writers like Swinburne and Kipling. Of particular interest for the present study Down says that Brandes "remained ignorant of Chaucer," despite having seen enough of Bierfreund's work to enter into a public dispute about Shakespeare with him (Downs 1948: 149). Brandes was on much better terms with another main Chaucer figure of this chapter, Otto Jespersen, who contributed to a Brandes *Festschrift*, where he concentrates on Brandes and English naturalism and Brandes on Shakespeare (146). Jespersen also shares an interest with Brandes in Browning, writing academically engaged about an Icelandic Browning article as plagiarism (163). This controversy about Browning seems to have interested Downs more than Jespersen's book about Chaucer, which he includes on one of his lists, but like some of the other listed material does not seem to have actually read. That Chaucer is of peripheral interest to Downs, compared to Browning, is illustrated also by another reference, this time to Niels Møller, whom Downs praises at length for introducing Browning in Denmark by translations as well as commentary, and for his work on Tennyson. Møller's role as a translator of Chaucer is mentioned only in passing and alongside praise for translations of two other well-known late Victorian poets: "Chaucer and the two Rosettis were, I believe, new to Danish readers." (Downs: 152-153, 162). As we have seen this estimate is not quite true about Chaucer, but of course Downs has reasons for providing his general picture of a 19th century Danish readership being largely unfamiliar with anything before Shakespeare. One exception to this rule is worth mentioning. N.F.S. Grundtvig, Brandes's predecessor as leading cultural figure in Denmark, translated *Beowulf*, a work of course set in ancient Danish land and also for that reason of interest. Grundtvig also published a critical edition of the poem (Grundtvig 1820 and 1861).

It is the same Grundtvig who, in a survey of 14th century England in his *Verdenskrønike* [World Chronicle], passes Chaucer by so quickly that we can be fairly sure that he has only come across him in a survey (Grundtvig 1812: 261). Somewhat later in the century, in a work translated from German, J. Rodenberg's *For Romantik og Historie* [For Romanticism and History], there is also only a brief mention of Chaucer (Rodenberg 1878: 461). We shall see in later chapters that after the turn of the century there are more literary histories and encyclopediae in Denmark with substantial entries on Chaucer. I will offer the explanation that this reflects a considerable change of status for Chaucer in the sources that the Danish literary historians used, i.e. their main sources from the English speaking world.

The main development in the international Chaucer scholarship ca. 1865-1900, and in medieval scholarship in general, is marked by the great efforts of central European, mainly German, textual editors, some of which we will return to in the section on Jespersen in this chapter and in the section on Brusendorff in chapter 7. Even more so, however, the field genuinely changes with the emergence of the Chaucer society and the Early English Text Society in Britain, culminating with W.W. Skeat's complete Chaucer edition of 1894-7 in six volumes. This monumental edition is based on the important manuscript work of the Chaucer Society that F.J. Furnivall had directed in the preceding decades (Skeat 1894-7). Skeat readily acknowledges his debt to Furnivall in his introduction (vol. 1,vii), and it is fair to say that the two of them are the English founding fathers of editing Chaucer. Skeat's edition is still in print and used as base text in cheap editions of *The Canterbury Tales*, but it is no longer the standard edition that it was for so long.[23]

With the availability of a trustworthy, well glossed Chaucer text and an exuberance of other medieval literature printed for the first time, the end of the 19th century becomes the first period since the Middle Ages themselves where readers can enjoy almost the real thing, with the import reservation of the language and culture barriers that still remain. This situ-

---

23   The standard edition is now Benson, gen. ed., 1987, new edition 2008, and before that Robinson, ed., 1933, second ed.,1957. The cheap *Wordsworth Poetry Library* edition from 1995 with Skeat's text and a foreword by Catherine Wells-Cole happens to be printed in Denmark (Benson 1987/2008, Robinson 1933/57, Chaucer 1995).

ation gradually affects the literary assessment of Chaucer and medieval literature in English critical writing and literary histories, and as recorded by Steve Ellis, the first couple of decades of the 20th century became a sort of golden age for Chaucer on both sides of the Atlantic with a flow of new popular editions and critical books (Ellis 2000: 17-8). In turn this is also reflected in the Danish reception. I will now turn to some of the first Danish writers that have registered a new paradigm on the way.

Theodor Bierfreund

Lorentz Christian Theodor Bierfreund (1855-1906) was an art historian, author and literary critic who obtained both a master degree (*magisterkonferens*) in English language and literature from the University of Copenhagen, and a habilitation (*dr. phil.*) also from Denmark's still only university. After his degrees in respectively 1890 and 1891 he wrote four novels, including the partly autobiographical *Ira* (1897), but he never earned much recognition as a novelist. His work as an art historian included a book on Florence, one on Rembrandt and one on Danish castles, and these works received more attention from the reading public, as did his book on Shakespeare's art from 1898 (Elling 1933). The two works considered here, his habilitation *Palemon og Arcite: En literaturhistorisk undersøgelse som bidrag til Shakespearekritiken* [Palemon and Arcite: A literary-historical investigation as a contribution to Shakespeare criticism] and *Kulturbærere* [Carriers of Culture] made it possible for Bierfreund to carry on a literary feud with Brandes, as noted above, and let it be no secret before I start my treatment of Bierfreund that there is every good reason why Brandes was the stronger of the two in that feud, and that most modern encyclopediae have excluded Bierfreund. Already in 1915 the Danish encyclopedia *Salmonsens Konversations Leksikon* called Bierfreund's doctoral dissertation "et ubetydeligt lille Arbejde" [an insignificant piece of work] and characterised him in general as "uden Kraft og videnskabelig Kritik" [without power and scientific criticism] (Clausen 1915: 207). These are blunt terms and of course no longer acceptable language for encyclopedia purposes, but I have to agree about the dissertation in question here and wonder why this was accepted for the Dr. Phil. degree at the University of Copenhagen.

Bierfreund's dissertation *Palemon og Arcite* is only 80 pages long, and the main problem with it is that no substantial scholarly work is undertaken. In essence most of it is a summary of the plot in the various versions from Boccaccio to Shakespeare. In the Chaucer part Bierfreund is working not only with *The Knight's Tale*, but also with a fragment no longer ascribed to Chaucer, "Queen Annelide and False Arcite." After two pages about Chaucer's relationship to his Italian sources, and a brief summary of this fragment, Bierfreund starts his summary of *The Knight's Tale*:

> "I Athen herskede en hertug, Theseus, der havde ført krig med Femenye: Amazonernes land. Cithea kaldtes det tidligere. Han har ægtet Hippolita, og dennes søster Emily er fulgt med hende til Athen. Hjemkommen fra sin bryllupsfærd møder han en skare sørgeklædte kvinder, ..." [In Athens the ruler was a duke, Theseus, who had led a war against Femenye: the land of the Amazones. It was earlier called Cithea. He had married Hippolita, and her sister Emily has followed her to Athens. On his homecoming from the wedding he meets a group of women dressed in mourning clothes, ...]
> (Bierfreund 1991: 20)

The passage here is quite characteristic of Bierfreund's technique, which neatly foregrounds the main plot elements, occasionally translating a line or two directly or indirectly from Chaucer's text. Thus "Cithea kaldtes det tidligere" echoes Chaucer's line "That whilom was ycleped Scithia" (Benson, gen. ed., I 867). In a later passage recording Palemon jumping from a bush to fight his rival, Chaucer's choice of words is echoed again as "Arcite bliver så 'vild som en løve', drager sit sværd" [Arcite gets as wild as a lion and pulls out his sword], which closely follows Chaucer's line "As fiers as leon pulled out his swerd" (Bierfreund 1891: 22, Benson, gen. ed., I 1598). In this instance, unlike most other examples of Bierfreund using near-quotation, he uses quotation marks, but he never quotes Chaucer's text from an edition, although it appears from the bibliography in *Kulturbærere* that he knows Furnivall's Six Text Print (Bierfreund 1892: 219).

Apart from the 5 page summary, which in a very poor way represents Chaucer's masterly *The Knight's Tale*, there is next to nothing to be gathered from this part of Bierfreund's dissertation. Characteristically, the one short passage following the tale summary before Bierfreund ends his chapter has him guessing, more than dubiously, that the reason for Chaucer's changes in relation to Boccaccio's *Teseida* are due to Chaucer having lost access to that text and not remembering well (25). My own published PhD dissertation *Chaucer's Narrative Voice in* The Knight's Tale (Klitgård 1995) is one of several scholarly works that refutes this fanciful theory by focusing on Chaucer's independent composition.

In *Kulturbærere* it is noteworthy that the title Carriers of Culture signals such importance of Chaucer and the other medieval authors treated there, but apart from that it is hard to find much of value also in this case. In his discussion of Chaucer's works Bierfreund arrogantly dismisses several of them, only too obviously not having read them at all. For instance according to Bierfreund *The Book of the Duchess* is "ganske uselvstændigt og interesseløst" [completely unoriginal and without interest] and *Troilus and Criseyde* "havde [for Chaucer] … ingen anden Betydning end den, at føie et Værk til hans andre" [had no other importance [for Chaucer] than that of adding one work to his other works" (Bierfreund 1892: 179 and 183). Bierfreund's ignorance is only demonstrated more clearly than this when he starts bestowing praise on the one work he has consulted, *The Canterbury Tales*. His complete misreading and secret mission of promoting an image of Chaucer in his merry England is perhaps not a lot worse than many native English speaking commentators before and after him, but it is pretty gross, as is his outspoken anti-semitism and racism in other parts of the chapter. One example will suffice to illustrate the unsubstantiated myth-making about Chaucer, here about the opening of *The Canterbury Tales*:

> "Chaucer iagttager Naturen, ikke med den Bagtanke, at den kan tage sig ud i hans Bog, men med en ren og umiddelbar Nydelse. Han elsker den engelske Sol, der varmer uden at brænde, og han kan skatte Skønheden i en "sød" Aprilbyge, der farer hen og lader Millioner af Perler tilbage på Blade og Træer. Han nyder det rette sjælelige Velbehag ved at lade Øiet glide henover og hvile på de skønne, fredelige, sydengelske Landskaber, hvor der aldrig ses en helt klar Himmel, aldrig en fri Horisont, hvor den lette Dis lægger en drømmerig Stemning over Høidedragene, der

fortoner sig bag hinanden med Borge på Toppene,..." [Chaucer regards Nature, not with the ulterior motive that it may appear nice in his book, but with a pure and immediate enjoyment. He loves the English sun, which warms without burning, and he can appreciate the beauty of a "sweet" April shower, which has the effect of leaving millions of pearls on leaves and trees. He enjoys the proper mental pleasure of letting the eye glide across the beautiful, southern English landscapes, where there is never a clear sky, never a free horizon, where the light mist creates a dreamy mood over the ranges of hills that loom into sight behind each other, with castles on top of them...]
(Bierfreund 1892: 188-9)

The sentence is twice as long, but this is quite enough. Readers familiar even with only the first famous lines of *The General Prologue* will know that Bierfreund's text is as far from the spirit of Chaucer as possible. More or less the only accurate observation in the whole piece is the remark about the sweetness of the rain showers in April.

The severe misrepresentation of Chaucer continues over more than 25 pages, and I shall spare my reader a more detailed analysis, except a couple of observations about parallels to other Chaucer representations in Denmark. Bierfreund interestingly, like Westergaard, uses oblique translation mixed with summary in his treatment of later parts of *The General Prologue,* and the portrait of the Prioress is more or less a direct translation (191-2). Like many others in the Danish and international reception, Bierfreund likes The Wife of Bath best among the pilgrims, and like many others he makes an effort not to get too close to anything indecent (195-7). He also manages to summarise the two fabliaux *The Miller's Tale* and *The Reeve's Tale* with next to no dirty references. The following summary of main plot in *The Reeve's Tale* triggers our imagination, but no more, and it is of course far from Chaucer's directness:

"Men på Grund af nogle mærkelige Komplikationer, en Storm, der tvinger dem til at blive Natten over i Møllen og et Anfald af Mavepine hos Møllerkonen, hævnede de sig blodigt om Natten, i hvilken Hævn Møllerens Kone og Datter spiller en betydelig Rolle. De fik hvad en Ynglings Hjerte kunde begære, og desuden alt deres Mel og frit Natteleie og gav Mølleren Prygl oven i købet." [However, because of some strange complications, a storm that forces them to stay at the mill overnight and an attack of stomach pain on the part of the miller's wife, they took a bloody revenge during the night, and in this revenge the miller's wife and daughter play a considerable part. They got all that a young man could desire, and moreover they got all their flour and a free night's stay and also beat the miller.] (Bierfreund 1892: 198)

Chaucer's text records no stomach pain on the part of the miller's wife, but has her snoring, then waking and going "out to pisse" (Benson, gen. ed., I 4214-5). Bierfreund's change of this point represents a clear avoidance strategy, whereas his effort to avoid naming the sex between the students and the wife and daughter can be seen as a typical euphemistic paraphrase. In an 1890s context Bierfreund is hardly to be blamed for this. I shall instead conclude this part by quoting Bierfreund on one of the many points where he can be blamed, writing about matters beyond his grasp and not bothering to investigate. The quotation, about Chaucer's contemporary John Gower's main work, may aptly be turned against himself and be used about *Kulturbærere*: "Der findes ingen mere søvndyssende Bog på Jorden end *Confessio Amantis*." [No book on earth is more sleep-provoking than *Confessio Amantis*] (Bierfreund 1992: 175).

Otto Jespersen and Niels Møller

At the same time as Bierfreund, Otto Jespersen was also working with Chaucer at the University of Copenhagen. Jespersen gave a series of lectures there in the autumn of 1891, and subsequently edited and published his study in 1893, including three translated poems and extracts by Niels Møller. Møller (1859-1941) is now best known in Denmark for his impressive three volume world literary history *Verdenslitteraturen* (Møller 1928), which he wrote single-handedly, and which is still available in many Danish libraries. I return to his Chaucer entry in *Verdenslitteraturen* in chapter 7. Møller also had a successful career in the insurance industry, having graduated as a law candidate in 1887. As noted above, he was a literary critic and translator, and like Bierfreund he also tried his hand at writing literature himself. His poems and stories did not earn him much fame in Denmark, but he was acknowledged by many Danes acquainted with English and classical studies, and he received a *Festschrift* on his 80th birthday.[24] Also Otto Jespersen acknowledges Møller's poetic translations very kindly as he includes them in his study of Chaucer's life and works, and this is quite in line with the general image we have of Jespersen as a very generous man. Otto Jespersen (1860-1943) is arguably the greatest international linguist of his time, and in a Danish context it is very fitting that he should also have produced a study of his great predecessor, Rasmus Rask (Jespersen 1918). Following in the footsteps of Rask, Jespersen grew to be a founding father of modern English grammar and phonetics, soundly based on his knowledge of historical linguistics. His autobiography *En sprogmands levned* from 1938 has been translated as *A Linguist's Life* in 1995 (Jespersen 1938/1995), and I refer readers to that for a further biographical context. I will mention here, however, that it contains entertaining accounts of the many internationally renowned scholars Jespersen came across and befriended, including Furnivall, Kittredge, Sweet and Bradley. Among the few scholars that did not become friends are German Chaucer scholar Zupitza, whose seminars Jespersen attended in Berlin in the 1880s, and English *docent* Stephens at the University of Copenhagen, who was also Jespersen's teacher in his student years. Jespersen disliked both and did not approve of their teaching methods (Jespersen 1938: 46-8, 59-60, 73).

Turning to Jespersen's work on Chaucer, one of the translators of the autobiography, Jørgen Erik Nielsen, told me personally that he was quite confident that Jespersen produced this work because he was worried about having a profile too narrow for a professorial seat in Copenhagen. This sounds plausible and is supported by a remark in Jespersen's autobiography, where Jespersen also makes a point of referring to it as not a scholarly study, calling it "den halvt-populære lille bog" [the half-popu-

---

24 The chief sources used for the biographical information about Møller are by Fr. Nielsen in *Dansk Biografisk Leksikon* (Nielsen 1887-1905) and a biographical note by Hakon Stangerup (Stangerup 1970: 215), but I have also used much of Møller's own published work. Among his merits as a critic are several reviews of the great contemporary novelist Henrik Pontoppidan.

larized little book] (Jespersen 1938: 70). *Chaucers liv and digtning* is not Jespersen's only venture outside linguistics, however. Among his publications we also find *The England and American Reader* (Jespersen 1903), which is a mixture of extracts from old and new mainly English literature, regrettably including nothing by Chaucer. I will return to this work and include further perspectives on Jespersen's many educational publications in chapters 6, 7 and 10, but let me also mention in this chapter that Jespersen added to his work on Chaucer by writing two further short academic articles, both concerning editing matters, and both in dialogue with the German philological tradition, one written in Danish and one in German (Jespersen 1893-4 and Jespersen 1899). In a recent article on lines 12-16 of *The General Prologue* kindly given to me before its publication, Chaucer critic Norman Klassen has reviewed the evidence of these articles and of Jespersen's German discussion partners. Klassen very convincingly demonstrates that Jespersen, Zupitza and Ten Brink between them worked out a correction to the hitherto accepted reading of these lines, but unfortunately their correction was lost in the language barrier that existed. The later English editors never took in the correction, and it has remained an error to the present day (Klassen, forthcoming).

Whereas Bierfreund creates a false image of a poet he has not bothered to read properly, Otto Jespersen's 1893 monograph is a serious study based on actual reading of several works by Chaucer and on the scholarly work of such eminent early Chaucer scholars as the German philologists just mentioned, but also English scholars like Lowell. This is a couple of years before Skeat's complete edition, but Jespersen cites other text editions by Skeat and Furnivall as well as Morris' Aldine edition in five volumes from 1885. He also makes use of the earlier editions by Tyrrwhitt and Wright, which I considered briefly in the previous chapter. First of all, however, Jespersen is himself quite able to discuss the quality of also Chaucer's works outside the *Canterbury Tales*, with well-selected extracts from *The Book of the Duchess*, *The Parliament of Fowls* and *The House of Fame*. He finds *The Legend of Good Women* "not funny, and marked by the fact that the writing was commissioned by someone" (Jespersen 1893: 32), which may in fact be true, but this is an example of Jespersen making qualified guesses at times. Another example of this is Jespersen's support of a claim made by Eilers in a German 1882 dissertation that Chaucer could not have written the *Retraction* to the *Canterbury Tales*

(56). Neither Eilers nor Jespersen can have been right, but they had the gut feeling to believe they were and frankly stated so.

Jespersen is generally well updated with contemporary research in Chaucer, not least the German philological tradition, and this also means that his study includes the first reasonably accurate account of Chaucer's life in Danish. It has to be considered that this is still some 50 years before the monumental work of Manly and Rickert on Chaucer's life records appeared with their 1940 complete Chaucer edition, but already here in the early 1890s Jespersen is able to correct Chaucer's date of birth to "nearer 1345" (5-6) and to recount and discuss scholarly corrections to the list of works that Chaucer wrote. The records establish that Chaucer was born in either 1340 or 1343, and we still do not know which of the two, only that the old assumption, 1328, is wrong. Jespersen takes his evidence for dating and for the Italian influence from various German philologists, but is for good reasons not quite certain. In 1916, when he publishes a Chaucer portrait in the second edition of *Salmonsens Konversationsleksikon*, he has reached the conclusion about Chaucer's birth date that it is "about 1340" (Jespersen 1916: 802).[25] Jespersen writes with enthusiasm about Chaucer's journey to Italy in 1372-3 and claims quite rightly that "den rejse fik större betydning for England, ja for hele den dannede verden, end nogen da kunne ane" [that journey came to have greater importance for England, indeed for all of the educated world, than anyone could imagine at the time] (Jespersen 1893:11). Jespersen is also right in being sceptical about earlier critical assumptions that Chaucer met both Boccaccio and Petrarca, but he decides to believe that he probably met Petrarca. Derek Pearsall, writing a hundred years later than Jespersen, on the sound basis of the life-records, does not believe that Chaucer ever met either of the two poets, and incidentally he corrects the length of the journey to six months rather than the 11 months believed at Jespersen's time (Pearsall 1992: 102 and 114).

---

25 Manly and Rickert's work on the life records was revised by Crow and Olson and published as *Chaucer Life-Records* in 1966 (Crow and Olson 1966). The German philological tradition will be more substantially treated in the Brusendorff section of chapter 7, where I will also discuss the work of Richard Utz about that tradition (Utz 2002). Jespersen's 1916 Chaucer portrait, two pages in *Salmonsens Konversationsleksikon*, will not be further treated, as except for the birth date discussion it adds nothing new to his far more substantial 1893 study.

Turning again from life to poetry, Jespersen's discussion of Chaucer's work is also marked by his familiarity with scholarship, as he voices opinions about Chaucer's gradually growing skills as a poet after his Italian journey. Discussing *The Book of the Duchess*, Jespersen quotes Ten Brink at length in his own translation into Danish, then disagrees with Ten Brink's positive attitude towards Chaucer's plot construction and simply calls the poem an artistic failure, the young poet's imagination running riot (Jespersen 1893: 19). To be fair, Jespersen acknowledges some elements of Chaucer's first dream vision poem as successful, and he includes his own prose translation of several lines (20), but it is as if Jespersen has wanted to insist that Chaucer lacked maturity in most of his work before *Troilus and Criseyde*. On a par with this Jespersen is quite unsentimental about the many fragmented and unfinished works Chaucer left behind, claiming after a discussion of various fanciful scholarly explanations of these loose ends that this simply reflects a mind that could not "fastholde en engang fattet plan energisk til slutningen" [energetically stick to a once conceived plan to the end] (35). Jespersen's estimate has some weight, but here and elsewhere he tends to be too categorical. Not all critical opinions offering other explanations of fragmented and unfinished Chaucer poems can be dismissed as fanciful, and Chaucer is hardly to blame for not being able to stick to a compositional plan, as witnessed by the strong internal coherence of the fragments in *The Canterbury Tales*.[26] In a similar vein, Jespersen is categorical when dismissing the admittedly less interesting Chaucerian works in prose as "hverken original eller interessant" [neither original, nor interesting] (16). This may be partly true from a modern point of view, but judging from the frequency of scribes copying Chaucer's two prose tales *Melibee* and *the Parson's Tale* in the 15th century, it seems that Chaucer's prose was among his most popular work in his own time.

Troilus and Criseyde is a work that appeals more to Jespersen than the

---

26 Jerome Mandel offers insight into the coherence of the fragments of *The Canterbury Tales* in his *Geoffrey Chaucer: Building the Fragments of* the Canterbury Tales (Mandel 1992). Discussing the abrupt or missing ending of *The House of Fame*, I have myself offered an explanation as equally simple as Jespersen's here, i.e. that the poem was composed in instalments for readings at court, and that some external event made it necessary to stop these readings, leaving an unfinished manuscript in Chaucer's desk. See Klitgård 1998.

prose tales from *The Canterbury Tales*, and his extensive commentary on that poem is among the finest in his study. He has wisely ignored Bierfreund's estimate of the poem, although he does quote Bierfreund in a couple of references elsewhere. Instead Jespersen takes his starting point in Kissner's comparative study of Boccaccio's and Chaucer's version of the story in his habilitation (Kissner 1867). Jespersen clearly feels well at home in Kissner's academic German and jokingly quotes Goethe's famous line in "Klärchens Lied", "himmelhoch jauchend, zum Tode betrübt" [on the top of the world, down in the dumps] to characterize Troilus' reaction after being hit by love-sickness through Criseyde (Jespersen 1893: 25). A second example of Jespersen demonstrating his characteristic independent touch in presenting the research of fellow academics is a comment he adds to Kissner's point that Chaucer is more interested in psychological analysis than Boccaccio: "En historie vinder altid ved at gå igennem Chaucers hænder" [A story always gains something by going through the hands of Chaucer] (26). This is certainly true of *Troilus and Criseyde*, and Jespersen appreciates Chaucer's psychological insight as well as his humour. The humour created through the character of Pandarus, according to Jespersen Chaucer's most original change from Boccaccio's dull friend to a real comedy figure, leads Jespersen to a comparison with the great Danish-Norwegian comic dramatist Ludvig Holberg (1684-1754), in my opinion very appropriately, showing his accurate understanding of Chaucer's poem as full of dramatic comedy as well as passionate and tragic love (26). I also endorse Jespersen's evaluation that compared to Boccaccio Chaucer has moved his characters "adskillige breddegrader nordligere" [several degrees of latitude north], losing some of the latino love intensities, and gaining more "virkeligt liv" [real life] (28).

The comparative approach to Chaucer's sources and analogues is applied by Jespersen in further examples from *The Canterbury Tales*. In a thorough analysis of the relationship of *The Reeve's Tale* to its sources, Jespersen's main scholarly source is again a German study, this time by H. Varnhagen.[27] Jespersen makes good use of Varnhagen's

---

27 Unusually for Jespersen, he forgets this source in his bibliography, but he does acknowledge the reference in-text as from *Englische Studien*, 9. The study is titled "Die Erzählung von der Wiege" [The story of the cradle] and is printed in *Englische Studien*, 1886, vol. ix, 240-66. I have checked the list of contents from this issue of

minute comparison of details from various cradle stories and other analogues, then focuses on Boccaccio 6th story of the 9th day in the *Decameron* versus Chaucer's *Reeve's Tale*, once again much preferring the latter. More significantly Jespersen is able to dismiss the claim by some scholars that Chaucer used Boccaccio as his main source (Jespersen 1893: 41-4). The summaries that Jespersen has to provide to point out differences are given in a sober tone, but he is less reluctant than Bierfreund, Bruun and others to talk about the sexual details, and he certainly manages to recount the plot without changing the crucial parts about the double seduction of wife and daughter. Not surprisingly for a linguist, Jespersen is fond of Chaucer's invention of letting the two students speak in dialect, and he even gives the details of their dialect words in an endnote (43 and 62).

After his thorough comparison of all the stories that are found both in the works of Boccaccio and Chaucer, Jespersen concludes that Chaucer is superior with respect to plot construction and characterisation, and in Jespersen's estimate also as far as the moral value of the stories is concerned. Moreover the individualisation of the tale tellers falls in Jespersen's taste, whereas he thinks less highly of Boccaccio's story-tellers: "Elisa, Lauretta, Emilia, hvem kan kende forskel på dem?" [Elisa, Lauretta, Emilia, who can tell the difference between them] (44-5). I have myself spent a considerable proportion of my research in Chaucer studies on the question of Chaucer's narrative voice, and I will agree with Jespersen's emphasis on the superiority of Chaucer's narration, but I will also point out that he is close to writing himself into a long tradition of critics who accept the narrators of *The Canterbury Tales* as *persona* narrators in the same way as Gulliver is a marked and unreliable narrator of his travel accounts. This is not the case in Chaucer's narrative poetry, but it is understandable that Jespersen should believe that it is. In the 1890s medieval texts had been well edited, but no scholarship had yet

Englische Studien and discovered accidentally that a grammar book in Danish by Jespersen from 1885 is reviewed in the same issue. This means he will have had one further reason to be acquainted with Varnhagen's study. Utz briefly records the study in *Chaucer and the Discourse of German Philology* (Utz 2002: 289), but readers interested in a fine comparison of seven versions of the cradle story should read the full study, which as so much else is now accessible on the internet.

determined the principles of medieval narrative to any degree of sophistication.[28] Despite a few reservations mainly due to the research that was available to Jespersen in his time, Jespersen's study is as indicated highly recommended and should really be translated into English in full.

Meanwhile, I will consider Jespersen's own translations from Chaucer, and also the three translated poems and extracts by Niels Møller that he has included. The first example is an extract that is translated both by Jespersen himself and by Niels Møller. Jespersen's translation is in prose and appears in the main text, whereas Møller's is added in an appendix with a note from Jespersen saying that he received it during the printing phase of the study. The choice of this extract for translation is at first sight slightly odd, since "Merciless Beauty", so named by Skeat, is one of the minor poems that cannot with any certainty be attributed to Chaucer. Jespersen's own student Aage Brusendorff, who will be considered in chapter 7, argues against it being Chaucer's (Brusendorff 1925: 440), and the argument over its authenticity has continued. Jespersen, well aware of the differences of opinion in textual scholarship, argues in favour of authenticity on the background of tone of voice, pointing out that the humour expressed in the third roundel of the three-part poem is Chaucer's. He explains that the exact reason for including it in his study is to draw attention to something typically Chaucerian (Jespersen 1893: 8). Agreeing with Jespersen that the poem sounds like Chaucer's humorous tone, let me quote the third roundel *in extenso* from Skeat and the two translations by Jespersen and Møller:

> Sin I fro Love escaped am so fat,
> I never thenk to ben in his prison lene;
> Sin I am free, I counte him not a bene.
> He may answere, and seye this or that;
> I do no fors, I speke right as I mene.
> Sin I fro Love escaped am so fat,
> I never thenk to ben in his prison lene.
> Love hath my name y-strike out of his sclat,

---

28 This is of course still a major issue in modern medieval scholarship. I have analysed Chaucer's narrative voice in several works listed in the bibliography. My most recent study in the field is Klitgård 2011.

And he is strike out of my bokes clene
For ever-mo; [ther] is non other mene.
Sin I fro Love escaped am so fat,
I never thenk to ben in his prison lene;
Sin I am free, I counte him not a bene.
(Skeat, *The Works of Geoffrey Chaucer*, 1.80-1)

Siden jeg slap bort fra Amor, er jeg så trind og fed; aldrig mer vil jeg mager være i hans fængsel; siden jeg blev fri, bryder jeg mig ikke en döjt om ham. – Lad ham kun svare, sige dit og dat, jeg er ligeglad og siger min mening rent ud: Siden jeg slap bort fra Amor, er jeg så trind og fed; aldrig mer vil jeg mager være i hans fængsel. – Amor har slettet mit navn af sin liste; Amors navn er slettet af mine bøger for bestandig; nu er vi to kvit. Siden jeg slap bort fra Amor, er jeg så trind og fed; aldrig mer vil jeg mager være i hans fængsel; siden jeg blev fri bryder jeg mig ikke en döjt om ham. [Since I escaped from Amor I have become so round and fat; I will never again be thin in his prison; since I escaped, I haven't much cared for him. – Let him only answer this or that, I don't care and give my opinion openly: Since I escaped from Amor I have become so round and fat; I will never again be thin in his prison. Amor has deleted my name from his list; Amor's name is deleted from my books forever; now we are quits. Since I escaped from Amor I have become so round and fat; I will never again be thin in his prison; since I escaped, I haven't much cared for him.]
(Jespersen, transl., 8)

Da jeg så fed af Elskovs fængsel slap, [When
I so fat from Love's prison escaped]
skal det mig aldrig mere göre mager; [It
will never make me thin again]
nu er jeg fri, hans ord mig ikke rager. [Now I am
free, his words are all the same to me]
Hvad så han siger er mig hip som hap;
[Whatever he says is all the same to me]
jeg svarer frit, så tit hans bud mig plager: [I answer
freely, as often as his bidding torments me]

da jeg så fed af Elskovs fængsel slap, [When
I so fat from Love's prison escaped]
skal det mig aldrig mere göre mager. [It
will never make me thin again]
Jeg har ströget ham af min bog, og knap [I have
erased him from my book, and barely]
Mit navn i sin han nogensinde tager; [ever
he includes my name in his book]
Nu er vi kvit; det nytter ej, han klager: [we are
quits; it is no use for him to complain]
Da jeg så fed af Elskovs længsel slap, [When
I so fat from Love's prison escaped]
Skal det mig aldrig mere göre mager; [It
will never make me thin again]
Nu er jeg fri, hans ord mig ikke rager. [Now I
am free and don't care about his words]

(Møller in Jespersen 1893: 63)

Jespersen's prose is generally more accurate as translation than Møller's poetic translation, which is not particularly surprising. Especially because Møller has decided to follow the metre, including the rhyme scheme of his source text, he is subject to more restrictions than Jespersen. Møller still gets away with this piece rather elegantly, certainly conveying the content well, and establishing the repeated rhyme words as the core of his composition. The rhyme words are essential in "Merciless Beauty" and form its core compositional structure, with only two sets of rhyme-words: "lene, bene, mene, clene" and "fat, that, sclat [slate]", which are matched by Møller's "mager, rager, plager, klager" "slap, hap, knap". Both Møller and Jespersen find Danish idiomatic expressions that suggest the playful tone of the poem well, Møller with "hip som hap" and Jespersen with "dit og dat", phonetically similar informal expressions that are still used in Danish. Jespersen correctly translates "sclat" with "liste", whereas Møller takes the liberty to let the poem's Love personified also have a book. The personification itself is translated by "Elskov" in Møller's version, whereas Jespersen chooses "Amor". I would suggest that this is a better solution than Møller's because Amor is a more conventionally poetic personification in a Danish context.

The most conspicuous change of meaning in both translations concerns line 10, "For ever-mo; [ther] is non other mene." The line can be regarded as a typical formulaic filler with little significant content, and can be translated into modern English as "forever; there is no other course of action", "mene" of course literally meaning "means". It may well be that Jespersen and Møller have discussed the poem before translating this line, because they both come up with a translation that is logical in the content, i.e. Danish equivalents of "we are quits", but there is no such phrase in the original. Jespersen avoids the content of line 10 altogether, whereas Møller, having to fill the line with something, invents "Nu er vi kvit; det nytter ej, han klager: [we are quits; it is no use for him to complain]. I suggest that both translators had problems with the admittedly difficult line 10 and took an easy way out, but the avoidance, respectively the replacement strategy does not seriously affect the overall impression. In fact both translations work well and help Jespersen demonstrate his point that we have a typical Chaucerian tone. I would add to Jespersen's argument that we also have a typical setting for Chaucer, who repeatedly in his works runs into playful controversies with figures like the God or Goddess of Love. "Merciless Beauty" is most likely composed by Chaucer, despite what Brusendorff has to say about the weak external evidence we have, afforded by the single copy in a manuscript not including Chaucer's name (Brusendorff 1925: 440).

Having thus used a translator and his commentary to argue for authorship of a poem, let us turn to one more piece translated by Jespersen. This is the well-known passage from the introduction to *Sir Thopas*, where the Host grabs hold of the next story-teller, Chaucer himself:

> "Hvad er du for en mand? Du ser ud, som om du ledte efter en hare, sådan stirrer du bestandig på jorden. Kom herhen og se muntert op. Pas nu på, mine herrer og damer, og lad denne mand få plads; han er lige så trind om livet som jeg. Det var en rigtig dukke til at omfavnes af en slank dejlighed. Han ser ud som var han elleskudt; han indlader sig ikke spøgende med nogen. Kom du nu frem med noget lystigt." [What man are you? You look as if you were searching for a hare, the way you continuously stare at the ground. Come over and look up cheerfully. Watch out, ladies and gentleman, and give space to

this man; he is just as round as I am. He would be a real doll to be embraced by a lovely woman. He looks as though he has been hit by the elvish people; he does not enter into any joking conversation. Do come up with something merry.]
(Jespersen 1893: 55)

Whereas the previous example was explicitly translated from Skeat's edition, Jespersen is unclear about which of his listed editions he has used here. I will again quote from the modern standard edition:

> …, "What man artow?" quod he;
> "Thou lookest as thou woldest fynde an hare,
> For evere upon the ground I se thee stare.
> Approche neer, and looke up murily.
> Now war yow, sires, and lat this man have place!
> He in the waast is shape as wel as I;
> This were a popet in an arm t'enbrace
> For any woman, smal and fair of face.
> He semeth elvyssh by his contenaunce,
> For unto no wight does he daliaunce.
> Sey now somewhat, syn oother folk han sayd;
> Telle us a tale of myrthe, and that anon."
> (Benson, gen. ed., VII, 695-706)

First of all the selection of this particular passage for translation again shows Jespersen's keen eye for Chaucer's humour. After his translation Jespersen well explains the context of Chaucer's ironic self-portrait and the ensuing parody of contemporary popular minstrel poetry, which I will return to in chapter 7. Jespersen strikingly characterises the rhymes of *Sir Thopas* as full of "klingklang-fraser", a Danish onomatopoeic idiom that equals "ding-dong phrases" (Jespersen 1893: 55). In the passage here Jespersen conveys the gently sarcastic tone of the merry Host with great precision, which I hope to have demonstrated with my back-translation. The choice of the now slightly archaic adjective "trind" [round] rather than "tyk" or "fed" [fat] carries the correct more positive connotations in the context of the Host himself being over-weight and playful about it. The contrast is neatly drawn up with the reference to an imagined "slank dejlighed," literally a "lean loveliness", which also well covers Chaucer's "woman, smal and fair of face." Finally, Jespersen's explication of "elvyssh" as "elleskudt", meaning hit or shot by the elvish people, is a very sensible slight change in the context, as there is no idiomatic adjective correspondence in Danish.

There are other bits of translation in Jespersen's study that focus on humorous elements, such as extracts from the prologue of *The Legend of Good Women* and *The Wife of Bath's Prologue,* but as at least the latter example is treated extensively elsewhere in the present study, I shall leave these examples without further comments, except to say that Jespersen is again not only a great linguist, but also a great prose writer in Danish. I shall also only note in passing that Jespersen manages more serious passages equally well, and that he manages to select important and illustrative passages from Chaucer to give a brilliant impression of the poet's versatility to his Danish readers. One example of a serious and also very moving passage that Jespersen chooses to include is the now famous preface to his 10-year-old son Lowys in *The Treatise of the Astrolobe,* a preface that shows Chaucer's dedication to write in plain English rather than the usual scientific language, Latin. In the context of Chaucer being the first great poet in the English language, this is an extremely important programmatic declaration from Chaucer, not least because he shows the same respect for his young son that he elsewhere shows for his adult reader. Jespersen is aware of the importance of speaking plainly, as he includes Chaucer's actual phrase in English in a parenthesis: "ligefremme ord (naked wordes)" (Jespersen 1893: 8, Chaucer in Benson, gen. ed.: *A Treatise of the Astrolabe,* 26).

My final example of translation in Jespersen's study is from Niels Møller. This is the passage first published five years previously in Møller's collection of poetry *Efterår* (Møller 1888). It is reprinted and commented on by Jespersen, who suggests that the poem might reflect Chaucer's personal bitter experience (14-5):

> O, kvalfuld kvide! Armods bitre plage! [O doleful
> agony! Bitter torment of destitution!]
> I sult og tørst og kuld din lod du kårer! [In
> hunger and thirst thy lot you choose]
> Du blues i dit hjærte for at klage, [In your

heart you are ashamed to complain]
men nøler du, den nøgne nød dig sårer, [but if
you hesitate, naked need will hurt you]
og snart den blotter de fordulgte tårer. [and
soon it exposes the hidden tears]
Din trang dig tvinger, vil du eller ikke, [your urge
forces you, whether you want it or not]
så du må stjæle, borge eller tigge. [so you
must steal, beg or borrow]

Du dadler gud, og bittert du forkynder, [You
blame God, and bitterly proclaim]
han skifter uden skøn de gode gaver; [that he
bestows his good gifts without judgment]
med kiv og skældsord du mod næsten synder, [with
strife and quarrel you sin against your neighbour]
for du har lidet, han så meget haver. [because
you have so little, he so much]
Men vent – du siger – snart hans grav de graver, [but
wait – you say – soon they will dig his grave]
da skal i lueglød hans legem brænde, [then
his body shall burn in flames]
ti han gav ej de arme hjælp i hænde. [for he
never gave the poor any helping hand]

Kom hid og hør den vises ord og stemme: [Come hither
and listen to the words and voice of a wise man]
"Bedre at dø end tiggerkost at tære". ["Better
to die than to live off beggar's food]
Selve din nabo vil dig såre skæmme; [Even
your neighbour will much despise you]
hvis du er arm, hvo viser dig vel ære? [If you
are poor, who will show you respect?]
Tag end af vismands ord mod denne lære:
[Learn from a wise man's words this:]
"Hvor ond hver dag, som fattigmand må stride!" ["How evil
is every day that a poor man must struggle through!"]

Forvar dig da, kom ej i denne kvide. [Defend
yourself, do not get into such trouble]

Hvis du er arm, din broder du forliser, [If you
are poor, you will lose your brother]
og hver en ven vil vige dine veje; – [and every
friend will turn off from your road]
o, rige købmænd, eders lod jeg priser, [oh,
rich merchants, your lots I praise]
I valgte kløgtig verdens bedste eje. [You wisely
chose the best property in the world]
Hos jer tog luvslidt vinding aldrig leje, [By
you there was never filthy lucre]
I øser af en strøm, som ej vil standse – [You
pour from a never-ceasing stream]
I kan ved julegilde glade danse. [You may
at Christmas dance merrily]
(Møller 1888: 84-5)

This poem, titled "Geoffrey Chaucer" in Møller's *Efteraar* from 1888, is translated from Chaucer's *The Man of Law's Tale, Prologue*, II, 99-126 (Benson, gen. ed.).[29] In this case I will make an exception and not include Chaucer's text for comparison, because my main point here is not chiefly about translation criticism, and I have found no unnecessary inaccuracies in Møller's translation, although compared to the other Chaucer poems translated by Møller, its choice of idioms is more archaic. The point I want to raise here is that Møller by naming it "Geoffrey Chaucer", placing it in a section of translations from among others Greek epigrams, Whitman and Shelley, and not quoting the original source precisely, gives his reader the idea that this is an independent poem by Chaucer. In Møller's translation it works rather well as an independent poem, but it is not until Jespersen's inclusion of it that his readers may know it is not. It is also remarkable that Møller should have chosen such an untypical piece by Chaucer, celebrating worldly richness and scorning poor people to an extent that will not have been pleasant for a medieval Christian audience.

---

29 The poem can also be found on an internet link (Møller, accessed May 2011).

Again it is important to note that the piece is spoken by the Man of Law as a dramatic representation of the man, a prologue that functions in relation to the portrait of him in *The General Prologue,* 309-30. Here he is portrayed as "ful riche of excellence" (311), exuberantly dressed, always busy, and totally occupied with legal matters. It is not one of the most satirical portraits in *The General Prologue,* but there is no doubt that the Man of Law is not a sympathetic character.[30] It is thus reasonable to assume that the words spoken in the prologue to his tale are not to be taken as the bitter wisdom of Chaucer's personal experience, as Jespersen suggests, but as a celebration of being rich and avoiding poverty offered by a man, who also in the Middle Ages held one of the most unpopular positions in society, that of a lawyer. It is regrettable that Møller ignores this context and presents what is really a dramatic monologue by a bitter lawyer as an independent poem composed by someone his readers have little chance of knowing in 1888, Geoffrey Chaucer.

Conclusion

To sum up the last three chapters very briefly, the Danish reception of Chaucer in the 19th century has two highlights with the studies by Westergaard and Jespersen, paving the way for further academic studies, translations and educational editions in the early and mid-20th century. Professor Bruun, who probably knew of Chaucer from his source text by Alexander Pope, is unwilling to share this knowledge with his 1823 audience, preferring instead to extend the humour of the Wife of Bath to domestic domains. Møller, although a highly skilled poetic translator, leaves an imperfect impression of Chaucer by translating him out of context. And finally Bierfreund with his hollow merry England agenda turns out to be incompetent at studying Chaucer.

30　The most thorough study of the satirical portraits in *The General Prologue* and the tradition that the prologue is part of is Jill Mann, *Chaucer and Medieval Estates Satire* (Mann 1973).

CHAPTER 6

VILHELM MØLLER, UFFE BIRKEDAL AND THE PERIOD 1900-20

In this chapter I will consider the period 1900-20, as already noted two decades that see a marked increase in Chaucer publications in English on both sides of the Atlantic. In Denmark the cultural climate is also slowly changing in favour of more English. This change will be treated in the first part of the chapter, which also includes a discussion of a Chaucer portrait in an English literary history by Adolf Hansen from 1901 (Hansen 1901), a second shorter portrait for secondary school children also by Hansen (Hansen 1929/1907), besides a couple of encyclopedia entries. The second part is devoted to three substantial Chaucer translations. First Vilhelm Møller's translation of about half of *The Summoner's Tale* in connection with a general presentation of *The Canterbury Tales* in the third of his volumes on *Verdenslitteraturens Perler* [The Pearls of World Literature] from 1901. Secondly Birkedal's translations published in 1911 and 1913 of respectively *The General Prologue* and *The Nun's Priest's Tale,* the latter including also the Hugolino section of *The Monk's Tale* and extracts from Langland's *Piers Plowman* (Birkedal, transl., 1911 and 1913). Besides *Verdenslitteraturens Perler,* Vilhelm Møller (1846-1904) is best known for his many translations, not least several of the works of Turgenev. These translations and Møller's importance in literary circles generally have been well discussed in an influential study of the period 1870-1900 in Danish literature, Johan Fjord Jensen's *Turgenev i dansk åndsliv* [Turgenev in Danish culture] (Fjord Jensen 1961: 52-77). Uffe Birkedal (1852-1931), a vicar and later principal of the folk high school in Rønde, was well-known for taking part in public religious and cultural debates, and was also the author of a book about William Morris. His translations include poems by Burns, Byron and Tennyson, and he also translated essays by Carlyle. His most important work was a complete translation of Milton's *Paradise Lost,* published in 1905 as the second Danish translation, the first one published in 1790. In 1908 Birkedal received a distinguished prize for this translation from *Selskabet for de skiønne og nyttige Videnskaber* [The society for fine arts and scholarly research], and the translation was re-published as late as 2006 (Birkedal, transl., 2006).[31]

English in Denmark ca. 1900-20

In his study *Modernitet eller åndsdannelse: Engelsk i skole og samfund 1800-1935* [Modernity or culture: English in education and society 1800-1935] Jens Rahbek Rasmussen has a special focus on the process leading up to the secondary school reform in 1903, where English becomes a compulsory main language in the Danish *gymnasium* for the first time (Rahbek Rasmussen, 2006).[32] As we have also seen in earlier chapters, the process was a slow one, with very few people competent in English a hundred years earlier, then gradually more schools including English as an option. In the last decades of the century, according to Rahbek Rasmussen, an increased number of schools taught English, and one important explanation for this was the fact that by the 1890s the UK had become clearly the best market for Denmark, importing two thirds of all Danish exports (Rahbek Rasmussen: 23 and 86). The reform in 1903 established a *nysproglig gymnasium* option (secondary school up to A levels with modern languages) to compete with the *gammelsproglig* option (classical languages) and the science- and math-based options, a *gymnasium* system known to most Danes still, because it lasted with

---

31 I have used information from Jensen, ed. at *http://www.litteraturpriser.dk/aut/bu.htm*, Lund, gen. ed., 1995: 44 and Downs 1948 as sources of Birkedal's life and works. In the case of the Milton translation I have given a sketch of the Danish reception in my Milton author portrait in *Forfatterleksikon: udenlandske forfattere* [Author encyclopedia: foreign authors] (Klitgård in Michelsen ed., 1999: vol. 2, 448). In the first section of this chapter I have drawn on other entries in this encyclopedia written by myself (Shakespeare, Wilde, Wells) and by author colleagues in the encyclopedia for whom I edited the bibliography sections with the assistance of librarian Carsten Ravn.

32 During the final editing process of this dissertation I received the sad news of the death of my good friend and former colleague Jens Rahbek Rasmussen (1949-2012). Let me take this opportunity to acknowledge his great inspiration as a thorough and dedicated scholar.

only minor revisions for approximately 100 years. In 1903 it was a bold and innovative reform, since the status of English was still that of a very foreign language. A professor at the University of Copenhagen, Professor Lütken, estimated that 10 per cent of the university students knew English, and as Rahbek Rasmussen points out, this will have covered a sound knowledge of grammar and some experience in reading English texts, but hardly fluent communicative competence in most cases (8-9 and 56). Symptomatically a planned invitation of English students to visit the University of Copenhagen in 1901 was cancelled because it was feared by many that communication would be too difficult, and in the same year and apparently for much the same reasons a public royal visit by the new king and queen was also changed into a private visit by the queen only (8-9). Edward VII's queen Alexandra had a proper chance to communicate with the Danes, being Danish of birth herself.

Culturally speaking the beginning of the 20th century was still a period where English in Denmark was mainly associated with England, even when that designation covered the United Kingdom or the British Isles. After the Boer War there were some anti-English voices in Denmark, but not only trade was going well, there were cultural imports as well. One such was the Boy Scout movement, which came to Denmark only two years after Baden-Powell had established the organization in 1907 (Kolind 2000: 573-4, Rahbek Rasmussen 2006: 23). American culture was still very secondary in influence, and even though such an important cultural symbol as the hamburger was invented in the year 1900 (Bredal 1999: 151), it was well after World War 2 that this and other American food became popular in Denmark. This tendency is also seen in the field of literature. Rahbek Rasmussen claims that Jespersen's English and American reader, which I mentioned in the last chapter, was used in the new *gymnasium* mainly for its predominant British content, and he uses the convincing argument that a later revision by Jespersen did away with the few American pieces altogether, renaming the collection *A British Reader* (Rahbek Rasmussen 2006: 96, Jespersen 1928).

Rahbek Rasmussen discusses Jespersen's role in the period leading up to the school reform at length, and for good reasons. Jespersen fights a strong battle from his professorial chair that he received in the year his Chaucer study was published, 1893. He writes diligently in the Danish newspapers, and although he is in opposition to many, his influence is very important in bringing about the reform. Jespersen is even prophetic, as he argues that English will become the international language of scholarship, as Latin formerly was (Rahbek Rasmussen 2006: 96 ff., especially 99). In connection with Birkedal's translations it is also worth noting that Jespersen is acknowledged for his help and advice by Birkedal, who also recommends Jespersen's study for a more thorough introduction to Chaucer's life and works (Birkedal 1911: 6).

Adolf Hansen, an anonymous encyclopedia entry, and Otto Andersson

Birkedal also includes a favourable reference to a Danish *docent* (associate professor) of English at the University of Copenhagen, Adolf Hansen (1850-1908), who wrote an English literary history that was used for many years in the new *gymnasium*, twice revised after his death by H. Helweg-Møller (Hansen 1929/1907). This 100 page literary history includes three pages on Chaucer with a further few pages on Old and Middle English literature, including *Beowulf*, which Hansen had translated, to be published posthumously (Hansen, transl., 1910). The treatment of Chaucer is generally fair as far as life and works is concerned, and Hansen tries his best to entertain by selecting details from the portraits in the *General Prologue* to give his young readers an impression of the diverse characters. The appearance of the Pardoner and Wife of Bath are foregrounded, but even these two characters have to be dealt with in a couple of lines. Hansen translates one quotation, from *The Knight's Tale*, 1491-96, about the lark as busy messenger of day, and whereas he does so in neat lyrical verse, he rather misleadingly uses the example to claim that Chaucer is a nature lover. Apart from that there are no obvious weaknesses in Hansen's Chaucer portrait, except a statement on the lines of Bierfreund claiming that "Der er over Chaucers første Ungdomsdigtning en vis Vaghed og Veghed og en Forkærlighed for allegorisk Fremstillingsmåde." [Chaucer's first, youthful poetry is marked by a certain vagueness and feebleness and a preference for allegorical presentation]. This is a generalization that fails to recognize Chaucer's unique talent even in his youthful poetry, but of course Hansen is not alone in his assessment.

Somewhat more successfully, Adolf Hansen worked on Chaucer a few years earlier for the third volume of Gyldendal's *Illustreret Verdens-Litteraturhistorie* from 1901, edited by Julius Clausen. There are two illustrations, one containing the Chaucer portrait from Harley MS 2866, folio 88, and the second a full page illustration from William Morris's Kelmscott edition containing the scene from *The Knight's Tale* of Emily in the garden with Palemon and Arcite behind prison bars. Altogether there are 10 pages on life and works, also including some short pieces of translation, including the famous opening of *The Canterbury Tales*. Hansen's translations are with only 30 lines translated too short for assessing his skills as a translator, but I analyse his opening lines later in this chapter and compare them to Birkedal's translation.

Hansen also translates a short bit from the beginning of *The Book of the Duchess* (lines 11-15 and 30-34), but makes the mistake of thinking that it expresses Chaucer's own melancholy or even a kind of "Verdenssmærte" [Weltschmerz or general feeling of pain] (Hansen 1901: 30). This confusion of Chaucer with some of his persona narrators is also found in Hansen's discussion of other works, such as *The Parliament of Fowls* and *The Legend of Good Women.* For example Hansen translates 10 lines from the F text of *The Legend of Good Women*, 175-82, in which the speaker conventionally praises the season of spring and in this case in particular the daisy flower. However, Hansen takes this as proof of Chaucer being a true nature lover rather than a poet skillfully making use of the proper poetic code for medieval love poetry (Hansen 1901: 32). I partly forgive Hansen his mistake, for unlike some of his fellow literary historians considered in this study Hansen has at least clearly read some of Chaucer's early works besides *The Canterbury Tales*, and he gives a generally balanced portrait of the poet. Hansen prefers generalizations about Chaucer's writing to discussing examples, although he does mention and discuss some of Chaucer's best known characters from *The General Prologue*, such as the Pardoner, the Monk and the Parson (36). No less than four times (notably on page 35) is Chaucer compared to the renaissance and Shakespeare, and in many ways Hansen constructs Chaucer as a kind of early renaissance writer, the implication being that not much else of any literary value came out of the late Middle Ages. This of course is a tendency often seen in literary assessments of Chaucer, even to the present day, but that does not make it any truer.

A short entry on Chaucer is found in *Allers Illustrerede Konversations*

Leksikon (Lütken, ed. 1906: 652), the first of several *konversationsleksika* [literally conversation encyclopediae] that appeared in the 20th century, where most Danes wanted to have one of these on their bookshelves, a tradition that has disappeared again in the 21st century with the internet generation. I will discuss these and similar short entries only briefly, but of course they are important in the sense that many Danes will have acquired their only general knowledge of Chaucer from them. As we shall see in many examples, the information we get from them is not always reliable or very accurate. The exception to this rule is *Salmonsens Konversationsleksikon*, the second edition of which from 1915-30 was briefly mentioned in the last chapter, with the Chaucer entry written by Otto Jespersen.

The 18-line entry in *Allers illustrerede konversations leksikon*, unsigned as all its entries, is not the worst example of a Chaucer portrait, but it has a prominent emphasis on life rather than works and only mentions one work, *The Canterbury Tales*, briefly at the end. This encyclopedia from 1906, edited by George Lütken (1839-1906), is the last I have seen printed in blackletter.[33] It uses phonetic transcriptions of most foreign names with a phonetic alphabet that looks like home-made. Chaucer thus becomes [tjaahs'r]. He is acknowledged as the father of English poetry, but the assertion that he actually created the English poetic language ("skabte det engelske Digtersprog", Lütken, ed. 1906: 652) is of course taking it too far. Furthermore, the author of the portrait is around 25 years wrong in claiming that Chaucer began his writing career as a translator in 1387. To his credit, he establishes that Chaucer was born "omtr. 1340" [around 1340], but he has not wondered about the fact that Chaucer according to his own estimate would have started writing in his late 40s.

The next encyclopedia entry, in *Illustreret Konversationsleksikon* from 1908 (Anderssen in Rørdam, ed., 1908: 344-5), also has an amusing phonetic transcription of Chaucer's name, here as [tŠå'sə]. This portrait is more substantial with its 50 lines. It was written by Otto Anderssen (1851-1922), who became the first Norwegian professor of educational studies and whose publications cover a broad field within the humanities

---

33 George Lütken was in the medical profession, but near the end of his life he edited both this encyclopedia and a dictionary for Carl Aller's press, still today a major Danish publisher of mainly popular magazines (Blangstrup 1924: 202).

(Skagen, accessed November 2011). Anderssen, unlike the anonymous author in the *Aller* encyclopedia, appears to have consulted an unnamed source, where he has found information about the framework of *The Canterbury Tales*. He mentions the diversity of the tales and talks about Chaucer's "fine fortællekunst" [sophisticated narrative art] (Anderssen: 345). Very little is included about Chaucer's remaining works. The only other work mentioned is *Troilus and Criseyde*, or *Troilus and Cressida* as also Andersson calls it, and this is mistakenly placed as an early work written before Chaucer became acquainted with Dante and Boccaccio. Andersson is also inaccurate about details in Chaucer's life, claiming that "Londons Borgere forærede ham et Hus og Kongen en Krukke Vin daglig" [The citizens of London gave him a house and the king gave him a daily pitcher of wine] (Andersson: 344). Chaucer's house in Aldgate was given to him rent-free in 1374 as part of the wages paid for his employment at court, but he still had to maintain it, and it was certainly not a gift from the people. As for the wine, this allowance was converted into cash a few years later, and although it was given as an honour, it may also be regarded as a part of his wages, as Ward noted in his chapter on Chaucer's life from 1880 (Ward 1880: 48-9, Pearsall 1992: 95-97). By including such simplified assumptions, Andersson manages to create an idealized image of Chaucer as a celebrity in his time. Combined with statements such as "Han elskede Naturen og Kunsten, Verdenslivet som Arbejdet og Ensomheden" [He loved Nature and Art, Life in the world, as well as work and loneliness] Andersson furthermore contributes to the wealth of life writing about Chaucer that constructs an image of him as he would be in the writer's own idealized picture.

Classics translations and translation from English in Møller's and Birkedal's time

Before turning to an analysis of Møller's and Birkedal's Chaucer, I will also briefly consider the context of the translations by looking at respectively translations of Chaucer's Italian inspirations into Danish and translations of other English language works in the period. Dante's *Divina Commedia* had been translated already in 1851-62 by Chr. K.F. Molbech, and in 1908 the 5th edition of this immensely popular classic appeared with an introduction by literary historian Valdemar Vedel. Boccaccio's *Decamerone* was translated by Sophus Prahl just a few years before this and published in a collection of three volumes in 1907. The third of the great Italian *trecento* poets, Petrarca, was translated by Fr. Moth and published in a small collection of poetry in 1924. Some psalms by Petrarca had been translated already in the 16th century, and as we have seen some English classics like Milton were translated relatively early, but we are now in a period where a lot more world literature appears either for the first time or in new translations. This includes also a number of works in the series in which Jespersen's Chaucer study and Birkedal's Chaucer translations appear, *Studier fra Sprog- og Oldtidsforskning* [Studies in Linguistics and Ancient Literature], with Birkedal's second translation in 1913 up to number 90.

At this point it is also worth noting that by 1911 the works of William Shakespeare have been published in Danish translation three times, a fourth translation begun in 1927.[34] The bard's popularity among English authors in Denmark can only be compared to that of Charles Dickens, who was obviously read by a broader segment of the population, although there is only one complete translation, by L. Moltke, mainly undertaken during his lifetime but collected in a revised complete edition in 29 volumes 1889-94.[35] Like Dickens, most of the prominent writers of the 19th century and early 20th century were translated soon after their works originally appeared. This is mainly true of the Brontë sisters, George Eliot, Rudyard Kipling, Robert Louis Stevenson, Arthur Conan Doyle and H.G. Wells, and also of American authors such as Mark Twain and Jack London. However, there are notable delays such as Jane Austen, as already noted, and one Brontë novel, arguably the most important of them all, Emily Brontë's *Wuthering Heights,* was not translated until 1919.

---

34 The translations, listed in the bibliography, are by Foersom and Wulff 1807-25, Foersom and Lembcke 1861-73, Lembcke 1897-1900 and 1910-11, and Østerberg 1927-48 and 1958. In the 1990s Niels Brunse began what will soon appear as a complete 5th Shakespeare translation in Denmark. Some of these translators are treated in Hjørnager Pedersen and Quale 1998, which also includes a brief survey of the translation history of English literature into Danish and Norwegian.

35 Eva Hemmer Hansen (1913-83) nearly finished a complete translation shortly before passing away in 1983. Both Moltke's and Hemmer Hansen's translations and the many translations by others of individual works have been treated in Nielsen 2009.

Other notable long delays in translation are the early modernists Joseph Conrad, Stephen Crane and Henry James, most of whose works were not translated until the 1950s and later. Another famous early modernist, D.H. Lawrence, was first published in Denmark in the 1930s, but as a noteworthy point *Lady Chatterley's Lover* appeared as the first translation in 1932. It was censored and abbreviated until a new complete translation was published in 1950, ten years before that infamous novel first passed through British censorship. One other writer unjustly pursued by public scandal, Oscar Wilde, had only one play, *Lady Windermere's Fan,* translated into Danish in his heyday, the 1890s, but most of his other works appeared in fairly quick succession from 1905-1927, his most popular play, *The Importance of Being Earnest,* first staged in Denmark in 1922 as *Bunbury* (Klitgård 1999).

The context of Vilhelm Møller's and Uffe Birkedal's translations in the first two decades of the 20th century is, to sum up, a remarkable flow of new and old English literature as well as world classics in Danish translation. In some cases, as with Shakespeare and Dickens, translations appear in high frequency, in other cases works get quickly translated, and in yet other cases not at all or with serious delays. Before turning to an analysis of Møller's and Birkedal's work, let me finally point out that among the "not at all" translated works before 1920 is more or less all literature from the age of Chaucer, including Gower and the Gawain poet, although by 1920 many late medieval works have been well edited. Langland is the only contemporary of Chaucer to have been translated, also by Birkedal.

Vilhelm Møller's Chaucer translation

It is most strange that someone who wants to introduce Chaucer to a Danish audience, and who is living in an age where farting is an absolute taboo, should want to single out *The Summoner's Tale* for translation. This is one of Chaucer's crudest fabliaux, and the tale's climax and meaning depends on the main character, an annoying and hypocritical friar, getting what he deserves after pestering a dying man for further money and goods: the gift of an enormous fart, which moreover he has promised to share with his monastery. This sharing of the gift takes place in a masterful scene of low comedy, as the fart is ingeniously divided in 12 parts by the friars.[36] In 1901 Vilhelm Møller publishes his tale translation in connection with an introduction to *The Canterbury Tales* in the third volume of his series *Verdenslitteraturens Perler* (The Pearls of World Literature) that was first begun in 1897 (V. Møller 1901: 44-55). About half of his text is a translation of about half of *The Summoner's Tale*, and since he so desperately wants to avoid mentioning farting, it is a necessary choice to cut the tale in half, which he does with the remark that his reader must turn to Chaucer if he wants to know what happened. This must surely have been frustrating for the many of his contemporary readers who did not read English, but perhaps this radical strategy was actually effective in relation to the readers who did. Vilhelm Møller may well have made these readers very curious and wanting to read some Chaucer. I will analyse Møller's translation at the end of this section, but first I briefly consider the first part of his article, a general Chaucer introduction.

Møller's introduction to Chaucer's *Canterbury Tales* starts with the sentence "Det var Skik i det 14de Aarhundredes England at valfarte til adskillige hellige Grave og Billeder" [It was custom in the England of the 14th century to go on pilgrimage to several holy graves and pictures] (Møller 1901: 44). Then follows a brief historical account of the murder of Thomas a Becket in 1170, but soon this introductory account becomes more directly influenced by Chaucer's text in the opening lines of *The General Prologue*:

> Saa kom de desuden saa fornøjeligt ud af de gamle Folder en Stund! April-Bygerne havde dæmpet Vejenes Støv, Blomster myldrede frem, Skoven sprang ud, og Fuglene sang den ganske Dag og sov af lutter Foraars-Uro med aabne Øjne om Natten. Den samme Uro drev Folk paa Pilgrims-Tog. [Moreover, this gave them a merry opportunity to experience something new for a while. The April showers had made the roads less dusty, there was a riot

---

36 That the idea and practice of farting was far from a taboo in the Middle Ages can be seen in Valerie Allen's brilliant study *On Farting: Language and Laughter in the Middle Ages*, where she also discusses Chaucer's *Summoner's Tale* extensively. See also my enthusiastic review (Allen 2007, Klitgård 2009).

of flowers, the forest had come out, and the birds were singing all day, sleeping with an open eye all night from sheer spring unrest. It was the same unrest that drove people on a pilgrimage].

[Møller 1901: 44]

Møller's text is an interesting mixture of summary and free interpretation of Chaucer's opening lines (Skeat A, 1-12). Chaucer's "Than longen folk to goon on pilgrimages" (12) is the basis for Møller's assumption that the pilgrims are motivated by the opportunity to get new experiences and by the same unrest as the birds, who also in Chaucer's text sleep with an open eye (10). However, the unrest is not mentioned by Chaucer, and the comparison between the birds and the pilgrims is likewise Møller's interpretation. In Chaucer's opening April showers are mentioned in the famous first line "What that Aprille with his shoures sote" (1), but there is no mention of dusty roads at all, so Møller is making his own logical deduction. Finally both flowers and new shoots are included in the description by Chaucer (4 and 7), but not connected with a riot of flowers or with the forest. Møller is adding his own details, and in many ways creating his own, more conventional version of the setting for a pilgrimage. Moreover, he does not acknowledge here that he is using Chaucer's text as the basis for his own, nor does he state any other sources, i.e. historical sources for his information about Thomas a Becket. Møller, unlike Jespersen, is not a scholar, but of course his strategy of representation is not uncommon for his age.

The description of the setting after this introduction is remarkably precisely given as "Aaret 1393, en af de sidste April-Aftener" in "Kroen 'Herolds-Vamsen' i Southwark nær London" [the year 1393, one of the last April evenings in the Tabard Inn in Southwark near London] (44). It may well be that Møller has the year 1393 from some of the contemporary sources making a game of guessing at an actual historical year for the pilgrimage, but the specification of the April date as one of the last days of the month appears to be his own guess. Neither year nor date can be confirmed by any real data, but we now know that Chaucer had started composing *The Canterbury Tales* several years before 1393, and consequently it is not a good guess, which is furthermore represented as fact here. Møller has also decided to translate the name of the inn where the pilgrims meet, the Tabard, as "Herolds-Vamsen". It is correct that "Tabard" means a herald's coat, but the name looks rather funny in translation, perhaps because it is no longer the convention to translate place-names. Birkedal uses the same strategy as Møller and translates even Chaucer's first name, so I will conclude that both translators felt it necessary to use such an extreme domestication strategy.

The introduction of the pilgrims takes up just a little less than one page, and Møller has made a very condensed version of the portraits in *The General Prologue*. The order of presentation is Møller's own, starting, perhaps in an effort to be polite, with the female portraits of the Prioress and the Wife of Bath, then offering a selection of the male characters. The details given are all taken from Chaucer's text, but have been edited and in some cases summed up by Møller, adding also his own comments, such as his concluding remark "Alle Slags Mennesker, i alle Slags Dragter. Der var noget at se paa, som de sad bænket dér i 'Herolds-Vamsens' Gæstestue!" [All kinds of people in all kinds of clothes. Certainly there was something to behold, as they were seated in the parlour of the Tabard Inn!] (45). Møller clearly wants to stay in control of the story-telling with such remarks, and it must be granted that he presents Chaucer's material with enthusiasm.

After a freely rendered presentation of the Host and his proposed contest of tale-telling Møller turns to Chaucer himself, giving some also partly imagined details about his appearance:

> ... "en kraftig, svær Mand, omtrent som Kroværten, med et Par nedslagne, tilsyneladende søvnige Øjne, men med den kloge Iagttagers lune Smil om en lille, bestemt Mund, der stak frem mellem det tynde og tvedelte Skæg..." [a sturdy, heavy man, almost like the Host, with a pair of downcast, apparently sleepy eyes, but with the sharp observer's mild smile about a small, firm mouth, which protruded between the thin and forked beard]
> (Møller 1901: 45-6)

We know from the Host's comments in the prologue to Chaucer's own tale, *Sir Thopas* (Benson, gen. ed., VII, 695-706) that Chaucer is represented as someone who looks down all the time, but to conclude from this humorous self-representation that he is a man with downcast and apparently sleepy eyes is taking it quite far. Møller may well have seen one of the Chaucer portraits suggesting a sturdy man, but again the rest of the details, apart perhaps from the beard, are his own imagination.

This imagined presentation of Chaucer leads Møller on to a summary of the real Chaucer's life and works, based on a source that could well be Skeat's edition, which had been published a few years earlier and from which Møller probably also took his base text for translation of *The Summoner's Tale* (Skeat 1894-7). This part gives the main points of Chaucer's life at court and also gives a brief account of his literary inspirations in France and Italy. Whereas there is nothing controversial in this account, there is a major surprise awaiting at least the modern reader in the next paragraph, where Møller claims that Chaucer really went on a pilgrimage to Canterbury with the characters he has described, and that his book *The Canterbury Tales* consists of his re-telling of the tales he heard on that journey, adding only "hvad der lige stod i Forbindelse dermed" [what happened to be connected with them] (46). Whereas many Chaucer critics, also in the Danish reception, have discussed Chaucer as a realist, I have never elsewhere come across a postulate about actual authenticity, a claim that the tales really were told on a journey, and that Chaucer just wrote them down. Maybe Møller has been misled by Chaucer's general fictive stance about his own role on the pilgrimage and his more specific warning at the end of *The Miller's Prologue* (Benson ed., I 3167-86) not to hold him responsible for some of the more dubious stories, because he just heard them and wrote them down. Still, he has been misled, and he is consequently misleading his own reader.

Møller continues his Chaucer introduction by commenting briefly on Chaucer's more serious tales, such as *The Prioress' Tale* and *The Clerk's Tale*, which he does not mention by title but by saying what they are about. He does not like any of the serious tales, and does not hesitate to say that they "indeholder intet særegent" [contain nothing special] and that Chaucer did not find "gribende Udtryk for den Art roligere Sindsbevægelser" [any moving expression for this kind of slowly progressing emotional development] (47). Louise Westergaard (chapter 4) and other serious readers of *The Clerk's Tale* could hardly disagree more, and apparently Møller has not really made an effort to read anything but the comic tales. Before turning to *The Summoner's Tale* he even quotes Niels Møller's short translation from *Efteraar* (Møller 1888, see chapter 5) as further evidence for his claim that Chaucer is no good except in writing comedy (47). He adds for emphasis, "Dét var det nye, han bragte. Han er Nytids-Literaturens først Humorist" [That was the new thing he contributed with. He is the first humorist of the literature of the new age] (48).

After a comparison between Chaucer and Boccaccio and an introduction to the dramatic interludes, Møller introduces us to the quarrel between the Friar and the Summoner, translating also a few lines from both the Friar's and the Summoner's *Prologues*. In the summary of *The Summoner's Prologue* Møller carefully avoids using Chaucer's direct word "ers" ("arse", Skeat, ed., D 1690), but at least he is not afraid to say that Satan's tail is lifted to show the actual whereabouts of friars in Hell (50). Then he turns to *The Summoner's Tale* itself. As indicated already, Møller translates about half of the tale, and more specifically he stops at line 1980, leaving out about 300 lines with the climax of the fart and the ensuing episode of the divided fart. His defence of this decision is, "Der er Ting, som det jo meget vel gaar an at læse selv, men som det ikke sømmer sig for andre at anføre" [There are things which can very well be read in private, but which it would not be suitable to recount to others] (54). This is followed by a page or so containing further examples of tales that should be read in private and not discussed in front of others, such as *The Wife of Bath's Prologue and Tale*. In what remains of this section I shall refrain from further comments on this in 1901 well-founded editorial decision and instead turn to the roughly 300 lines that Møller does include in his translation. There are some further cuts in the translation, mainly some short interludes that are replaced by Møller's own summary, but also some of the Summoner's representations of the friar's biblical stories that Møller has probably found tedious. The longest section that is cut out is 1851-1937 with among others the story of Moses fasting in the desert.

Møller turns out to be quite a competent translator, and unlike in his summaries he does not generally invent his own details or cut corners, although he is not afraid to opt for a fairly dynamic equivalence. It also appears that he has worked with commentary by Skeat and perhaps others, as he is able to translate such concepts as "trentals" (1724) correctly, using the Danish term "Tredivedages-Messer" [thirty days' masses] for these masses sung for thirty days to rescue a soul in Purgatory (51). Møller obeys rhyme and rhythm very well, and his poetic flow is quite genuine in Danish. This is even more impressive since many of the passages he translates consist of dialogue spoken in common idiom, including some humorously rendered conversations between the friar and the wife of the dying man. A single passage will serve to illustrate this point:

> Slog arm om hendes Liv, i hendes Kind
> [Embraced her, and on her cheek]
> Han med et Trykkys pressed Munden ind,
> [he pressed his mouth with a smack]
> Og kvidred: […] [and chirped:]
> "En Kvinde ej jeg saa' saa smuk som I!" [I never
> saw a woman as beautiful as you]
> "Aah som I snakker!… maa vi være fri!
> [How you're talking! Stop it now!]
> Nej hvor det dog var morsomt, at I kom!"
> [Well, such fun that you came]
> "*Mercy, madame*! – jeg tvivler ej derom!" [Mercy,
> madame – I don't doubt you think so]
> (Møller 1901: 52)

> And hir embraceth in his armes narwe,
> And kiste hir swete, and chirketh as a sparwe,
> With his lippes […]
> "Yet saugh I nat this day so fair a wyf
> In al the chirche, god so save me!"
> "Ye, god amende defautes, sir," quod she,
> "Algates wel-come be ye, by my fey!"
> Grante mercy, dame, this have I founde alwey.
> (Skeat ed., D 1802-4 and 1808-12)

Møller accurately represents the embrace, the kiss and the chirping, although he gives up translating literally, e.g. leaving out the detail of the sparrow in line 1803. This is all very well in a poetic translation, and Møller hits the talkativeness of the tone spot on. The wife's "god amende defautes" means "God correct my faults" and is her polite Middle English self-deprecating answer to the friar's flattery. Møller's wife is equally self-deprecating, even though he lets her use a very different remark "Aah som I snakker!" [How you're talking], which is just the right kind of idiom for playing the game of flattery and rebuttal. Finally it is an acceptable, if less obvious solution to retain the word "mercy" in the final line of the quotation, although Møller has to defend this French term by using it in italics.

Another example of Møller finding a creative solution is the line "Thomas, that jape nis nat worth a myte" (1961), which I would translate more or less directly as "Thomas, that joke is not worth even a small coin", as a myte or mite refers to a small Flemish coin. Møller has "Thomas, hvor har – hvor har Du din Forstand" (53) which covers the sense very well, as the repetition stresses the Friar's insistence that Thomas has really lost the point here. In the ensuing sequence the Friar goes on to explain that Thomas' mistake consists of dividing his presents and money between several convents and friars, and in Chaucer's middle English that becomes a list of "that covent", "that covent", "that frere" (1963-5). Here Møller very sensibly translates by "Kloster A", "Kloster B", etc. (53), which makes the listing principle more easily understandable in Danish.

In sum Møller offers a very good piece of translation to introduce Chaucer's *Canterbury Tales* to a Danish audience, but his choice of a tale that he cannot finish is unfortunate. Furthermore his general presentation of the *Tales* and Chaucer is marked by his serious blunder with respect to the way Chaucer composed his work, because Møller seems to believe or at least pretends to believe it is a record of an authentic experience. Moreover there are serious flaws in his presentation of Chaucer himself and in Møller's reading, or lack of reading, of his serious works.

Uffe Birkedal's Chaucer translations

As Birkedal's two translations appear with only two years between them and both concern parts of *The Canterbury Tales*, I have decided to analyse them in the same section. Birkedal's two introductions are relatively short, as he is able to refer to Jespersen's study in the same series for further introduction to Chaucer. There are four pages on Chaucer in the 1911 publication and one in the 1913 publication, the remainder of that introduction being devoted to Langland and his *Piers Plowman*.[37] Most of the introduction is about Chaucer's life and times, and as with Bierfreund and Jespersen again with a strong focus on the Italian visit and inspiration. Very little mention is made of earlier works than the *Canterbury Tales*, and only a couple of these works are even given a title, all of them in Danish translation: "Bogen om Hertuginden" [*The Book of the Duchess*], "Troilus og Kressida" and "Rygtets Hus" [*The House of Fame*] (Birkedal 1911: 4-5). Birkedal does not rate these works as anything but "Forberedelsen til hans Livs Stordaad" [preparation for his life's great feat] (5), and it is a fair guess that he has not read them. However, Birkedal acknowledges his source text as Skeat's and he also mentions that he has used Skeat's notes supplemented by Ward's book *Chaucer* (Ward 1880). Birkedal's translation includes notes and glosses that show that he has in fact made diligent use of these sources, and I shall consequently quote Chaucer from Skeat's edition in this chapter.

Birkedal's short Chaucer introduction in the 1913 translation includes a noteworthy passage where, like many in the Danish reception before and after him, he tries to evaluate Chaucer's poetry in general:

> Hist og her er hans Skemten vel drøj efter vore begreber, men han er aldrig slibrig. Der ligger et halvt Aartusinde mellem Dickens og Chaucer, men den Maade, hvorpaa Digterlandsmændene tager de menneskelige Naragtigheder og Daarskaber under Behandling, er væsentlig ens og saa helt ud engelsk. [Here and there his jesting is somewhat coarse according to our notions, but he is never lubricious. There is half a millennium between Dickens and Chaucer, but the way the two poets and countrymen treat the follies and antics of human beings is by and large the same and so very English].
> (Birkedal 1913: 3)

Birkedal, who by choosing *The General Prologue* and a beast fable for translation has avoided all the frivolous passages in Chaucer's work,

---

37 Birkedal translates Piers Plowman first by *Per Plovmand*, then by *Peder Plovmand* (Birkedal 1911: 4 and Birkedal 1913: 5) whereas Bierfreund refers to this work as *Peter Pløjemands vision* (Bierfreund 1892: 173).

seems to know these well enough, and he is on a par with Bruun (see chapter 3) in ascribing a certain coarseness to Chaucer that is not easily acceptable to the Danes. This may be true from an early 20th century point of view, but actually there is also an older Danish tradition for rascal stories in the *fabliau* genre, most notably the dramatic fabliau from the 1530s *Den utro hustru* [The Unfaithful Wife] with a main plot comparable to Chaucer's *Shipman's Tale* (Birket Smith, ed., 1874). This may not have been known to Bruun and Birkedal.[38]

Birkedal's other main point in the quotation, the comparison between Chaucer and Dickens as both exponents of a very English treatment of human follies, is not a deeply original one, but still absolutely true in my opinion. Both writers share a sharp eye for the central vehicles of narrative, character and plot, and both are exquisite users of the English language to such an extent that they become emblematic of their respective literary periods. In what ways the works of these two eminent authors reflect Englishness specifically is a more complicated matter than Birkedal wants to acknowledge here, but let me at least agree that there are more national identity markers in their works than the language itself.

Turning to questions of translation again, the 1911 publication includes a brief introduction to the general framework and setting of *The Canterbury Tales* as presented in *The General Prologue*, and in this connection Birkedal, like Møller, chooses to translate the name of that setting, the Tabard Inn in Southwark south of London, as "Heroldkappen" [the herald's coat], both in the introduction and his translation of line 20. This follows his line of translating not only titles in full, but also in the case of his main text the names. Birkedal's title, "Kanterborghistorierne", changes the "C-" to the corresponding "K-" in Danish, translates "bury" as "borg", and chooses "historierne" in preference of "fortællingerne" for "tales". All can be warranted in Danish, which does prefer "k" for "c" in especially initial position, and "borg" does correspond to "bury" in actual parallel place names such as Newbury/Nyborg. Also, "historierne" [the stories] is acceptable, if a less natural choice than "fortællingerne". However, the domestication strategy goes over the top as the first name of the author is also translated as "Got-

---

38 I witnessed a splendid performance of the play at Bellahøj in Copenhagen in the early 1980s, with Danish actor and singer Maria Stenz as the unfaithful wife.

fred", to be sure a Danish and German parallel name, but not quite the same as Geoffrey. Birkedal, fortunately, remains the only Danish translator to date that has called the father of English literature Gotfred. Admittedly, early printers spelled Chaucer's name in funny ways, such as Geffrey Chavser (Speght) and Geaffrey Chaucer (Thynne), but this is well in line with spelling practice before spelling was standardized, and also Shakespeare's name has been spelled in several variants. This does not make Birkedal's name translation any more reasonable, and it is also a real change, not a spelling variant. The practice of translating names was more prevalent in Birkedal's time generally, whereas more recently it has been restricted to only a few genres, notably young children's literature. However, in publications from *Studier fra Sprog- og Oldtidsforskning* that follow relatively closely after Jespersen's study, it is very surprising that Birkedal settles on Gotfred.

Another unusual translation strategy is Birkedal's occasional choice of poetic Danish words that are so archaic that he has to explain their meaning in a footnote. Birkedal says in his 1911 introduction that "Jeg har givet min Oversættelse en let gammeldags Sprogtone, som kan minde Læseren om Digtets ærværdige Alder" [I have given my translation a slightly old-fashioned language tone that may serve for the reader as a reminder of the venerable age of the poem]. This is certainly the case, as we shall see in the analysis, and this is only to be expected in Birkedal's time and age. The extracts I have read from his *Paradise Lost* translation also have a venerable, archaic ring. However, it seems an extreme solution to introduce certain idioms that are no longer understood by even educated readers. Two examples will suffice. In the portrait of the Prioress in *The General Prologue*, 134, it says that "In curteisye was set ful muche her lest." (Skeat, ed., A 132), which Birkedal translates rather freely as "og hendes största Fryd var Tugt og Somme" [and her greatest joy was discipline and honour] (Birkedal 1911: 13, line 134), adding an explanatory note saying that "Tugt og Somme" is an expression from the ancient Danish folk songs *Kæmpeviserne* and referring to a word list by the editor of these, Axel Olrik (Olrik, ed., 1877-90). "Somme", out of use also in the early 20th century, means "honour" and is now only echoed in the also archaic adjectival use "sømmeligt", meaning "honourable". The second example is from the portrait of the Friar, line 218, "For he had power of confessioun" (Skeat, ed., A 218). Birkedal says "ti han havde Skriftemagt" [for he had the power to take confession] (16, line 225), preferring the older conjunction "ti" to "for", which is in line with his strategy. The problem word is "Skriftemagt", which is not an idiomatic expression and cannot be found in *Ordbog over det Danske Sprog*. It sounds both over-archaic and as something constructed for the purpose, which is supported by Birkedal putting it in inverted commas in his explanatory note.

To be fair, Birkedal was not the only practitioner of obsolete archaisms in the poetry of his time. One of the leading Danish poets of the day, Holger Drachmann (1846-1908), wrote a poem in 1877 called "De vog dem, vi grov dem en grav i vor have" [They killed them, we dug them a grave in our garden], also known as "De sønderjydske Piger" [The girls from Southern Jutland] (Drachmann 1877). The verbs "vog" and "grov" are deliberate archaic choices, and whereas "grov" would have been recognized as an old strong verb alternative to the ordinary weak form "gravede", "vog" would hardly have been recognised at all and only understood from the context. The use of "vog" goes back to Danish folk songs like "Niels Ebbesøn".[39] A poet like Drachmann would have been much admired by Birkedal, not least because, like Birkedal himself, he spent years translating English poetry. Drachmann's translation of Byron's *Don Juan* appeared in full in 1902, but was begun in 1879 and published gradually from 1880 (Dahl 1996: 230, Drachmann 1880-1902).

The archaic features in Birkedal's translations are first of all a number of idioms, some of which appear in passages analysed below. However, there are also examples of morphological changes, such as the occasional use of ancient Danish inflections. One example is the modal verb "skalst" [shall/must] (Birkedal 1913: 28), which here adds the second person singular "-st" still in use in German, but obsolete in Danish. Also the number system is from time to time archaic, as in "Dage treti to" [thirty-two days] (Birkedal 1913: 32), which would also in Birkedal's time have been "to og tredive Dage". Here it is not German, but Swedish that Birkedal can rely on for his audience to understand what number he is talking about, as the modern Swedish number system is quite similar to the archaic Danish one. Most of the changes in the formal system are, however, more easily recognisable as simply old Danish forms, e.g. "hvi"

---

39 I am grateful for this example from Drachmann's practice to *Politikens Oplysning*, the information service of the Danish newspaper *Politiken*, 26 March 2011: 20.

instead of "hvorfor" [why] and "eders" instead of "jeres" [your/yours] (Birkedal 1913: 35 and 37).

Selecting a few passages for closer inspection, let me start with Birkedal's translation of the opening of *The Canterbury Tales*. The analysis here will be restricted to the first six lines of *The General Prologue*, comparing them to Adolf Hansen's translation:

> Saa tit April med Regnen mild og god [So
> often April with rain, mild and good]
> Marstørken vædet har til dybest Rod [the drought
> of March has wetted to deepest root]
> og badet alle Aarer med en Saft, [And
> bathed every vein with a liquid]
> hvoraf hver Urt og Blomst faar Voksekraft, [From which
> every herb and flower receives growing power]
> og Zephyr aander med sin søde Mund [And
> Zephyr breathes with his sweet mouth]
> paa Vaarens Spirer trindt i Mark og Lund, [on the
> shoots of spring all around in field and grove]
> (Birkedal 1911: 7, 1-6)

> Naar i April de friske Byger trænge [When in
> April the fresh showers penetrate]
> Ned i den tørre Muld paa Mark og Enge [into
> the dry mould of field and meadow]
> Og alle Rødder bade sig i Regn [and all
> roots bathe themselves in rain]
> Og skyde Blomster frem som Livsenstegn,
> [and shoot out flowers as signs of life]
> Naar Zefyr med sit friske, milde Pust [When
> Zephyr with his fresh, mild blow]
> Hen over Krat og Hede lunt har sust [has
> whistled across thicket and heath]
> (Hansen 1901: 28)

> Whan that Aprille with his shoures sote
> The droghte of Marche hath perced to the rote,

> And bathed every veyne in swich licour
> Of which vertu engendred is the flour;
> Whan Zephirus eek with his swete breeth
> Inspired hath in every holt and heath
> (Chaucer in Skeat, ed., A 1-6)

Both Birkedal and Hansen have taken care to obey the metre with iambic pentameters in rhymed couplets, and they both write even more regular verse than Chaucer. This means that they look for new words in rhyme position, here "god/Rod", "Saft/Voksekraft" and "Mund/Lund" (Birkedal) and "trænge/Enge", "Regn/Livsenstegn" and "Pust/sust" (Hansen) to match "sote/rote", "licour/flor" and "breeth/heath" in Chaucer. Both translators are successful in maintaining as many important words in rhyme position as possible. Also both translators very sensibly sacrifice absolute accuracy for poetic flow, as in Birkedal's first line, where "Saa tit" [So often] is not the same as "Whan that", but close enough to convey the general meaning. Correspondingly Hansen lets the root actively shoot out the flowers, which also covers the original denotative meaning. The insertion of the unparallelled "Urt" [herb] in line three is an example of Birkedal's general strategy, which includes addition as here, but also deletion, as in line 4, where "vertu", which could have been translated by Danish "sandelig", is not translated. Regarding addition and deletion strategies, both Birkedal and Hansen in my estimate follow a highly commendable practice in poetic translation, because they manage to compose poetry that flows well, while at the same time remaining loyal to the source text with only insignificant changes of meaning. The opening of *The Canterbury Tales* is in fact somewhat untypical of Chaucer in that it opens with a rather complicated, long sentence, and Birkedal and Hansen are able to translate all 12 lines of that sentence into one long corresponding Danish sentence, while maintaining both its lyrical quality and its general sense. And as the first six lines here indicate, Birkedal is certainly not more difficult to understand than Chaucer, at least not here, where he almost avoids his often unfortunate archaisms. Only the adverb "trindt" (6) is here used in its archaic meaning "all around". Hansen's version, although he has made some different choices than Birkedal, is equally commendable, and he would have been the obvious choice for further Chaucer translations had ne not died so relatively young.

Extracts from just a few other passages in *The General Prologue* will suffice to amplify my analysis of Birkedal's translation strategy in the 1911 publication, as some further bits are used for comparative analysis in later chapters. Here is the beginning of the portrait of the Summoner:

> En *Stævningsmand* var og til Rejsen mødt [A
> *Summoner* had also turned up for the journey]
> Hans ansigt var kerubisk luerødt [His face
> was like a cherub's red as fire]
> Og fuldt af Blegner. Øjnene var smaa, [And
> pimpled. His eyes were small,]
> Rask var han, og saa gejl som Spurven graa, [He was in
> good shape, and as lecherous as the gray sparrow,]
> med tjavset Skæg og Skorpesaar helt mange,
> [with a wispy beard and lots of scabs,]
> saa for hans Aasyn Børnene var bange. [so the
> children were afraid of his countenance.]
> (Birkedal 1911: 33, 654-9)

> A Somnour was ther with us in that place,
> That hadde a fyr-reed cherubinnes face,
> For sawcefleem he was, with eyen narwe.
> As hoot he was, and lecherous, as a sparwe;
> With scalled browes blake, and piled berd;
> Of his visage children were aferd.
> (Skeat, ed.: A 623-8)

Again here Birkedal is rather successful with this horrific portrait of one of the villainous characters. Rhyme and rhythm work immaculately, even with an alliteration, "Skæg og Skorpesaar" (658), to match one in Chaucer's text, "browes blake". The details of the Summoner's child-frightening looks are conveyed with great precision. "Kerubisk" is an adjectivization of "kerub" [cherub] and is rare in Danish, but it fits the construction "kerubisk luerødt" well and can be readily understood, "lue" in "luerødt" [red as fire] being the archaic and colourful choice in preference for the stylistically neutral "ild" [fire]. The Middle English expression "sawcefleem" (625) finds a fine equivalent in the now archaic "fuld af Blegner" [pimpled], "Blegner" in modern Danish having been replaced by "bumser". The only slight criticism would be the translation of Chaucer's "hoot" in line 626 with "rask" [in good shape/fit] which perhaps deliberately avoids the sexual connotation. However, Birkedal includes that connotation later in the same line by using the unequivocally sexual reference of the word "gejl" [lecherous], a word now only used in Danish in its verb form with a preposition, "gejle op", a more innocent idiom meaning "provoke to action".

Birkedal's fine ability to translate Chaucer's colourful style and find the devil in the detail is also seen in some other portraits of unsympathetic characters. Examples include the line about the Shipman that "Of nyce conscience took he no keep" (Skeat, A 398), which Birkedal translates by "Til øm Samvittighed han ikke kendte" [he did not know of any tender conscience] (23, 411). The adjective "nyce" in Middle English can mean "foolish", but is glossed in the *Riverside* edition as scrupulous (Benson, gen. ed., 1987: 30). Birkedal hits the nail on the head by "øm" [tender], which in Danish has connotations to a softness that would be both foolish and too scrupulous in a character that makes stealing from others part of his living. Also in the portrait of the Pardoner Birkedal renders the details well, as when he translates "A voys he hadde as small as hath a goot" (Skeat: A 688) by "Hans Stemme var saa fin som Gedens Bræg" [His voice was as fine as a goat's bleating] (35, 718). In Danish "Bræg" is an onomatopoeiac expression referring to a goat's bleating, and it thus replaces "voys" well in this connection. Secondly, it works for Birkedal as a new rhyme-word to rhyme with "Skæg" [beard] in the next line, at least if both words are pronounced with a soft "-g", which for "skæg" in modern Danish is only the case in some dialects.

Birkedal, like Chaucer, knows how to be careful when addressing issues to do with the female sex. The gentle satire of The Wife of Bath in *The General Prologue* is one of the most elegant parts of Birkedal's translation, and he rounds it off by showing a fine ability to find idioms matching Chaucer's:[40]

---

40 For the sake of academic honesty it should be noted that not all scholars have interpreted the Wife of Bath portrait as a gentle satire. Most notorious is the view promoted by the patristic critic D.W. Robertson in his in many ways otherwise commendable study *A Preface to Chaucer*. He sees the Wife as "hopelessly carnal

Den Tid hun var udi en munter Flok, [The time she spent in a jolly party]
Hun kunde le og tale lystigt nok. [She could laugh and talk quite merrily]
Hun Elskovs Veje nøje kendte til, [She knew the ways of love accurately]
Og hun forstod helt vel det gamle Spil. [And she well understood the old game]
(Birkedal 1911: 27, 490-3)

In felawschip wel coude she laughe and carpe.
Of remedyes of love she knew perchaunce,
For she coude of that art the olde daunce.
(Skeat, A 474-6)

It should first be noted that this is an example that partly explains why Birkedal's General Prologue is 41 lines longer than Chaucer's. Here and several other places he translates one line (474) by two (490-1), and he apparently does so because he is in need of appropriate rhyme-words. I think he should be forgiven for this, and as can hopefully be seen from my back translation, he catches the essential meaning well and only explicates idioms like Chaucer's "In felawschip" (474). The corresponding Danish expressions are certainly idiomatic, notably "Elskovs Veje" [the ways of love] for "remedyes of love" (475) and "det gamle Spil" [the old game] for "the olde daunce" (476).

Issues about women are also on the agenda in Birkedal's 1913 translation of *The Nun's Priest's Tale,* where the following aside to the audience or reader is given by the narrator:

Ved Kvinderaad vor Jammer først er bleven [a woman's council first made our misery]
Ti derved Adam blev fra Eden dreven, [For this is how Adam was driven from Eden]

---

and literal" and is not much amused by her (Robertson 1962: 317). A more balanced reservation about her character and type can be found in Alistair Minnis' study *Fallible Authors: Chaucer's Pardoner and Wife of Bath* (Minnis 2007).

> Hvor han henleved udi idel Lykke. [Where
> he dwelled in sheer happiness]
> Men da jeg véd ej, hvem det kan mistykke, [But since
> I do not know who might be offended by it]
> Hvis Kvinders Raad at laste her jeg vover [If
> I dare blame the council of women]
> i Gammenstale, jeg det springer over. [in
> joking speech, I will let it pass]
> (Birkedal 1913: 35. This edition does not contain line numbers.)

> Wommannes counseil broghte us first to wo,
> And made Adam fro paradys to go,
> Ther-as he was ful mery, and wel at ese.-
> But for I noot, to whom it mighte displese,
> If I counseil of wommen wolde blame,
> Passe over, for I seyde it in my game.
> (Skeat ed., *The Nun's Priest's Tale*: B2 4447-52)

This is of course intended as a lighthearted remark about original sin and the unreliability of women's advice, spoken in jest by the male narratorial voice. Chaucer, as is his general, very sound habit, uses plain English, and the narrator notes explicitly that he speaks "in… game" (1452). In his translation Birkedal is not as successful as Chaucer in conveying the simplicity of the joke, because the crucial word he uses about it is "Gammenstale" [joking speech], which I had never heard before. Worse, nor had most of Birkedal's readers about 100 years ago, since *Ordbog over det Danske Sprog* records only a couple of examples of archaic, poetic usage. Part of the term, "Gammen" is occasionally used in Denmark in the idiom "fryd og gammen" [joy and bliss], but Birkedal's contemporary readers can hardly have been expected to read the correct meaning from the compound "Gammenstale", and he does not provide an explanatory note. His strange idea of digging out obsolete, archaic idioms is further developed in the passage, as he also uses the word "mistykke" [offend], which in his time had long since been replaced by "mishage", also now archaic. With a few other language elements reflecting old Danish and lofty rhetoric, such as the complicated grammatical construction of the first two lines of the quotation and the expression "udi idel Lykke" [in sheer happiness], Birkedal manages to spoil Chaucer's joke almost completely and share a different joke only with readers who might want to consult a dictionary and a library of ancient Danish poetry.

Apart from this gross example, Birkedal usually gets away with his archaisms in a way that makes him understandable, at least if the reader consults his explanatory notes. Again let us not forget that he undertook his translation during a time where poetic ideals in Denmark were different, and also let Birkedal be praised here for including the many sensible explanatory notes that he found in his sources, mainly from Skeat. As we shall see in chapter 9, Birkedal's notes were used by at least one later translator, Mogens Boisen. Birkedal, in sum, provides some splendid pioneer work in the field of Danish Chaucer reception and translation with the first substantial translation of parts of *The Canterbury Tales*, based on a reliable edition. He is a fine re-composer with his ear well tuned in to the possibilities of Chaucer's poetry, and I will have to forgive him for writing in a time where also Chaucer's work is regarded as the sort of vintage poetry that needs an archaic, high-flown tone.

CHAPTER 7

AAGE BRUSENDORFF, NIELS MØLLER AND MARGRETHE THUNBO. 1920-40

Between 1913 and 1943 I have not been able to trace any new Chaucer translations published in Denmark, and I conclude with some certainty that there are none. However, in the course of the 1920s, three publications appear that are such an important part of Chaucer reception in Denmark that they will be discussed thoroughly here. The first one of these, Aage Brusendorff's *The Chaucer Tradition* from 1925, is arguably the most important book on Chaucer ever published in Denmark. It was first written in Danish as a thesis for the University of Copenhagen and defended for the degree of Dr.Phil. in 1921, and it is included in this study because it was conceived in this Danish context. However, in order to do justice to Brusendorff, I turn to the international, fundamentally revised version, which was soon recognized as a foundational study in Chaucer criticism (Brusendorff 1925). Thus Dorothy Everett notes in *The Year's Work in English Studies* for 1925 that Brusendorff's study is "easily the most important book in English Studies for 1925" (Everett 1925: 83). I shall discuss this study mainly in the context of international Chaucer scholarship. I will start, however, by establishing a broad context of English in Denmark for 1920-40. Then follows the section on Brusendorff, and in the two final sections I consider the two other publications from respectively 1928 and 1929, Niels Møller's 16 pages on Chaucer in his *Verdenslitteraturen* [World literature] and another presentation of Chaucer, 30 pages on *Canterburyfortællinger af Geoffrey Chaucer* in a series written by Margrethe Thunbo for young readers, titled *Glimt af Verdenslitteraturen* (Glimpses of world literature). Both of these texts at points include text transformation, especially Thunbo's, which consists mainly of summaries of a number of *The Canterbury Tales*.

Hakon Stangerup

One further Chaucer text from the period, an encyclopedia entry in *Illustreret Dansk Konversationsleksikon* from 1934, will be briefly mentioned here in extension of the discussion of encyclopedia entries started in the last chapter. With just over 60 lines, this is a comparatively substantial entry written by well-known literary critic, Dr.Phil. Hakon Stangerup (1908-76), and it was reprinted slightly revised in *Vor Tids Konversationsleksikon* in 1942 and again in the second edition of that from 1950. In the 1950 edition Stangerup has added a sentence stating that among the pilgrims especially the Wife of Bath has been immortalized, and this could well be because Stangerup has now read her prologue and tale in one of the two Danish translations from the 1940s (see chapter 8). The rest of Stangerup's text suggests that he has looked into life and works in other sources, and he has most likely read some Chaucer texts as well. His mistaken claim that Chaucer became "en Slags Æresborger i London" [a kind of honorary citizen of London] seems to be taken from Anderssen's portrait in the 1908 edition of the same encyclopedia, which I discussed in chapter 6. Comparatively, however, Stangerup appears to be more knowledgable of Chaucer than Anderssen. For instance Stangerup convincingly emphasises Chaucer's epoch-making role in English literary history with his "Virkeligheds-digtning" [poetry true to real life] that establishes English firmly as a written language with "fremragende Menneskeskildring" [outstanding characterisation]. Stangerup goes even further and says that Chaucer "grundlægger på imponerende Maade den eng. moderne, det vil sige: efter-middelalderlige Litteratur [lays the foundation for the modern English, i.e. post-medieval literature] (Stangerup 1934: 123-4, 1942: 649-50, 1950: 44-5). In sum, this is not a bad presentation of Chaucer at all, given the conditions of writing for an encyclopedia.

English in Denmark 1920-40

The period leading up to World War II and the German occupation of Denmark sees a gradual development in the education system towards more English. German is still an important modern language in schools, but in 1930 it is possible to register for the first time that there is more English than German taught in Danish schools. This does not mean that English is the first foreign language, as the older generations have still learned German rather than English, and many more do not speak foreign languages at all. An interview investigation in 1945 resulted in only 9 per cent of the adult population saying they could speak English, whereas the corresponding number for German was 14 per cent (Rahbek Rasmussen 2006: 114-159). An investigation where people assess their own language proficiency and make a general judgment should naturally be taken with a pinch of salt, but the figures give a good indication of the general language situation, French being the third foreign language. For a small country like Denmark foreign languages have always been important, not least for the still growing industries, and also in the field of culture. The period sees increasing cultural influences from abroad, not least from the US with its film industry. A high point of this influence is reached with Victor Fleming's 1939 film version of Margaret Mitchell's bestselling novel *Gone With the Wind* from 1937, which cultural historian and literary critic Hans Hertel has described as the breakthrough of the American entertainment industry in Europe (Hertel 1992: 191). As far as English language culture is concerned, however, Britain is still the closest and strongest influence, and it is a still growing trading partner. Danish bacon and Danish butter are among the many popular imports in Britain, whereas coal is among the Danish imports from Britain.

Literary translation of English books is also a growing market. Among the most often translated writers from the period we find Somerset Maugham, whose novels are very quickly translated, with a few exceptions. Graham Greene, another immensely popular English writer in Denmark writing in this and later periods, is as opposed to Maugham not translated until the 1940s, with the exception of his 1929 novel *The Man Within* which appears as *Manden i Tågen* in 1931.[41] The English and Irish modernists attract little attention until much later. Forster's *A Passage to India* is translated in 1935 and again in 1985, but none of his other works

---

41 As in several other chapters, I have, unless otherwise stated, used my own and librarian Carsten Ravn's work, looking up translations in library catalogues. These are entered for each writer in Michelsen, ed., 1999.

appear until the 1950s. Even more remarkably, Virginia Woolf is almost completely ignored in her own life-time. *The Years* appears in 1941 and *Mrs Dalloway* in 1945, whereas most of her other works are not translated until between 1973 and 1994. In a study of the Danish reception, Ida Klitgård states that Woolf is really discovered in Denmark by the feminists when *A Room of One's Own* is translated in 1973 (I. Klitgård, 2002: 166 and 173-4). James Joyce has followers in Denmark, such as poet, novelist and journalist Tom Kristensen, who already in his main work *Hærværk* from 1930 [*Havoc*, English transl. 1968] is inspired by *Ulysses*, but none of Joyce's work is translated before the 1940s, the first of three translations of *Ulysses* appearing in 1949 (I. Klitgård, 2007, Greve and Klitgård Povlsen, 2004).

Also the American modernists are translated very late, e.g. Fitzgerald's *The Great Gatsby*, which is published in Danish in 1948. Faulkner is first translated in the 1940s, whereas Hemingway first appears in Danish in 1936 with *Farvel til våbnene* [*A Farewell to Arms*]. Most of his early short stories are translated much later, but after the huge success of *Farvel til våbnene* seven years after the American publication, his novels are translated immediately. In Danish literature the influence of the great modernists is accordingly so delayed that the corresponding Danish modernism coincides with the triumphs in drama of a related international wave, the absurd theatre of the 1950s. At this point, also T.S. Eliot's monumental modernist poem *The Waste Land* from 1922 has been translated, as *Ødemarken* in 1948. The delays of course have to do with Denmark's relations with the English-speaking world. As we shall see in the next chapter, the situation after the Second World War means that English books are by and large translated very quickly.

Aage Brusendorff

Aage Brusendorff (1887-1932) finished his *gymnasium* education in Aarhus in 1906, and since the University of Aarhus did not open until 1928, the only university choice in Denmark was still Copenhagen. Brusendorff first studied History and Archeology, before studying for a *magisterkonferens* in English, which he obtained in 1916. In 1921 the Danish version of his main work, *The Chaucer Tradition*, was accepted as a doctoral thesis, and he was employed as *docent* (Associate Professor) the same year. In the year of the English publication of his revised thesis, 1925, he followed Otto Jespersen as professor of English, working like his predecessor also in the field of linguistics. Unhappy personal circumstances made his promising career short, as he committed suicide in 1932 (Haislund in *Dansk Biografisk Leksikon*, 1934: 222-3).

It is important for understanding the background of Brusendorff's contribution to international scholarship that he was a student of Otto Jespersen, to whom he very naturally dedicates his book (Brusendorff 1925: 1). Jespersen in turn referred to Brusendorff as "den bedst begavede av alle mine elever" [the most gifted of all my pupils] (Jespersen 1938: 154). As we have seen in the previous two chapters, Jespersen has a hand in more or less all publications on Chaucer during his period as professor of English 1893-1925, and his expertise as Brusendorff's supervisor has clearly been very fruitful for such a talented student. That Brusendorff has been enabled to visit "numerous libraries in England, Scotland and Denmark" (Brusendorff 1925: 7) has been a second deciding factor for *The Chaucer Tradition* to come about. Brusendorff's firm acquaintance with and training in the manuscript and print traditions as well as his familiarity with the great editors and commentators on Chaucer makes his work rest on the firmest ground.

The most ground-breaking general result of Brusendorff's thesis is his success in establishing a canon of Chaucer's work, which, with the exception of a few minor poems and a possible inclusion of the treatise *An Equatorie of the Planetis*, still stands and becomes the basis for both F.N. Robinson's standard editions of 1933 and 1957, the editions that are the basis also for the present standard edition, *The Riverside Chaucer* (Benson, gen. ed. 1987/2008).[42] Brusendorff becomes the first scholar that is able to correct Skeat's work with the canon, the evidence of which was summed up in Skeat's study *The Chaucer Canon* from 1900 and of course in his complete works edition (Skeat 1900 and 1894-7). Brusendorff's task is accomplished in dialogue with Skeat, but more

---

42 The most important study to have examined the arguments for Chaucer's authorship of *An Equatorie of the Planetis* is Kari Anne Rand Schmidt's doctoral thesis from 1993 *The Authorship of The Equatorie of the Planetis* (Rand Schmidt 1993). See also my review of this study in *English Studies* (Klitgård 1996).

significantly by thoroughly digging out more evidence. In an age as the present one, where the Chaucer manuscripts and most editions are available in electronic form, and where library catalogues from all over the world can be viewed on the internet, Brusendorff's bibliography and list of manuscripts studied may at first glance seem unimpressive, but this is misleading. Brusendorff is extremely well acquainted with international, mainly German and English Chaucer scholarship of the 60-70 years leading up to his seminal study, both in books and journals, and he has carefully scrutinised 28 Chaucer manuscripts (Brusendorff 1925: 14 and bibliography 494-6). As Richard Utz has shown in his study of the German Chaucer scholarship 1793-1948 (Utz 2002), the German research tradition has been ignored by many in present-day scholarship, and even the standard editions no longer acknowledge original German discoveries about datings and authorship. Utz very convincingly demonstrates that lack of knowledge of German and Anglo-German hostilities even in the age of Furnivall and Skeat led to research communities almost entirely isolated from each other, even though between 1860 and 1900 German philologists produced almost as many academic studies of Chaucer between them as British and American scholars put together (Utz 2002: 173-4). Besides much improved, carefully edited Chaucer texts, e.g. Ten Brink's 1871 edition of *The General Prologue*, a number of important discoveries were made in Germany, such as Kissner's demonstration of the Italian influence in 1867 (see my chapter 5 and Utz: 267 and 271). In one case Skeat, according to a review by the early 20th century Chaucerian Flügel, was accused of plagiarising Koch in his edition, not acknowledging that the historical, occasional context of *The Parliament of Fowls* was in fact discovered, not only discussed by him (Utz: 110). Brusendorff, like Jespersen before him, found it natural to turn to the work of such eminent German scholars as Zupitza, Ten Brink, Kaluza and Koch as well as to such German journals as *Englische Studien* and *Jahrbuch für romanische und englische Literatur,* and he is certainly aligned with the thoroughness (*Gründlichkeit*) of that research tradition. Moreover, he writes admirably clearly and argues very convincingly for his points, and writing in English, Brusendorff comes to bridge the gap between the German and the Anglo-American scholarship. I have found only one occasion to correct Utz, whose impressive and thorough record of the German Chaucer tradition is quite invaluable, and that is his lack of acknowledgement of Brusendorff's own contribution to scholarship. Utz rightly says that Brusendorff discusses and comprises earlier German studies (173), and I agree that Brusendorff does that, but he does not simply reproduce the evidence. Rather he continuously holds it up against English and American scholarship, and he draws his own, well-argued conclusions. Utz could perhaps have taken more into account that Brusendorff through his own manuscript studies and historical investigations is able to form a thesis that moves scholarship significantly further. I will try to establish the essence of Brusendorff's work below.

It is beyond the task I have set myself in this reception study to review Brusendorff's *The Chaucer Tradition* again, and this would indeed seem pointless, considering how famous it is. I personally have not visited a university library anywhere that does not hold a copy of it, it was re-printed in 1968, and it is still available. What I shall do here besides considering its position in a Danish as well as international context is to focus on a couple of illustrative points indicating what exactly it is that made this study a seminal one. Near the end of his introductory chapter "The Problems", which contains a fine, if not exactly brilliant treatment of "The Chaucer Portraits" and "The Family Tradition" based on available manuscripts and biographical evidence (Brusendorff 1925: 13-43), Brusendorff approaches the crucial point of his study for the first time in a section of the chapter titled "The Canon" (43-52). In the following passage he addresses this point very precisely:

> The unsettled state of the Canon is really due to the comparative neglect of our most important body of evidence, the ascriptions of the scribes. It is true that their testimony has never been entirely lost sight of; still it is generally counted as supplementary evidence only, and even now the existence of a definite scribal tradition during the first two generations after the poet's death, practically never erring in its attribution of a definite body of work to Chaucer, is hardly sufficiently recognized. This tradition I should rank as our most valuable test in cases of doubtful authorship, ...
> (49, footnote not included in quotation)

The ingenious idea of trusting the scribes copying Chaucer's text to know what they were copying, while not excluding other relevant evidence, turns out to be a breakthrough for Brusendorff, and it becomes the basis of his overall strategy. Much about the Chaucer canon is given, since we have Chaucer's own references to works he wrote in *The Legend of Good Women* and in the *Retraction* at the end of *The Canterbury Tales,* as well as accounts by contemporary or slightly later English poets. Brusendorff now completes the list of works by critically reflecting on scribal notes and comments in the light of earlier scholarship and historical evidence. After long considerations, not least of the shorter poems and Chaucer's translation of a part of the *Roman de la Rose*, he comes up with a conclusion in the form of a list of Chaucer's works, 27 altogether, listed in seven categories (Brusendorff 1925: 445-6). This is the list that more or less still stands, and this is Brusendorff's most important contribution to Chaucer scholarship.

It is perhaps idle to speculate about what would have happened to the status of Chaucer in Denmark, had not Brusendorff died so young. First of all for international Chaucer scholarship it was a severe loss. I have inspected 20 pages of notes in Brusendorff's hand preserved by the Royal Library of Copenhagen in a collection otherwise consisting of letters to and from Otto Jespersen and thus probably left to him after Brusendorff's death. From a hand-drawn genealogical table and notes under the headline "Chaucer's levned" [Chaucer's life] it appears that Brusendorff was researching for an expansion of his Chaucer life portrait in *The Chaucer Tradition* or perhaps planning a Chaucer biography. These notes were written in or after 1928, as a *PMLA* issue from that year is included among them, whereas a second series of note sheets concerns Brusendorff's work with H.M. Cummings's study from 1916 of Boccaccio's influence on Chaucer, suggesting that Brusendorff was also preparing a study in this area (Brusendorff 1928?, Cummings 1916).

At the University of Copenhagen and in Danish academic circles generally, it is also clear that the loss of an international capacity in the field of English studies was a severe one, and Brusendorff did not have anyone to take over from him. Later professors of English in Denmark were eminent in many ways, but not one of them had specific expertise in Chaucer, except for the historical linguistics angle on his works.

Following Brusendorff's death Chaucer was only studied at university level from this angle. As we shall see later, it is not until the 1970s that something happened to change this situation.[43]

Niels Møller

From Brusendorff we turn to another Dane who really discovered Chaucer, if at a different level of insight. Niels Møller was introduced in chapter 6 as a diligent poet, translator and literary critic in his spare time, and after a long life in the service of especially Greek, English and Danish literature, he decides to embark on his ambitious world literary history, *Verdenslitteraturen*, which appears in three huge volumes in the late 1920s. Here I will restrict my further comments to the part of the second volume that is devoted to Chaucer (Møller 1928: second volume, 300-16).

Møller turns to Chaucer after a brief consideration of Langland, whose *Piers Plowman* he misleadingly calls full of "knudret sprog" [rugged language] and written by someone who is not "en fin Kunstner" [a fine artist] (298). Fortunately Møller's knowledge of Chaucer is much better, as he has clearly read most of his works. Thus Møller becomes the first writing Dane to bestow praise on *The Book of the Duchess* and also explain what it is about (303), and he is also able to draw on lines from

---

43   I have been able to trace the destiny of one student of English during Brusendorff's period as professor, since my second-hand copy of a first edition of *The Chaucer Tradition* bears the front page owner inscription "Margrethe Buch, stud. mag." [M.B., student for the degree of cand. mag., [MA]]. Buch unfortunately is not included in *Dansk Kvindebiografisk Leksikon*, but she appears in an internet article by Lars Kirkegaard as the "cand. mag." who founded Nyborg Studenterkursus, later Nyborg Gymnasium, becoming its first headmaster in 1939. Before that she had taught at Høng Studenterkursus for some years, but had to move because of disagreements about the running of the school. This conflict is briefly described in a letter by Bent Frandsen to the Høng school society, also available on the internet. The former headmaster had died, and his wife bought the school, but could not agree with the newly appointed headmaster, Buch (Frandsen 2003). Buch took 20 students with her to Nyborg. A picture from 1940 shows her happy and proud with her first class of students leaving school after their final exams (Kirkegaard, accessed May 2011). This only goes to show that the study of Chaucer can lead to much good.

The House of Fame. This is the funny, ironic image Chaucer conveys of himself in conversation with the eagle he is allegedly dreaming of, an image of a dry bookworm, who also likes a drink at the end of the day. Møller provides a short prose translation of the passage:

> Naar du er færdig med dit Kontorarbejde og har gjort Regnskabet op, søger du ikke hvile og spør om nyt, men går lige hjem til dit Hus, og der sidder du stum som en Sten over en anden Bog, til dine Øjne er ganske matte; saadan lever du som en Eremit (skøndt du ellers ikke er synderlig asketisk). [When you have finished with your office work, and have done your accounts, you don't seek rest and ask for new things, but go straight home to your house, and there you sit as mute as a stone with another book, till your eyes are quite dull. In this way you live like a hermit (although you are not particularly ascetic)]
> (Møller 1928, transl.: 301)

> For when thy labour doon al ys
> And hast mad alle thy rekenynges,
> In stede of reste and newe thynges
> Thou goost hom to thy hous anoon,
> And, also domb as any stoon,
> Thou sittest at another book
> Tyl fully daswed ys thy look;
> And lyvest thus as an heremyte,
> Although thyn abstinence ys lyte.
> (Benson, gen. ed. 1987/2008: *The House of Fame*, 652-60)

Møller has translated the passage very well, except for the explication "spør om nyt" [ask for new things], where the asking is not found in Chaucer's text. This is a free interpretation, if not a direct mistake. However the idea of using this piece to give us an impression of the man Chaucer is fine, even though this is an image constructed by Chaucer to break the illusion of the fiction. It is known that Chaucer was working in the London customs office while composing *The House of Fame* around 1380, and it is also known that he had had an allowance of wine, so there is every reason to believe that what Chaucer is doing here is to step out of the fiction for a while and pull a joke about himself for his listeners or readers.[44] Møller on his part seems to be less sure that Chaucer means it as a joke, as he adds the comment that Chaucer was "en Drømmer og Bogmand" [A Dreamer and a Book-man]. I do not think we know whether Chaucer was a dreamer, and it is certainly not evidence that he composed dream visions.

After fine summaries of and brief commentary on all of Chaucer's three early dream visions, *The Book of the Duchess*, *The Parliament of Fowls*, and *The House of Fame*, and a short discussion of *The Legend of Good Women*, Møller turns to a four page long treatment of *Troilus and Criseyde*. The opening statement shows from the start that like Jespersen, Møller has read, enjoyed and then studied Chaucer's masterly poem, not read about it and dismissed it as others in the Danish Chaucer reception: "Men Chaucers fuldkomneste Kunstværk er Bogen om Troilus og Criseyde." [But Chaucer's most complete work of art is the book about Troilus and Criseyde]. Møller opens his treatment with a competent comparison with Boccaccio's version, and then focuses on the character of Pandarus and his role in the plot construction, before turning to a consideration of the lovers. I will quote the high point of Møller's analysis in full:

> Det siger Folk, ikke jeg, tilføjer Chaucer. Han er forelsket i hende som de andre, ønsker at undskylde hende, nænner ikke at dømme hende. Og han har levendegjort hende med en Ynde og Sødme, saa hans Læsere er enige med ham. Men al sin Ynk vier han den forladte Troilus. Skildringen af hans Længsel og Sorg og Savn højner sig til tragisk Poesi, der dog har Virkelighedsfarve, som i det Stik af Smærte, han føler, en Dag han kommer forbi Criseyde's Hus med de lukkede Skodder, eller hvor han den 10. Dag sammen med Pandarus venter hende ved Bymuren, stadig tror at se hende, skuffes, fatter nyt Haab og

---

44 I have argued elsewhere that *The House of Fame* was composed for Chaucer's own real performance, and that the missing ending of the poem is indicative of composition in instalments, the final instalment never composed because of some disturbance at court. The occasional nature of *The House of Fame* was first established by John A.H. Koch, summed up in Utz 2002: 348. See Klitgård 1998, Koch 1916 and Utz 2002.

hitter paa Undskyldninger for hende, selv da det stunder mod Natten. Og da han omsider faar Vished om, at hun har svigtet ham, taler han ikke et ondt Ord om hende; han kan ikke drive sin Kærlighed ud, kun sørge og lide. Han søger Døden i Kampene og finder den for Achilles' lanse. [People say so, not I, Chaucer adds. He is in love with her as the others, wants to excuse her, does not have the heart to judge her. And he has made her alive with so much grace and sweetness that his readers agree with him./But all his pity is bestowed on the deserted Troilus. The depiction of his longing and grief and loss is elevated to tragic poetry, yet poetry with the colour of realism, as in the stab of pain he feels when one day he passes Criseyde's house with the windows shuttered, or when on the 10th day in the company of Pandarus he awaits her at the city walls, hoping still to see her. He is disappointed, finds new hope, and makes up excuses for her, even as the night is approaching. And when he finally realizes that she has deceived him, he does not speak a bad word about her; he cannot make his love go away, only mourn and suffer. He seeks death in battle and finds it at the lance of Achilles] (307-8).

The first line of this quotation directly echoes Chaucer's narrative voice saying "Men seyn – I not – that she yaf hym hire herte." (Benson, gen. ed., *Troilus and Criseyde*, book V, 1050). This is when she has been exchanged to the Greek camp and finds a new lover, Diomede, and Møller is right in saying that the narrator is so much in love with Criseyde that he excuses her, or as in this example distances himself from the painful knowledge of her deceit by questioning the authority of this knowledge. In another often quoted narratorial comment from the same sequence of the poem the urge to excuse and pity Criseyde is spelled out: "And if I myghte excuse hire any wise,/For she so sory was for hire untrouthe,/Iwis, I wolde excuse hire yet for routhe" (1093-5). Møller is also right in stating that Chaucer "har levendegjort hende med en Ynde og Sødme…" [has made her alive with so much grace and sweetness], and I will add that it is exactly because Criseyde is so cleverly made to be alive as a realistic human being that she stands out as a rounded character superior to the Criseyde character in all other versions of the tragedy. It is going too far to characterize *Troilus and Criseyde* as "the first psychological novel in English," first of all because it is not a novel, but modern readers have understandably responded warmly to Chaucer's Criseyde, because the psychological traits of the woman are so nuanced and real.[45] Møller is mistaken about Criseyde and her narrator in only one respect, which is his last remark about the reader agreeing with him. Had Møller known of Henryson's terrible personal vendetta on Criseyde in his late 15th century palimpsest, *The Testament of Cresseid*, where Criseyde ends up as a leper, he would have known that not all readers respond in the same way to Chaucer's most interesting female character (Henryson, Dickins, ed., 1925). However, among the so-called Scottish Chaucerians, Møller only briefly mentions Dunbar and the anonymous author of *The King's Quair*, so my guess is that he does not know Henryson at all (317-19).[46]

Møller's treatment of the character of Troilus is even more engaged, and he very successfully conveys the deeply moved emotion he, like many other readers of the poem, has felt. Møller's response to Troilus' longing, grief and loss is well pronounced in the quoted passage, which also follows in Troilus' restless footsteps, so to speak. All in all Møller's presentation and general analysis of *Troilus and Criseyde* is by far the most convincing I have come across in the Danish Chaucer reception, and it is only a pity that nobody has ever taken on the task of translating

---

45 The quotation is taken from S. Stephenson Smith, *The Craft of Fiction* from 1931 (Stephenson Smith 1931: 157), which is the earliest occurrence of this description I have been able to trace. The phrase "the first psychological novel" has been used a great number of times about *Troilus and Criseyde*, also on sleeve covers in popular editions like the 1959 Vintage Book edition. This does not make the genre label "novel" any more true. On the question of narrative genres before the novel see Bayer and Klitgård, eds., 2011.

46 I use the expression "Scottish Chaucerians" with caution and hesitation. It is still widely used about at least Dunbar and Henryson, but in 1997, in a splendid lecture on Scottish literature by Douglas Gifford, recently appointed to the first-ever Chair in Scottish Literature, at the University of Glasgow, a group of students and I were told that the term is misleading and somewhat derogatory, as these poets compose splendid, independent poetry.

the poem into Danish. There are translations into many languages, but Denmark still needs one.[47]

Møller's section on *The Canterbury Tales* is no longer than that of *Troilus and Criseyde*, which is after all remarkable. Not least because a considerable proportion of this section is taken up by summaries rather than analysis. This is especially true of all Møller's portraits from *The General Prologue*, where his text is really of the same type as Westergaard's (see chapter 4), i.e. a mixture of summary and translation. One example will suffice, and I have chosen a few lines from Møller's presentation of the Prioress:

> Madame Eglantine var en særlig Priorinde med en anden Nonne og 3 Præster til Følge. Hun smilede blysomt og brugte kun en pæn lille Ed. I Kirken sang hun sødelig gennem Næsen, hun talte pyntelig fransk, efter Skolen i Stratford-at-the Bow (ved London), for pariserfransk var hun ikke kendt med. Hun spiste saa dannet: tog pænt af Maden, førte den sirlig til Munden, tabte aldrig en Bid eller dryppede den paa sit Bryst, dyppede kun Spidsen af Fingrene i Saucen og tørrede sin Mund, før hun drak af Bægret…[Madam Eglantine was a special Prioress with a second nun and 3 priests following her. She smiled coyly and only used a nice little oath. In church she sang sweetly through her nose, she spoke neat French, after the school of Stratford-at-the Bow (near London), for she did not know the Parisian French. She ate in such a well-bred way: she helped herself gently to food, led it meticulously to her mouth, never lost a bite or let it drip on to her breast, she only dipped the tip of her fingers in the sauce and dried her mouth, before drinking of her cup] (311).

All the details of the Prioress' French and her table manners have been picked from *The General Prologue*, 118-33 and 163-4, but Møller has ar-

---

47 One of the more bizarre examples of translation is that of Sir Francis Kynaston, (1587-1642), who translated both Chaucer's and Henryson's Troilus and Criseyde poems into Latin verse. These translations have been treated in a doctoral dissertation by Helmut Wolf (Wolf 1997).

ranged them in his own order and left out some parts of the portrait, although my quotation does not include his full text. In a few instances he has used added explication for his Danish reader, such as adding to Stratford-at-the Bow that it is near London, but otherwise all the details from the portrait have been translated and constructed as a prose summary. This is very neatly done, and Møller has taken care to select the most entertaining portraits, such as this one, for substantial presentation. Almost needless to say, The Wife of Bath also gets due attention, and interestingly she is presented alongside the Prioress, which is not the case in Chaucer's text (311). Møller must have had his good reasons, most likely thinking that the contrast would work as appetizers for his readers, who he so obviously wants to read some Chaucer themselves. A noble purpose.

The tales themselves are mainly rendered briefly through their dramatic function in the story-telling contest, Møller reporting that the drunken Miller tells a story about a carpenter who is fooled and is answered by the Reeve, who used to be a carpenter, and who accordingly tells a story of a duped miller (312). The only tale selected for a summary of more than two lines is *The Pardoner's Tale,* which as Møller rightly points out is a moral story told by an immoral character and marked by Chaucer's "mesterlige fortællekunst" [masterly narrative art] (313). This story of the three topers, who find death while unknowingly asking for it, has fascinated many more in the Danish reception and translation history, as we shall see later.

Although not as prominently as in Bierfreund's portrait (see chapter 5), Chaucer is also regarded as a sort of Mother Nature's son by Møller, who in his finishing, general remarks about Chaucer's poetry says that it follows the reader like "en Bæk, der risler og blinker i Solen, hopper kruset over Stenene og snor sig med smaa underfundige Hvirvler, …" [a brook, babbling and glinting in the sun, rippling over the stones and winding along with small, subtle eddies] (314). It may be that also some modern readers share this very sensuous experience of reading Chaucer, but this particular kind of natural metaphor is in my mind an empty sublimation that has little to do with Chaucer's poetry. I will of course forgive Møller, since he can write with such insight about *Troilus and Criseyde* as we have seen, and after all Møller is no worse than many other literary historians who make this kind of vague generalizations.

Margrethe Thunbo

There are no entries about Margrethe Thunbo in any of the Danish biographical encyclopediae, and very little comes up on electronic searches. The only reference I trust enough to reproduce here is the inclusion of her name among the pre-subscribers to Thøger Larsen's translation of the Icelandic saga *Heimskringla* into Danish in 1926. Here her name appears as "Bibliotekar Frøken Margrethe Thunbo, København" [Librarian Miss Margrethe Thunbo, Copenhagen], so in 1926 she was unmarried, worked as a librarian in or near Copenhagen and was interested in a literary classic. Thunbo is the author of one publication in 10 small volumes, *Glimt af Verdenslitteraturen* [Glimpses of World Literature] (Thunbo 1929). The series consists of summaries of literature as different as Hans Christian Andersen, Tolstoj and Goethe, besides folk and fairy tales from Ireland, Wales, Japan and Austria. The volume on *Canterbury Fortællinger* [Canterbury Tales] is the second in the series, which in all its diversity shares one trait, which is that it is told for children. In the Chaucer volume, there are two full-page, hand-drawn illustrations, one of a crying Constance in a boat with a baby, and one of Griselda reunited with her children and Walter the Marquis, no illustrator's name given (Thunbo 1929: 11 and 23). In a very unfortunate case of literary theft, this volume was re-published in 1984 with the same text by Thunbo, set in a different font, but with the same two illustrations, and with her author's name removed and replaced by "Geoffrey Chaucer" as well as a reproduction of one of the Chaucer portraits. There is also a new drawing, of a horseman who could be Chaucer, although the drawing is poor. The publisher, Brage, for very good reasons no longer existing, has replaced "copyright Thunbo", by "copyright Brage". This copyright violation has been reported to the Danish author's union by me, but unfortunately it has proved impossible to take the case further. I have, however, excluded the plagiarized version from my bibliography.

Thunbo takes her audience very seriously and is a good story-teller in the genre. To make it more lively for her young readers, she frequently inserts dialogue in her summaries, also in places where Chaucer has none. For this reason, and because the prose summaries are rarely based on close parallels to Chaucer's text, I will not attempt to analyse Thunbo's text as translation. Instead I will give a characterization of her text and select a few examples for further comment. One of these is the remarkable idea that Thunbo has decided to open her text with what looks like a historical account of "En yndig Foraarsdag i 1387" [a lovely spring day in 1387], during the reign of Richard II, as she explains. It is certainly around the time that Chaucer would have started his work with *The Canterbury Tales*, but of course we do not have a specific year for the setting in Chaucer's text.[48] Thunbo goes on to explain that pilgrimages were quite normal, but the roads were bad and there could be robbers hiding in the woods (3). She does not mention Robin Hood, but she certainly evokes his image in this passage. After her introduction Thunbo spends a couple of pages on the pilgrims, and again it is easy to see whose portraits are most fascinating, as Thunbo goes into detail with only two of them, the Prioress and the Wife of Bath. Finally in her prologue she says that she has had to choose only a few tales, but "de andre kan I læse andetsteds" [you can read the others somewhere else]. Unless Thunbo imagines that the children and young people reading her book are able to read English, this is actually a truth with some modification. Thunbo also says that she unfortunately does not know who won the prize for the best story, for Chaucer died before he could finish *The Canterbury Tales*. It is again a fine service to answer a question that many, not only children, might wonder about.

The tales Thunbo has chosen are *The Man of Law's Tale*, *The Nun's Priest's Tale*, *The Wife of Bath's Tale*, *The Clerk's Tale*, *The Franklin's Tale* and *The Canon Yeoman's Tale*. From a children's literature point of view this is an understandable selection. Thunbo avoids the problem of telling dirty stories by excluding the fabliaux, and she is still able to tell some dramatic stories with a childish appeal, including a beast fable, *The Nun's*

---

48 In 1880 John A.H. Koch argued that the historical date of the pilgrimage is April 18th 1391, but this claim is highly dubious and has not been accepted in later scholarship (Koch 1880, summarized by Utz 2002: 279). Whereas this might theoretically have been a date Chaucer once had in mind, Thunbo certainly gets her date from out of the blue.

Priest's Tale, and a romance, *The Wife of Bath's Tale.*[49] That tale has one problem, which is that the knight is a rapist, but Thunbo gets around that by the euphemism that he "søgte at føre hende bort med magt" [sought to take her away with force]. After a short girl's scream, order is soon restored by the king and queen, and the knight is sent out on his quest to find out what women desire most (16). The *denouement* of the tale, that women desire to have the upper hand in marriage, is loyally rendered by Thunbo, who lets the old hag exclaim, "Saa har jeg sejret!" [Then I have won!], an example of the sort of dialogue that Thunbo makes up herself. It is also part of a general strategy to use explication, an understandable strategy in communication with children.

Compared to Westergaard (see chapter 4), Thunbo renders *The Clerk's Tale* with relatively little involvement, and of course also in a much shorter space than her. Thunbo uses the adjective "grusom" [cruel] three times, but otherwise not much of Chaucer's narratorial skepticism is maintained. Only towards the end is there implicit criticism of Walter the Marquis, as Thunbo writes: "Da Griselda hørte dette, faldt hun i Afmagt, og I nogen Tid var det hende umuligt at tro, at hendes Husbond virkelig havde elsket hende hele Tiden." [When Griselda heard this, she fell into a swoon, and for some time it was impossible for her to believe that her husband had really loved her all the time]. This is Thunbo's moment of realistic insight, but it would have been a very good idea if she had also included a summary of Chaucer's concluding remarks at the end of the tale, where he explains that the moral is not that women should be like Griselda, and that no husband should act as Walter (*The Clerk's Tale*, 1142-1182).

Whereas Thunbo fails to explain the main point of *The Clerk's Tale* to her readers, she is concerned with the moral of another tale, Chaucer's venture into alchemy, *The Canon Yeoman's Tale*. She ends her summary in this way:

---

49 Richard Utz cites the early German philologist Bernhard ten Brink for regarding Chaucer's fabliaux as "the pinnacle of the poet's achievement", while acknowledging that they cannot be retold for a contemporary audience. As Utz explains, ten Brink is rather alone with this positive attitude and certainly does not share it with British Victorian readers and critics (Utz 2002: 97, ten Brink 1893: II, 35-7). I will add that ten Brink's view is equally unmatched in the Danish reception up to Thunbo, except for Jespersen and, up to a point, both Niels Møller and Vilhelm Møller.

> Det er unødvendigt at sige, at da han undersøgte Recepten og gav sig til at lave Sølv, fik han ikke noget ud af sine Anstrengelser, men opdagede, at han var blevet bedraget. Moralen af Historien er naturligvis, at vi alle bør vogte os for Begærlighed. [It is unnecessary to say that when he examined the recipe and started making silver, he got nothing out of his efforts, but realized that he had been deceived. The moral of the story is naturally that we should all take care not to be greedy] (32)

One might at first sight argue that if something is unnecessary to say and natural in the sense of given, then why say it, but this is exactly the kind of redundancy that is needed when writing for children. Sometimes it is as necessary when writing for adults, and as a former colleague of mine, the Danish literary critic Søren Schou has said, we would all get terrible headaches if we had to read only minimalist literature and sharp academic prose. We would also lose our readers outside the academy if we tried to write too sharply all the time. This is the present writer saluting redundancy of a certain, elegant kind, like Thunbo's here.

Chapter conclusion

This has been a chapter covering some very different publications on Chaucer, the most unifying context being the time period in which they were published. Brusendorff is undoubtedly the most influential Danish Chaucerian ever, but from the point of view of the present study, both Stangerup's, Møller's and Thunbo's Chaucer texts are important too. It is all a question of readers, and whereas Brusendorff's effort in international scholarship is the most important and long-lasting of them, let us not forget the broad appeal of a well-considered and insightful literary history like Møller's, still available in public libraries, and the fine communication to children in Thunbo's summarized Canterbury Tales, made more long-lasting through the illegal reproduction by a Danish publisher in 1984.

CHAPTER 8

BERGSØE, THORBJØRNSEN AND SONNE. THE 1940s

In this chapter we consider several Chaucer publications in the decade that begins with the German occupation of Denmark during World War 2 and ends with a full paradigm shift in cultural and linguistic orientation following the victory of the allied forces. The context of this paradigm shift will be the subject of the first part of the chapter, with sections English in Denmark and English literature in Denmark. After this there is a short section about two encyclopedia entries and a schoolbook by Niels Alkjær and Kaj Bredsdorff. Then I turn to a verse translation from 1943 of *The Wife of Bath's Prologue and Tale* titled *Geoffrey Chaucer, Konen fra Bath*, translated by Flemming Bergsøe, with an introduction by Kai Friis Møller, illustrated by Poul Christensen. Following this, I analyse a prose translation of *The Pardoner's Prologue and Tale* from 1946, titled *Geoffroy Chaucer, De tre drikkebrødre* [The three topers], by Lis Thorbjørnsen, illustrated by Ib Spang Olsen and with an introduction by Paul V. Rubow; further prose translations by Thorbjørnsen of *The Merchant's Tale* and *The Wife of Bath's Prologue*; and finally Jørgen Sonne's prose translations from the late 1940s of *The Manciple's Tale, The Physician's Tale, The Reeve's Tale, The Franklin's Tale* and *The Nun's Priest's Tale*, the last three appearing in a booklet titled *Geoffrey Chaucer: Canterbury Fortællinger* with woodcuts by Erik Christensen. Sonne's first versions of *The Reeve's Tale* and *The Franklin's Tale* had been illustrated by Ib Spang Olsen in connection with their first publication in the magazine *Cavalcade*, and Spang Olsen also illustrated his translation of *The Manciple's Tale*. I have decided to include introductions to the encyclopedia writer, to the three translators and to illustrators and introducers in the sections which follow my treatment of the cultural-historical context in which they produce their works.

English in Denmark in the 1940s

There is a host of literature on World War 2 and Denmark, a considerable amount of which is devoted to Anglo-Danish relationships during the war, including treatments of Danish diplomats and politicians operating in respectively the United States and Britain during the war, the Danish resistance movement and its connection to Britain, Danish government relations to Britain, and many other points.[50] While drawing only in a broad sense on historical representations of the occupation period, I have for my purpose decided to focus more narrowly on English language and culture in Denmark, especially the status of education in English and of English literature in the 1940s. This is a continuation of a similar focus in earlier chapters. For this purpose I am fortunate enough to be able to draw on some specialized studies. Firstly, Inge Kabell and Hanne Lauridsen's *Den belejrede humanisme* [the occupied humanism] on the occupation years in Denmark seen from the point of view of English studies at the University of Copenhagen.[51] Secondly, Jørgen Sevaldsen's "Culture and Diplomacy: Anglo-Danish Relations 1945-49", with a glance also at his somewhat broader study from 2003, "Trade Fairs and Cultural Promotion c. 1930-1970: Visualising Anglo-Danish Relations." And thirdly Hans Hertel's "Armstrong, Bogart, Churchill… Penguin: the Danish Turn to Anglo-American Cultural values from the 1920s to the 1950s" (Kabell and Lauridsen 1995, Sevaldsen 1992, Hertel 2003). I shall present and discuss these studies, drawing also on a couple of other sources that help provide a platform for more specifically understanding the renewed interest in British and American culture and literature, including the Chaucer translations treated in this and the following chapter. Whereas it is rather obvious that the victory of the allied forces would have led to a general anglification of Danish culture, it is less clear what this anglification consisted of, and what

---

50 Two of the most important Danish publications in the field are *Den 2. verdenskrig 1939-45* [The 2nd World War 1939-45] by Hans Kirchhoff, Henning Poulsen, and Aage Trommer (Kirchhoff, Poulsen, and Trommer 1989/2002) and *Kampen om Danmark 1933-45* [The fight about Denmark 1933-45] by Bo Lidegaard (Lidegaard 2006).

51 Kabell and Lauridsen have also published a book chapter in English based on their investigation, much abridged compared to the full study. See Kabell and Lauridsen 2003.

were the specific manifestations of the paradigm shift. This chapter will provide some of the answers.

Kabell and Lauridsen's *Den belejrede humanisme* is based on an empirical investigation in the shape of questionnaires received from 19 respondents, who were all students of English at the University of Copenhagen between 1940 and 1945. Further qualitative interviews with a few respondents, and a consideration of course catalogues, events lists for the student organisation *The Union*, biographical information and other evidence has been provided, adding up to a book-length, very thorough study of university English studies in these difficult years.[52] The nature of these difficulties can be illustrated by the fact that tutorials and classes especially in the last two war years had to be carried out in private apartments, public restaurants such as the still existing Peter Liep in Klampenborg, north of Copenhagen, or Kunsthåndværkerskolen [the artist craftsman school] in the centre of town (Kabell and Lauridsen 1995: 98). Many students were involved in illegal activities, such as the spreading of resistance movement information, and some were more directly active in the resistance. By and large without their knowledge, so was their professor, C.A. Bodelsen, who managed to keep up his impressive academic activities while secretly working in the resistance movement, from 1944 as a member of *Frihedsrådet* [the freedom council], the alternative Danish government of the last war years.[53]

English books for study purposes were hard to retrieve, and some were smuggled in or printed illegally, including a resistance movement translation of Steinbeck's *The Moon is Down* (as *Månen er skjult*) in the year of its original publication, 1942 (Kabell and Lauridsen: 28-30). It helped English students in Copenhagen that remaining books were sold

---

52 The study does not include English at the University of Aarhus, but Kabell and Lauridsen refer to a visit of a theatre production of *The Union* to the University of Aarhus in 1942, where the local hosts are professor of English Torsten Dahl and associate professor in general and comparative literature Jens Kruuse (Kabell and Lauridsen 1995: 85).

53 As one of the two professors of English, Bodelsen is a dominant figure in Kabell and Lauridsen's study generally, and his activities are cited frequently. Kabell and Lauridsen also reprint an obituary by Bodelsen's war-time student, later professor of English Eric Jacobsen, which includes a consideration of Bodelsen's time in *Frihedsrådet*. Jacobsen 1979, reprinted in Kabell and Lauridsen 1995: 128-35.

after the closing of the British Council and also that Otto Jespersen's collection was offered for sale after his death in 1943 (26). Furthermore, grammar books such as that by C.A. Bodelsen's professor colleague Niels Bøgholm, and other works produced in Denmark were still available. And as we shall see below there were also new literary translations from English, especially in the first war years. The missing contact with the English-speaking world, including the opportunity to travel, was partly compensated for by employing native speakers resident in Denmark for readings and dramatizations, and by frequent readings and performances by students themselves (34-45, 72-93). The student *Union* also invited knowledgeable speakers for a series of evening arrangements, for example the author and journalist Kai Friis Møller, who will be dealt with below in connection with his preface to Bergsøe's Chaucer translation. In December 1941 Friis Møller spoke on the topic "Stemningsbilleder fra London efter den forrige krig" [Report on public feeling in London after the last war], apparently a topic that was not too controversial (83). Many other activities in *The Union* bear witness to a very engaged Anglo-Danish society in a time where much had to be kept secret. The activities in *The Union* formed a strong basis for the growth of Anglo-Danish societies in both Copenhagen and provincial towns after the war, where by 1947 the revived British Council estimated that there were 37 societies with around 5000 members in Denmark (Sevaldsen 1992: 22).

The Copenhagen University course catalogues investigated by Kabell and Lauridsen reveal a number of cancellations especially towards the end of the war, where for instance a planned semester course on Chaucer taught by Professor Bøgholm was never carried out. Chaucer was actually very frequently on the agenda in Bøgholm's classes, but this does not mean that the students were brought to an understanding of Chaucer as an author. Chaucer was taught exclusively as part of historical linguistics, and the main focus would be on sound changes and dialect patterns. One student, the later well-known author Elsa Gress had enough of this already in 1940, where she changed from English to General and Comparative Literature. She records in her autobiography *Fuglefri og Fremmed* [Bird-free and Estranged] that she fled from "gennemgangen af de middelengelske dialekter der blev brugt til at destruere smukke og ejendommelige tekster med" [this way of going through middle English dialects, which was used to destroy beautiful and extraordinary texts]. This remarkably sharp and appreciative remark is supported by a statement by Eric Jacobsen, who records that his later professor colleague Knud Schibsbye was also employed to teach in this line: "sproghistorie var næsten kun lydhistorie, og de old- og middelengelske tekster blev kun studeret som prøvekasser med eksempler på lydovergange, ikke som litteratur" [historical linguistics was almost entirely sound history, and the old and middle English texts were only studied as sample cases of sound transitions, not as literature]. (Kabell and Lauridsen 1995: 40-67; Gress 1972: 76-7, Jacobsen 1990: 12, quoted by Kabell and Lauridsen: 113 and 64). It should be stressed that Jacobsen himself made a successful effort to teach old literature as literature when employed at the University of Copenhagen a few years later, but as noted by Kabell and Lauridsen in their conclusion, not a lot changed in the study regulations for English between the 1930s and 1970s (185). Chaucer for this reason was most often not studied as Chaucer, but as the sound system of Middle English, and that did not change until the 1970s.

Turning to the rest of the educational system, we have already seen in earlier chapters that from 1903 English had become firmly established in both primary and secondary school, alongside German and to a lesser degree French. In 1945 German was still the foreign language best known in Denmark. Sevaldsen quotes statistics saying that 47 per cent of the population according to themselves had ability in German, the corresponding figure for English being only 30. According to Sevaldsen English was already taking over as more popular in the younger generation from the late 1930s, and of course the allied victory boosted English education further (Sevaldsen 1992: 12).

After the war both economic and cultural ties between Denmark and Britain were strengthened significantly. British imports of Danish farm produce grew to such proportions that in 1947 there was a major farmer protest against the prices and a stop to exports until a new trade agreement was established (Sevaldsen 1992: 20), but the protest was an exception to the general impression registered by British Council Representative H.M. Keyes in May 1951 that "there exists … a pro-British feeling, in this sense, of the greatest cordiality and a widespread sense of respect for and kinship with British civilization" (report quoted by Sevaldsen

1992: 10).⁵⁴ This is certainly also the image evoked by the welcoming in Copenhagen of respectively Montgomery in 1945 and Churchill in 1950, both greeted with a massive public turnout in the streets of Copenhagen.

The British Council played a significant part in strengthening the cultural links in the postwar years, from 1946 in a central location next to the Town Hall Square of Copenhagen. A lending library with British books and music was opened, increasing their stocks of books to 8300 by the end of the 1940s, and in 1948 followed an American library at the US embassy. Furthermore, the "English Bookshop" opened in late 1947 in the Town Hall Square itself (Sevaldsen 1992: 22 and note, 32). Another important cultural manifestation was the British Exhibition of September 1948, which included not only an exhibition of "English television" in the *Tivoli Gardens* a few years before TV reached Denmark, but also politically tainted events such as a speech in the *Odd Fellow Palæ* by Anthony Eden on unity in Western Europe. The events were matched by exhibitions on Danish Art Treasures at the Victoria and Albert Museum in London, October 1948 (Sevaldsen 2003: 84-93). Danish design was gaining a name abroad, and the English speaking world welcomed it. Also, one author from Denmark, writing her stories in Danish and translating them into English herself, made a big name for herself in Britain and the USA in this period: Karen Blixen, who, under the pseudonym Isak Dinesen, had debuted in the USA already in 1934 with *Seven Gothic Tales,* her own Danish translation of the tales, *Syv fantastiske fortællinger,* having been published in 1932.

English Literature in Denmark in the 1940s

Blixen is not the worst starting point for further establishing the Anglo-Danish literary ties, as she was notoriously admired by one of the most

---

54 Rasmus Mariager has analysed the extent of Danish trade with Britain and the USA 1945-1955. Britain is by far the major trade partner, roughly 30-40 per cent of all Danish exports going to Britain in the period, with import figures also nearly at the same percentage level. The corresponding figures for US exports and imports are with a few exceptions in single figures, in most years around 5 per cent (Mariager 2003: 542-5). Mariager also considers the temporary breakdown in Danish-British trade relations in 1947 (551-7).

translated and read writers in English in Denmark in the 1940s, Ernest Hemingway. As noted in the previous chapter modernism hit Denmark somewhat belatedly, but the 1940s was full of translations from Hemingway and other modernists, although far from all of them were translated. *A Farewell to Arms* had been translated as *Farvel til vaabnene* in 1936, and now followed translations of *The Sun Also Rises* (*Og solen gaar sin gang*), 1941, *For Whom the Bell Tolls* (*Hvem ringer klokkerne for?*), 1941 and *Green Hills of Africa* (*Afrikas grønne bjerge*), 1945. Also some of Hemingway's short stories were translated in the 1940s. *Sans comparison* one other fine author in the English language, Evelyn Waugh, was also belatedly discovered in Denmark during the war. No less than six of his satirical works were published between 1942 and 1945, including his debut novel from 1928 *Decline and Fall*, which appeared as *Forfald og Fald* in 1945. In 1946 followed translations of Waugh's two novels published during the war, *Put Out More Flags* (1942, translated as *Flere Flag* [more flags]) and his masterpiece *Brideshead Revisited* (1945, translated as *Gensynet med Brideshead*).

Turning back to the modernists, James Joyce also reached Denmark in translation for the first time in the war years, probably because of the interest after his death in January 1941. *A Portrait of the Artist as a Young Man* was translated as *Portræt af kunstneren som ungt menneske* in 1941, whereas *Dubliners* appeared as *Dublinfortællinger* [tales from Dublin] in 1942.[55] In the case of Joyce there is a more direct connection to Chaucer translations, which I will also return to in the next chapter. This is because the first official translator of Joyce's *Ulysses* into Danish is Mogens Boisen, one of the two *Canterbury Tales* translators from the 1950s considered in chapter 9.

In his brilliant survey article Hertel provides more detailed information about British and American authors translated in the 1940s than I will do here, but let me emphasise one of Hertel's central points, which is that the war actually saw an increase in the share of translations from the English-speaking world, despite the censorship on certain publica-

---

55 For the author bibliographies in this chapter I once again rely on Knud Michelsen, ed., *Forfatterleksikon: Udenlandske forfattere* (Michelsen, ed., 1999), and again I have good reason to do so, as I myself and librarian Carsten Ravn retrieved or checked the information in library catalogues.

tions. Whereas proportionally the share of translations dropped during the 1920s and 1930s to a still high 44 per cent, it rose again from the early 1940s and reached a peak of 72 per cent by the end of the 1950s (Hertel 2003: 448). Considering that the figures also take translations from other Nordic countries into account, this is a remarkably high figure, which underlines the dominance of Anglo-American culture in postwar Denmark. The statistics are supported by a survey from *Aviskronikindeks* (here: newspaper article index) from 1945-49 quoted by Sevaldsen, showing percentage distribution of book reviews, which in 1945 was 18 per cent both for British and American books, and in 1949 had risen to 31 and 25 per cent respectively, with translations from Scandinavian, French and German going down in percentage (Sevaldsen 1992: 14 and note). It is tempting to conclude that the increased number of Anglo-American books on the Danish market reflected a silent protest during the war, and this may well have been the case for many. Certainly the statistics also for the postwar period show that a paradigm shift was taking place from prominence to dominance.

Alkjær and Bredsdorff

The first encyclopedia article considered here is by Niels Alkjær and appeared in *Raunkjærs Konversationsleksikon* in 1948 (Alkjær 1948). Alkjær (1909-82) was at the time of writing an associate professor of English at the University of Aarhus, and later published mainly on Blake (Disen 2007). He also translated Blake's *The Marriage of Heaven and Hell*, and this translation has been well analysed and compared to a more recent translation by Niels Brunse in an article by Maria Witting Lund (Witting Lund 2005). Alkjær's 60-line article focuses on Chaucer's life and works. It is a fairly neutral presentation, and it is generally competent. Alkjær is, however, on slippery ground in his estimate of Chaucer's changing life conditions, but this inaccuracy is something we see in many sources. He possesses more sound judgement when he is skeptical about evidence of Chaucer's postulated unhappy marriage to Phillippa, and he should also be praised for counting Chaucer as only second to Shakespeare in English literature (Alkjær 1948: 1031-2).

Also in 1948 Kaj Bredsdorff is registered as the author of an encyclopedia entry in *Hagerups Illustrerede Konversations Leksikon* (Bredsdorff 1948: 392-3). Bredsdorff (1880-1970) was a *gymnasium* teacher and at one point teaching assistant at the University of Copenhagen. He wrote several articles about English literature, especially in the periodical *Edda* (Anonymous internet source, accessed November 2011). *Hagerups Illustrerede Konversations Leksikon* is the new name of *Illustreret Konversationsleksikon* and its 4th edition. It turns out that despite the new author name, the Chaucer article is not really new, but is effectively a reprint of Andersson's 1908 article with a few revisions and some added references, presumably provided by Bredsdorff. Bredsdorff thus adds his name to most of Anderssen's weaknesses and mistakes discussed in chapter 6. He has corrected one point, so that Chaucer's plan for *The Canterbury Tales* is now given as 128 tales rather than Anderssen's 64, but with 29 pilgrims and the Canon Yeoman joining on the way, the actual number is 30 times four tales, i.e. 120. This means that the only praise for Bredsdorff must be that he has clarified that *Troilus and Criseyde* is a poem and not among Chaucer's earliest works, and that he has given references to further reading, naming five very good sources: Ward, Pollard, Jespersen, Birkedal and Brusendorff.

Bredsdorff actually knew at least a little more about Chaucer than suggested by this unfortunate encyclopedia entry. This is shown in his schoolbook written in English for the Danish *gymnasium*, *From Beowulf to Kipling: A Survey of English Literature* from 1943 with revised editions in 1948 and 1956 (Bredsdorff 1943/1948/1956). With its five pages this is a fairly substantial introduction to Chaucer for young readers, and in the 1956 edition he has even got the number of planned tales right (Bredsdorff 1956: 14). Furthermore, Bredsdorff has worked so much with at least *The General Prologue* of *The Canterbury Tales* that he is able to quote from it, discuss Chaucer's metrical skills and characterise the pilgrims, including text quotations to illustrate his much abbreviated portraits. However, he is much less convincing in his cursory treatment of the tales themselves, e.g. arguing that the best known tales are those told by the Knight, the Prioress, the Clerk, the Pardoner and the Wife of Bath. Thus he leaves out all the fabliaux in favour of a pious tale, *The Prioress' Tale*, and also excludes obvious candidates like *The Nun's Priest's Tale* and *The Franklin's Tale*. Other weaknesses include the once again repeated image of Chaucer as nature's son, and the very shakily founded suggestion that

Chaucer's Parson and Ploughman refer to respectively John Wyclif and William Langland (Bredsdorff 1956: 13-17). It would have been good to know what source Bredsdorff has used for the latter fanciful suggestion, but he does not state his sources.

Before turning to the translations, I conclude this part by noting that Alkjær has written a short and sober Chaucer portrait, whereas Bredsdorff has copied and written two rather problematic contributions to the Danish Chaucer reception.

Flemming Bergsøe

Among the translations from English during the war Flemming Bergsøe's *Konen fra Bath* [The Wife of Bath] from 1943 falls within the central concerns of this study. Flemming Bergsøe (1905-68) was an educated sculptor and became a well-known naturalist painter. His interest in literature and his versatility and enterprise ran in the family, as his grandfather was Vilhelm Bergsøe (1835-1911), author, zoologist and numismatist. One of Vilhelm Bergsøe's main works, the short story collection *Fra Piazza del Popolo* [From Piazza del Popolo], was in fact inspired by Boccaccio's *Decameron*. Flemming Bergsøe's father Paul Bergsøe (1872-1963) was a chemical engineer, who also became well known to the public by writing popular introductions to chemistry. His brother Svend Bergsøe (1902-85), also an engineer, was at least as well-known a public figure, among other things as the first chairman of *Rådet for Større Færdselssikkerhed* [The council for better traffic security] (Bostrup, Andersen, Kondrup and Kristensen in Lund, gen. ed., 1995: 513). Flemming Bergsøe's other writings include *Det underlige år* [The strange year] (Bergsøe 1945), a report from the last occupation year, where he had been a contact person in Copenhagen for leading member of the resistance movement Mogens Fog.

The translation had first been begun in connection with an article from the art magazine *Aarstiderne* from 1941 titled "Chaucer bør oversættes" [Chaucer ought to be translated] (Bergsøe 1941). Bergsøe was the co-founder and chief editor of this magazine, which focuses on painting, film and literature and is of remarkable quality with its rich illustrations, although it should be noted that Bergsøe and his co-editors would have done well to employ a professional proofreader, as seen also in the extracts below. The very first issue of *Aarstiderne* from March 1941 contains two contributions by Bergsøe, an obituary about painter Erik Raadal and the Chaucer article of five pages. Both pieces are written with great empathy and involvement, and I will quote Bergsøe's concluding remarks about Chaucer *in extenso*:

> "Hvad Chaucer siger om Mennesker, om deres Kærlighed og Had, om deres Glæder og Sorger og om deres Krige er evigt aktuelt. Vi gaar i dag anderledes klædt, vi spiser Daasemad og vi benytter Vand-Closetter, men vore Følelser og Tanker, selve det menneskelige, er uforandret fra hans Dage. Og den gamle Englænder beskæftiger sig netop med det menneskelige. – Vi er i Familie med ham, og det halve Aartusinde skiller os ikke mere fra ham, end vi er skilt fra vores Far. 'Canterbury Tales' bør oversættes til Dansk. Den er en Inspirationskilde, vi ikke har Raad til at undvære. Læsningen af den, efterlader et lignende Indtryk som Læsningen af Bibelen, 'Don Quiqote' [sic] og Shakespeares Skuespil. I de Bøger staar alt om Mennesker."
> [What Chaucer says about human beings, about their love and hate, about their joys and sorrows and about their wars, is eternally topical. Today we dress differently, we eat tinned food and we use water closets, but our feelings and thoughts, our human existence itself, are no different from his time. And the old Englishman is precisely concerned with being human. – We are members of his family, and the half millennium does not separate us more from him than we are separated from our fathers. *The Canterbury Tales* ought to be translated into Danish. It is a source of inspiration we cannot afford to do without. Reading it leaves a similar impression to reading the Bible, *Don Quixote* and Shakespeare's plays. These books contain everything about human beings.]
> (Bergsøe 1941: 16)

These are big words from Bergsøe, but apart from wanting to include Joyce's *Ulysses* to this list and considering a few more candidates, no protest from the present writer. It is remarkable how inspired Bergsøe is here, and in the remainder of the article, and it may well be that his sincerely expressed wish was heard in publishers' and translators' circles, as a few years later the two full translations of *The Canterbury Tales* were begun (see chapter 9).

Bergsøe starts his article by rendering the plot of *The Pardoner's Tale*, which he says he remembers from an English reader at school. This will have been the summary "The Three Drunkards" from Otto Jespersen's schoolbook reader series published in its first edition in 1895, which I treat further in chapter 10 through Nørfelt's 1965 translation of it (Jespersen in Brüel, ed., 1957-60: 70-3, Nørfelt 1965: 134-8). Bergsøe then moves on to a general consideration of the importance of classics in all fields of art, and he regrets the scarce representation of Chaucer in Denmark. In a footnote it becomes clear that Bergsøe knows Birkedal's translation of *The General Prologue*, but not his translation of *The Nun's Priest's Tale*. He also refers to Jespersen's study from 1893 and adds rather vaguely that "endvidere er vistnok en enkelt af Fortællingerne blevet oversat af Margrete [sic] Thunbo" [besides one of the tales has been translated by Margrethe Thunbo, as far as I know] (Bergsøe 1941: 14, note 1). In other words Bergsøe only knows of a fraction of the works on Chaucer considered in this study so far, but obviously his main claim is true, that *The Canterbury Tales* had not been made available in Danish.

Bergsøe gives a short account of the idea of *The Canterbury Tales* and an extremely brief account of Chaucer's life, before embarking on his main errand, a summary with two extracts in translation from *The Wife of Bath's Prologue and Tale*. I shall return to the extracts in connection with my translation analysis below, but let me say here that the short summaries of both prologue and tale show Bergsøe's fine sense of Chaucer's tone and acute understanding of the entertainment value. For Bergsøe the Wife is first of all a "Livsstykke" [a live wire] (Bergsøe 1941: 14), and he attaches no sinfulness to her behaviour.[56] It

---

[56] Monty Python's Eric Idle would probably have translated it as "a goer", as in the sketch "Nudge, Nudge" (Idle *et al.* 1969/1989: 40). Idle's insinuation in the sketch about a wife who is "a goer" and has "been around" is actually a joke used already by Chaucer, who says about the Wife of Bath in *The General Prologue*, 467, that "She koude muchel of wandrynge by the weye", meaning that she has been going around on amorous adventures.

is not surprising that the article with its appealing rendition of arguably Chaucer's funniest tale caused Kai Friis Møller to ask Bergsøe to translate the whole text, as Friis Møller explains in the preface to the full translation (Friis Møller in Bergsøe 1943: 12). Given a few weak points in Bergsøe's article, it was also probably a good idea to let Friis Møller write the introduction. Besides the inaccuracies about the previous Danish translation and reception, Bergsøe is clearly unfamiliar with the linguistic side of Middle English, which is revealed in another footnote (14, note 3), where he ponders that the *Canterbury Tales* must be a treasure for linguists. He adds: "Man genfinder mange rent danske Ord og, saavidt jeg kan se, maa det have været talt med en udpræget jydsk eller skotsk Akcent." [One recognises many purely Danish words, and as far as I can see, it must have been spoken with a distinct Jutlandish or Scottish accent]. This is not altogether wrong, to be sure, but it is also clearly a point made through an amateur's impressionist gaze. Other non-professional details in Bergsøe's article include a misspelling of Boccaccio's name and another wrong count of the number of Canterbury tales. All these weak points should be forgiven in a context where Bergsøe successfully says something very important about Chaucer, as in the quotation above.

The author of the introduction, Kai Friis Møller (1888-1960), was a well known author and journalist, as indicated above. Living a few years in Brooklyn in his early childhood, he was fluent in English, and he translated Kipling, Eliot and also medieval ballads into Danish. He became an almost legendary reviewer for the Danish newspapers Ekstra Bladet and Politiken (Lund, gen. ed. 1997: 138). At Politiken he was a colleague of author Tom Kristensen for some periods, but fortunately this did not prevent Kristensen from writing a very appreciative review of *Konen fra Bath,* where both translator, illustrator and introducer were praised highly (quoted on the back sleeve of later imprints). His introduction, 8 pages long, focuses on Chaucer as the *grand translateur,* who, inspired by his French, Italian and Latin sources, brings existing European stories into the English language. Interestingly Friis Møller remarks that Chaucer does for English poetry what the Danish poet and psalmist Thomas Kingo did 300 years later for Danish poetry, i.e. "bragte den paa europæisk Højde" [took it to the standard of European poetry] (Friis Møller in Bergsøe 1943: 8). Friis Møller's comparisons with

English writers include Fielding and again Dickens (10), but also Dryden is mentioned as Chaucer's translator into modern English (11-12). It does not look as if Friis Møller knows Dryden's translations, but generally his introduction is fairly competent, and he refers to the work of both Niels Møller, Aage Brusendorff and Uffe Birkedal in such a way that his familiarity with their work is clear. However, Jespersen and the remaining 19th century reception and translation are not mentioned at all.

There are six full page black and white illustrations by Poul Christensen, showing a marriage scene, two domestic fight scenes and a burial in the prologue, and in the tale respectively the young knight and the old hag. Whether they will have pleased the art connoisseur who is the translator is unknown to me, but they certainly function well and make the short book even more reader-friendly.

Reader-friendly is an expression that can also be applied to the translation itself, as Bergsøe uses uncomplicated Danish without unnecessary archaisms (cp. Birkedal's translation, chapter 6), and he also makes everything more simple by only giving necessary bits of information in footnotes, such as noting the medieval tradition of weddings taking place at the church door (Bergsøe 1943: 15). Furthermore Bergsøe shows real poetic talent in not only obeying Chaucer's metre, but also catching the talkative tone of the Wife's monologue in the prologue, as well as the romance language of the tale. Here is the opening of the prologue with my back translation in prose, and Chaucer quoted from Skeat's edition. It is not mentioned which source text Bergsøe has used, but I have checked some passages in Skeat's and Robinson's editions and can say with some certainty that Skeat is Bergsøe's text:

> Var der paa Jord Autoriteter ej [If there
> were no authorities on earth]
> Saa var Erfaringen dog nok for mig [Then
> experience would be enough for me]
> Til Snak om Ægteskabets drøje Kaar; [For talking
> about the hard conditions of marriage]
> Thi, bedste Venner, fra mit tolvte Aar,- [For,
> my friends, from my twelfth year]
> Og evig priset være Herren god!- [And

ever praised be the good Lord]
Med fem Mænd jeg ved Kirkedøren stod; [With
five Men I stood at the church door]
Saa ofte holdt jeg nemlig Bryllup der, [So
often, you see, I was married there]
Og hver en Mand var god paa sin Manér. [And
every man was good in his manner]
(Bergsøe transl.1943: lines 1-8)

'Experience, though noon auctoritee
Were in this world, were right y-nogh to me
To speke of wo that is in mariage;
For, lordinges, sith I twelve yeer was of age,
Thonked be god that is eterne on lyve,
Housbondes at chirche-dore I have had fyve –
For I so ofte have y-wedded be –
And alle were worthy men in hir degree.
(Skeat, ed., *The Canterbury Tales,* D 1-8)

At first sight "drøje kår" (3) and "bedste venner" (4) appear to be rather free translations of respectively "wo" and "lordinges", but actually they are very idiomatic solutions that work well in the context. Bergsøe could have chosen something more solemn and old-fashioned for "lordinges", such as "ærede tilhørere" [noble listeners], but "bedste venner" is straightforward and accurate. The whole passage convincingly establishes a voice talking intimately to an audience, and Bergsøe is able to stay in this voice throughout the prologue.

Bergsøe's strategy of avoiding archaic language works especially well since he makes sure that the language is not too modern, either. Occasionally this involves choosing a word or idiom that is only slightly old-fashioned, but still in use, as opposed to Birkedal's strategy of finding completely obsolete archaisms (see chapter 6). Examples are "inden Kvæld" [before evening] (1012), more poetic and old-fashioned than the standard expression "inden aften". Also the adjective "ful" [foul] (1082) about the old hag is more colourful and unusual in Danish than its English counterpart. And finally "gør han Haneben" [literally: if he shows cock's legs] (932) is a well chosen if not exactly modern idiom for flirting.

Bergsøe strikes a fine linguistic balance in his poetic translation, and it is only regrettable that we only have this one tale from his hand.

In Bergsøe's case we have an opportunity to look into the translator's process of working with his material, as there are two passages of respectively 16 and 62 lines that appear as part of his article "Chaucer bør oversættes" (Bergsøe 1941: 15-16). In the finished version from 1943 these passages have been heavily revised and much improved with regards to poetic quality and linguistic accuracy. I will analyse just a few lines as examples:

> Jeg dansede vidunderligt til Harpers Klang, [I danced wonderfully to the sound of harps]
> Og som den bedste Nattergal jeg sang [And as the best of nightingales I sang]
> Naar jeg var fuld af kraftig Vin [When I was drunk from strong wine]
> Matellius, den usle Karl, det Svin, [Matellius, the wretch, the pig]
> Sin Kone med en Dolk han stak ihjel
> [stabbed his wife with a dagger]
> Fordi hun drak; hvis jeg var hende, ved min Sjæl!
> [because she drank; If I were her, by my soul]
> Han skulde ej ha' holdt mig væk fra Vinens Gud; [He should not have kept me away from the god of wine]
> Og efter Vin jeg bøjed mig for Venus Bud, [And after wine I gave in to the bidding of Venus].
> (Bergsøe 1941: 15)

> Jeg kunde danse til en Harpes Klang, [I could dance to the sound of a harp]
> Saa godt som nogen Nattergal jeg sang [as well as any nightingale I sang]
> Naar jeg mig tog en Slurk af kraftig Vin.
> [When I took a gulp of strong wine]
> Metellius, den usle Karl, det Svin, [Metellius, the wretch, the pig]
> Som med en Knippel tog sin Kones Liv, [who took his wife's life with a cudgel]
> Fordi hun Vinen drak; var jeg hans Viv, [because

she drank the wine; if I were his wife,]
Mit Drikkeri han skulde aldrig krænke; [he should
never be allowed to infringe on my drinking]
Thi efter Vin jeg maa paa Venus tænke: [For
after wine I must think of Venus]
(Bergsøe 1943: 457-64)

Wel coude I daunce to an harpe smale
And singe, y-wis, as any nightingale,
Whan I had dronke a draughte of swete wyn.
Metellius, the foule cherl, the swyn,
That with a staf birafte his wyf hir lyf,
For she drank wyn, thogh I hadde been his wyf,
He sholde nat han daunted me fro drinke;
And, after wyn, on Venus moste I thinke:
(Skeat, ed., D 457-64)

First of all Bergsøe has adjusted the metre in the revised version and avoided a clumsy rhythm such as in the first line of the 1941 version. Secondly some of the rhyme words have been changed, so as to allow improvements both in sound and in accuracy. "Vin" and "Svin" rhyme equally well in Danish and English, and this is also the case for "Liv" and "Viv", although the latter is now archaic in Danish. In the 1941 version, however, the rhyme words are "ihjel" and "Sjæl", and because of the Danish glottal stop in "Sjæl" and not in "ihjel", this is a poor rhyme substitute. The 1943 rhymes "krænke" and "tænke" that replace "Gud" and "Bud" come closer to Chaucer's, allowing also a more accurate translation than in the 1941 version. Accuracy is also obtained by spelling Metellius correctly and by letting him kill his wife with a cudgel rather than a dagger, as in the story from Valerius Maximus referred to in a footnote in the 1943 version. "Naar jeg mig tog en Slurk af kraftig Vin" is idiomatically far better in relation to the source text than the 1941 version, which does not go into detail with the Wife's rather vulgar manners ("dronke a draughte"), but only states that she was drunk. Both Danish versions have "kraftig" [strong] wine rather than Chaucer's sweet wine, but logically this is a reasonable solution, as the focus is on getting drunk rather than tasting something sweet.

As opposed to many other translators of Chaucer, Bergsøe does not employ euphemisms or avoidance strategies when dealing with the Wife of Bath's direct references to sexual organs. The French expression for the female sexual organ *belle chose* (447 and 510) is left unchanged, a very sensible solution. And in line 116 "membres … of generacioun" are equally clearly translated as "Redskaber til Avling" [tools for breeding], following the Wife in leaving nothing to the imagination, just as in line 149, where "myn instrument" becomes "mit Instrument". Parallel to this, Bergsøe calls a spade a spade in his translation of the rape scene in the *Tale*, where the line "By verray force he rafte hir maydenheed" (888) is translated by "Med skændig Vold han hendes Mødom tog" [With shameful violence he took her maidenhood]. Here the adjective "skændig" [shameful] is not matched directly in the corresponding line from Chaucer, but the context in Chaucer's tale makes it a very forgivable explication.

A final example from Bergsøe's highly successful translation will be the climax of the *Tale*:

> "Da har jeg Herredømmet over Dig, ["Then I have the mastery over you]
> Naar jeg maa vælge, som jeg vil, og raade?" [When I may choose as I wish and decide?"]
> "Ja," sagde han, "bedst er det paa den Maade."["Yes", he said, "it is best this way."]
> Hun sagde: "Kys mig, lad vort Had da være,
> [She said, "Kiss me, let our hate be,]
> Thi Du skal faa mig baade-og, paa Ære, [For you shall have me both-and, truly.]
> Forstaar Du, altid smuk og god mod Dig. [You see, always beautiful and good to you.]
> Og lad Vorherre blot forbande mig, [And let our Lord throw a curse on me]
> Om ej jeg bli'r saa god og tro en Mage; [If I do not become as good and faithful a mate]
> Som man har kendt fra Verdens første Dage;" [As has been known from the first days of the world]
> (Bergsøe 1943: 1236-44)

> 'Thanne have I get of yow maistrye,' quod she,
> 'Sin I may chese, and governe as me lest?'
> 'Ye certes, wyf,' quod he, 'I holde it best.'
> 'Kis me,' quod she, 'we be no lenger wrothe;
> For by my trouthe, I wol be to yow bothe,
> This is to seyn, ye, bothe fair and good.
> I prey to god that I mot sterven wood,
> But I to yow be al-so good and trewe
> As ever was wyf, sin that the world was newe.'
> (Skeat, ed., D 1236-44)

This is one of Chaucer's finest twists to the ending of a well-known medieval romance. Whereas the standard ending in other versions of the same medieval romance has the knight saying that he will choose virtue, before the old hag transforms into a beautiful young girl, the transformation is here provoked by a *denouement* which corresponds to the message of *The Wife of Bath's Prologue*, i.e. that women desire to have the upper hand in marriage. Only when the hag knows that she is in power, does she give her love and beauty to the knight. This feminist message is well carried through by Bergsøe, who translates Chaucer's "maistrye" by "Herredømmet", a word that literally means "man's judgment", but is used broadly about both sexes when in power. Still the literal meaning carries funny connotations when used in a connection like this. The idiom "sterven wood" [die mad] is rendered by Bergsøe as "forbande mig" [throw a curse on me] (1242), which is not quite accurate from a formal point of view, but still it is acceptable in this context, because it covers the same meaning, i.e. it has dynamic equivalence in Nida's sense (Nida 1964/2000). Bergsøe also manages to convey the dialogue between the knight and the hag in idiomatic Danish showing that we have to do with spoken language. "Baade-og" [both-and] (1240) is one such idiom, and another is the communicative gambit "Forstaar Du" [you see] (1241), which well translates Chaucer's "This is to seyn".

With this fine finale, Bergsøe manages to keep up the impressive work he has undertaken in this translation. The extracts from his 1941 article show that he moved a long way in quality over the next couple of years, taking the utmost care to obey rhyme and rhythm, find a natural flow of language fitting to Chaucer's wife and selecting appropriate idioms that carry the sense of the original accurately. A translation strategy that avoids archaic Danish and lets the Wife appear more as a timeless character works very well, and Bergsøe should also receive full praise for letting the Wife remain vulgar at certain points. It is remarkable that this work was carried out in difficult circumstances during the war, by someone who is not known otherwise for being an expert in medieval studies, in English literature, or in English language, but of all the translations I have investigated in connection with this study, including modern English ones, Bergsøe comes closest to my own absolute ideal of a Chaucer translator. Fortunately *Konen fra Bath* has been reprinted so many times that it is still available in antiquarian bookshops and libraries. The last available reprint is from 1967 (Bergsøe 1967), and the same year an extract from the prologue, lines 587-827, appeared in an anthology of translated French, German, Italian and English medieval poetry, edited by Anker Teilgård Laugesen. His afterword only mentions Chaucer once (188), and he has reprinted Bergsøe's translation without revisions except for modernized spelling. (Laugesen ed. 1967).

Lis Thorbjørnsen

Our next translator, Lis Thorbjørnsen, also produced a translation titled "Geoffrey Chaucer, Konen fra Bath", published in the literary magazine *Cavalcade* in 1948 (Thorbjørnsen transl. 1948), but this is very far from the quality of Bergsøe's translation, and since it is a much abbreviated translation of *The Wife of Bath's Prologue*, it will be treated only briefly at the end of this section together with her also abbreviated translation of *The Merchant's* Tale, titled "Maj og Januar". Thorbjørnsen's main Chaucer translation is from 1946 and is titled *Geoffroy Chaucer, De tre drikkebrødre* [The three topers]. This is a full text translation of *The Pardoner's Prologue and Tale* (Thorbjørnsen transl. 1946). The alternative spelling of Chaucer's first name has probably been chosen by the writer of the introduction Paul Rubow, who as a professor of general and comparative literature at the University of Copenhagen was highly competent in a variety of fields. Why he should have chosen this now unauthorized spelling is unclear, but of course the variant is found in some, older sources. Paul V. Rubow (1896-1972) was a particular expert in Nordic literature and in Shakespeare, whereas the five-page introduction to Thorbjørnsen's translation is to my knowledge all he ever published on Chaucer.[57] The short introduction is mostly competent, with references to the way Shakespeare, Dryden and Pope carried the Chaucer tradition, and to how Chaucer himself was inspired by earlier traditions from France and Italy. Rubow's section on Chaucer's life covers ground well, but here he allows himself some speculation that is at points very dubious. This involves a claim that Chaucer probably studied in Paris, which if true would be important news in Chaucer studies. Also the assumption that Chaucer's works are marked by the pub atmosphere of his father's combined pub and wine shop is free imagination, to say the least (Rubow in Thorbjørnsen, transl. 1946: 9). Rubow has a better hand with his final short evaluation of Chaucer's *Canterbury Tales*, which leaves an impression that Rubow has understood the general idea of them quite well.

The seven illustrations by Ib Spang Olsen (1921-2012), later a much loved Danish painter and illustrator, not least for children, are dramatic and cover episodes like the initial pub scene and the meeting with the old man, but the murder scenes are not represented in any scary detail. Spang Olsen's distinct style of drawing can be recognized, but I would rate these illustrations as no more than promising work, marked by lack of experience compared to his later mastery.

Turning to the translator herself, Lis Thorbjørnsen (1918-) was already an often used translator when she turned to Chaucer, including an abbreviated translation of Dickens's *Oliver Twist* published in 1944, reviewed briefly by Jørgen Erik Nielsen (Nielsen 2009: 46-7). Later she also published her own work on for example feminist issues, mysticism and ecology, besides writing reviews for the Danish newspaper *Aktuelt*.[58] All in all she has had a very productive and versatile writing career.

Thorbjørnsen's *De tre drikkebrødre* starts with the last part of *The Introduction to the Pardoner's Tale* (title in Benson, gen. ed., *The River-*

---

57 I have checked factual information on Rubow in Rømhild 2000 and below about Ib Spang Olsen in Liza W. Kaaring and Peter Kühn-Nielsen 2000, both in Lund, gen. ed., *Den Store Danske Encyklopædi*.

58 There are no entries on Thorbjørnsen in the standard reference works, but she is included in the literature site http://www.litteraturpriser.dk/aut/tl.htm#TLisThorbjoernsen. I have also used library catalogues for my references to Thorbjørnsen's work.

side Chaucer), known in Skeat's text, which Thorbjørnsen has probably used, as *Words of the Host*. Her prose translation does not leave out those references in Chaucer's text that are glossed in most editions, including the reference in the first lines to "Sankt Ronans Knogler" [St. Ronan's bones], where a note to this Scottish saint spelled as "Ronyan" in Chaucer (Skeat, ed.: C 320) might have prevented the modern reader from being puzzled from the beginning. However, the decision in this translation has been not to include explanatory notes of any kind. The opening of the Thorbjørnsen's text otherwise makes sense, since this is the part where the Host calls for the Pardoner to tell a tale with the words "Thou bel amy, thou Pardoner" (Skeat, ed.: C 318), translated somewhat freely as "Halløj du Afladskræmmer" [Hey you Pardoner] (Thorbjørnsen 1946: 13). This catches the general derogatory tone of the Host a little less clearly than the implications of the French term for "good friend", which might well be intended to hint at the Pardoner's effeminate appearance as described in *The General Prologue*. Also the conclusion to the introduction, where the Pardoner agrees to tell "som honest thyng" rather than "ribaudye" (324-8), is somewhat freely translated as "noget opbyggeligt" [something edifying] rather than "grove historier" [coarse stories] (13). Somewhat freely, certainly, but also quite acceptable in the context, and Thorbjørnsen generally takes very sensible liberties in trying to communicate well with her Danish readers. In the same effort, the Pardoner's latin motto, three times used in his *Prologue*, "*Radix malorum est cupiditas*" (Skeat: subheading, 334 and 426) is translated into Danish as "Griskhed er Roden til alt ondt" [Avarice is the root of all evil] (Thorbjørnsen 1946: 13-15).

The strategy of leaving out explanatory notes while still trying to avoid too many difficulties for the Danish reader is generally quite successful, although explanatory notes would have helped, as in the example with St. Ronan. I have also registered a few strange choices that might easily leave readers bewildered, such as "Disse Belials huler" (19), requiring knowledge of that devil's nickname, where Chaucer just has "that develes temple" (470). Equally a couple of the many swear words are translated peculiarly by Thorbjørnsen, e.g. the expression "Guds Dros" [literally "God's bubo", meaning "I'll be damned"] (24), where "for pokker" would have been a more elegant, idiomatic choice. "Guds dros" is quoted both in this spelling and as "Guds dross", and it is registered in *Ordbog over det Danske Sprog* as only archaic usage. Let me, however, stress that Thorbjørnsen is most often very good at finding corresponding Danish idiomatic expressions. For instance she calls the old man "gamle knark" [old geezer] when he is addressed derisively by one of the rioters as "olde cherl" (Thorbjørnsen: 27, Skeat, ed.: 750), and in the same passage she translates "if that yow be so leef" (760) by "hvis I er saa forhippede på" [if you are so keen on] (27). Also the expression "min Sjæl og Salighed" for "al-so god my soule save" (860/30) sounds quite right in Danish. This idiom would also in 1946 have had a slightly old-fashioned ring, and Thorbjørnsen clearly likes to maintain a somewhat archaic tone.

I will single out just one substantial passage for further consideration, since Thorbjørnsen's translation is after all only a 20-page prose tale with a clear focus on plot, compared to the more refined poetic narrative by Chaucer. My choice here will be a passage that I hope will illustrate just that point, a disturbing, puzzling and poetically intense piece that has led critics to speculate over many years, the matter in question being, who exactly is the old man that the rioters meet? I will not provide the many fanciful answers here, but only remark that the mysterious quality of the character is exactly what is fascinating.

> This olde man gan loke in his visage,
> And seyde thus, 'for I ne can nat finde
> A man, though that I walked in-to Inde,
> Neither in cite nor in no village,
> That woulde change his youthe for myn age;
> And therefore moot I han myn age stille,
> As longe time as it is goddess wille.
> Ne deeth, allas! Ne wol nat han my lyf;
> Thus walke I, lyk a restelees caityf,
> And on the ground, which is my modres gate,
> I knokke with my staf, bothe erly and late,
> And seye, "leve moder leet me in!
> Lo, how I vanish, flesh and blood and skin!
> Allas! Whan shul my bones been at reste?
> Moder, with yow wolde I chaunge my cheste,
> That in my chamber longe tyme hath be,
> Ye! For an heyre clout to wrappe me!"

> But yet to me she wol nat do that grace,
> For which ful pale and welked is my face.
> (Chaucer, *The Pardoner's Tale* in Skeat, ed., C 720-38)

Den gamle mand saa ham ind i Ansigtet og sagde:

> "Jeg har vandret lige til Indien, men hverken i By eller paa Land kan jeg finde et Menneske, der vil bytte sin Ungdom med min Alderdom. Derfor maa jeg stadig bære paa min Alder saa længe det er Guds Vilje.
> Ak, heller ikke Døden vil have mit Liv. Derfor vandrer jeg som en hvileløs Stakkel. Tidlig og silde banker jeg med min Stav på Jorden, der er min Moders Dør, og siger: "Kære Moder, lad mig slippe ind! Se hvor jeg svinder hen, hvor Kød og Blod og Hud tørrer ind. Ak, hvornaar skal mine Ben finde hvile? Moder, jeg vil bytte min Dragkiste, der saa længe har staaet i mit Værelse, med dig for et Ligklæde til at dække mig!" Men endnu vil hun ikke vise mig den Naade, og derfor er mit Ansigt vissent og rynket. [The old man looked him straight in the face and said: "I have wandered all the way to India, but neither in town nor in the country can I find any person who will exchange his youth with my old age. For that reason I still have to carry my age as long as it is God's will. Woe is me that Death does not want my life either. This is why I wander like a restless wretch. Early and late I knock my staff to the earth, which is my mother's door, and say: "Dear mother, let me in! See how I dwindle, how flesh and blood and skin is drying up. Alas, when shall my legs find rest? Mother, I would like to exchange my chest of drawers, which has for so long been in my room, with you, for a shroud to cover me." But she has not yet shown me the mercy and that is why my face is withered and wrinkled.]
> (Thorbjørnsen transl., 1946: 25)

There is little doubt that Thorbjørnsen has translated the passage correctly in almost every detail, and again she should be praised for finding matching Danish idioms like "hvileløs stakkel" for "resteless caityf" (728) and the poetical, in 1946 only slightly archaic "tidlig og silde" for "erly and late" (730). The old man in all his mysterious wretchedness stands clear to us also in Thorbjørnsen's depiction. Still the passage illustrates how impossible it is to transfer Chaucer's beautiful and horrid image of the old man to another language without the backing of the full poetic effects. Poetic narrative, unfortunately a rare genre in the age of the novel, is dependent on the interplay between plot and poetry, and *The Pardoner's Tale* has its high point exactly in this meeting between the three rioters and the old man, because the plot is drawn to a temporary halt in this haunting linguistic and poetic presentation of its main theme, death. The Middle English original acquires its strength through a combination of content and form, the striking image of the old man seeking death in vain, combined with the poetic forcefulness of Chaucer's language. No translator can transfer such a passage successfully to prose without enormous loss.

Thorbjørnsen's *Konen fra Bath* from 1948 is abbreviated to just over three pages, which may very well not be her own fault. The literary magazine *Cavalcade* published both full translations and extracts, as well as abbreviated material, so this will probably have been part of an editor's policy. Orla Lundbo, having taken over from Ole Storm as editor, was by 1948 in the third year of the magazine, which promoted itself as "Maanedsmagasin for litterær Underholdning" [Monthly magazine for literary entertainment], and was actually the first magazine of its kind in Denmark, with a strong preference for British and American literature in translation, but also with classics translations of e.g. Boccaccio and Machiavelli, as well as new Danish literature. The three *Cavalcade* years with Chaucer translations, 1947, 1948 and 1949, present Chaucer in a context of the magazine's emphasis on intelligent entertainment. Storm and Lundbo's editorial quality is high, and besides many quite brilliant texts, there are adverts for such important publications as Danish translations of *Pepy's Diary* and Joyce's *Ulysses* (*Cavalcade* 1948, no. 1: 81 and 1949, no. 2: 50). *Ulysses* was also presented to the *Cavalcade* readers the year before Boisen's full translation appeared, with two brief extracts translated by Jørgen Sonne, whose Chaucer translations are treated below (Sonne in *Cavalcade* 1948, no. 2: 78-80 and no. 3: 37-9).

For the Chaucer translations in *Cavalcade* the general editorial question will have been for Storm and Lundbo what to do in a magazine with mainly short stories when including something that is not a short story. The answer for them was apparently to change Chaucer's poetic tales into short stories. Thus Thorbjørnsen's abbreviated *Wife of Bath's Prologue* focuses entirely on the story of her life with five husbands with a strong emphasis on the climactic episode of the fight with Jankyn, the fifth husband. The Wife's private reflections on Christian morality in the first part of the *Prologue* have simply been cut out, and worse, so have all her reflections on bodily, including sexual functions. We do meet her in bed with a husband, but Thorbjørnsen has avoided reference to most of the elements of the *Prologue* that have bothered Danish translators going back to T.C. Bruun, except Bergsøe. Thorbjørnsen's text is in many ways as much transformed as that of Bruun, her most characteristic translation strategies being, like his, omission, summary and avoidance. However, unlike Bruun she translates some parts straight from Chaucer, and the episode with Jankyn includes translation of substantial passages, including the *denouement* where Jankyn hands over the bridles to his wife. Only Thorbjørnsen has cheated a little bit by using a line from *The Wife of Bath's Tale* as the final line of the *Prologue*: "Gud sende os Ægtemænd, der er føjelige, unge og livlige i Sengen!" [God send us husbands that are yielding, young and vigorous in bed!" (Thorbjørnsen, transl. 1948: 35). This is a sensible translation of "Jesu Christ us sende/Housbondes meke, younge, and fresshe a-bedde" (Skeat, ed., D 1258-9), but it belongs in another context, although admittedly it fits in well here.

Just a few more details will be treated here. In Thorbjørnsen's first line, she lets the wife be married five times at the altar, rather than the church door (32). Whereas this is inaccurate, she is more accurate than Bergsøe in at least one case, which is the correct translation "sød Vin" [sweet wine] for the wine that makes the Wife amorous (33). However, this detail is rather unimportant compared to the translation of such lines as Chaucer's "I had the best *quoniam* mighte be" (608) as "ingen Kvinde kunde være bedre at sove hos" [no woman could be better to sleep with] (34). Thorbjørnsen's wife, having lost her frivolous language and provocative religious attitudes, becomes a shadow of the real thing, although the basic plot in Thorbjørnsen's version is still funny in its own way.

Thorbjørnsen's "Maj og Januar" from the year before (Thorbjørnsen 1947) of course takes its Danish title from the two main characters of *The Merchant's Tale*. It appears as the first of several *Canterbury Tales* translations in *Cavalcade*, and probably for this reason there is a page-long portrait of Chaucer. The author of this page is Elsa Gress, who as we saw earlier in this chapter had been a student of both English and comparative literature. Her general familiarity with Chaucer is clear from her short portrait, and her suggestion that Chaucer is "Realismens pioneer" [the pioneer of realism] can certainly be accepted in a broad sense, although with some reservations. Worse is her claim that Chaucer's language is "det endnu kantede, ubehjælpsomme og højst ufuldkomment udviklede Middelengelsk" [the still awkward, clumsy, and highly incompletely developed Middle English] (Gress 1947: 74). Gress is not the only one to pass such ignorance on to Danish readers, as witnessed by several examples in this study, but relatively speaking this is still an extremely incompetent statement.

Gress notes at the end of her Chaucer introduction that Thorbjørnsen's translation is from verse to prose and "let forkortet" [slightly abbreviated] (Gress 1947:74). It turns out that it is actually substantially abbreviated, as the long marriage debate at the beginning of Chaucer's version is completely left out. With roughly 500 lines of debate and reflection on the nature of old January's marriage to a young girl missing, the tale in Thorbjørnsen's version becomes a fairly simple *fabliau*, not a complicated and nuanced mixture of *debate* and *fabliau* as in Chaucer. Once again a Danish translator, perhaps after instruction from the editor, violates Chaucer's composition and reduces a Canterbury tale to its main plot.

This said, Thorbjørnsen is a skilful prose narrator, and she picks up the dialogue between the main characters very well. For instance this is the case at the dramatic moment when January regains his sight and reacts impulsively at seeing his wife May having sex with her lover Damian in a pear tree. In Chaucer it says, "Out! help! allas! harrow! he gan to crye,/O stronge lady store, what dostow?" (Skeat, ed. E 2365-6) Thorbjørnsen writes, "Han gav et Brøl fra sig og raabte, 'Hjælp! Ned med dig! Hvad gør du, frække Kone?'" [He made a roar and cried, Help! Get down from there! What are you doing, shameless wife] (Thorbjørnsen 1947: 79). Changing the word sequence slightly, Thorbjørnsen certainly covers the sense well, and she catches the drama as well as the humour of the passage. In her translation we are also in no doubt that the humour is about sex, even though she avoids translating Chaucer's very explicit sexual references, such as "in he throng" (2353) and "in it wente!" (2376) These references to penetration are left out, but can still be deduced from the context. In the case of "swyved thee" (2378), Thorbjørnsen gives up the avoidance strategy and uses the Danish euphemism "belaa dig" [lay by you] instead (80). Both the avoidance strategy and the euphemism are understandable, as correct translations of Chaucer's sexual terms might well have led to charges of pornography in the late 1940s. Furthermore, Thorbjørnsen is by no means a squeamish translator, and all her translations of Chaucer demonstrate that she has enjoyed working with her material. Only it is a pity that she has not allowed herself, or been allowed to be more loyal to Chaucer's composition.

Jørgen Sonne

The Danish poet Jørgen Sonne (1925-) has had a life-long passion for European medieval poetry, which has so far culminated with a translation of a wide selection of English, French and Italian lyrics 1100-1700, including a section with poetic translations of Chaucer (Sonne 2007). These Chaucer translations will be discussed in chapter 10, whereas this chapter section will deal with Sonne's prose translations of Chaucer from the late 1940s at a time when he also made his debut as one of Denmark's most distinct poetic voices. Sonne's works have been widely treated in Danish literary criticism, but to my knowledge the present study is so far the first to consider Sonne as a translator of medieval poetry except in short newspaper reviews, although his inspiration from his great predecessors has been acknowledged in criticism. The most important collection of Sonne criticism is a *festschrift* published on the occasion of his 70th birthday in 1995, edited by Per Olsen and Søren Schou (Olsen and Schou, eds., 1995). This collection contains critical articles by a range of Danish literary critics including the editors, and contributions by poet friends and admirers such as Klaus Rifbjerg and Benny Andersen. For the purpose of the present study one of the most useful contributions is a nearly complete bibliography 1946-1995 compiled by Orla Pedersen (Olsen and Schou, eds., 1995: 217-40), which well demonstrates that not only does Sonne have a massive own production, but he has also edited, commented on and translated a wide range of literature, besides being translated himself, into German, English, French, Italian, Hungarian and Macedonian.

The publication history of Sonne's early Chaucer translations is somewhat complicated. The most substantial publication is *Geoffrey Chaucer, Canterbury Fortællinger*, published by the printing house L. Ihrich in a *de luxe* numbered edition as a present to its customers on New Year's Day 1950 (Sonne 1949-50). This contains a one-page preface by Sonne himself (according to Pedersen in Olsen and Schou, ed., 1995: 218), and woodcuts by Erik Christensen.[59] As mentioned in the chapter introduction, the tales translated are *The Reeve's Tale, The Franklin's Tale* and *The Nun's Priest's Tale*. The Danish titles are "Forvalterens fortælling", "Fribondens fortælling" and "Munkens fortælling om Hanen og Hønen, Chantecler og Pertelote" [The Monk's tale about the Cock and the Hen, Chantecler og Pertelote]. However, Sonne had already published two of these translations in the literary magazine *Cavalcade* in 1947 and 1949. His first translation, of *The Reeve's Tale*, had the same title as later revised editions, "Forvalterens fortælling", whereas *The Franklin's Tale* was first titled "De sorte klipper" [The black rocks]. Two further Chaucer translations appeared in *Cavalcade* the same year, "Den syngende hvide ravn og Føbus" [The singing white crow and Phoebus], a slightly abbreviated translation of *The Manciple's Tale*, and "En ung piges hoved" [a young girl's head], an abbreviated translation of *The Physician's Tale*. The translation of *The Reeve's Tale* was revised again by Sonne and published in a collection titled *Humor fra hele verden* [Humour from all over the world], edited by Mogens Knudsen and Orla Lundbo and first published in 1952. A further minor revision was undertaken by Sonne for the second, abbreviated edition of this publication, which appeared in 1967 (Knudsen and Lundbo, eds., 1952/1967). There is also a sound recording by Jørgen Ask from 1975, reading the collection in a publication by *Danmarks Blindebibliotek* [The Danish library for the blind]. In the analysis below the main focus will be on *Geoffrey Chaucer, Canterbury Fortællinger* from 1949/50, including the revisions. However, I shall start by considering the *Cavalcade* translations that were not revised.

First of all it is remarkable that Sonne selects *The Manciple's Tale* and *The Physician's Tale* among his first Chaucer translations, as they are

---

59   Eric Christensen (1920-74), also known as "Spjæt", had a versatile career as an artist and ended up as artistic advisor for the Tivoli Gardens in Copenhagen (Hartmann et al., eds., 1994: vol. 1, 505).

generally not among the most frequently reprinted and translated tales. The titles "Den syngende hvide ravn og Føbus" and "En ung piges hoved" de-contextualise the tales from the tale-telling contest of *The Canterbury Tales*, especially since Sonne does not translate the introductions and prologues to the tales. He also leaves out the interludes at the end of the tales where the pilgrims react to the stories. Apart from that only a few rather insignificant lines near the beginning have been left out, and the lacunae are marked with dots in Sonne's text. *The Manciple's Tale*, with its story of how the white raven got its black colour as a revenge from Phoebus because it witnessed his wife's infidelity and sang to him about it, is well transformed into prose by Sonne, who also has a talent for translating spoken language, as in the dramatic climax of the tale: "Hvadfornoget, Fugl! udbrød Føbus, hvad er det for en sang du synger" [What on earth is this, Bird, exclaimed Phoebus, what song is this you are singing] (Sonne, transl., 1949 b, 78). Chaucer has the slightly simpler if also dramatic 'What, brid?' quod Phebus, 'what song singestow?' (Skeat, ed., H 244), but actually Sonne does well to pull out the dramatic idiom "Hvadfornoget?", which exactly represents Phoebus's embarrassed and frustrated outcry in the scene. More surprising, and less successful is the translation of what the crow actually sings to evoke this response, in Chaucer "cokkow! cokkow! cokkow!" (243). Sonne has "bøh, bøh, bøh" (78), a Danish exclamation used to frighten young children gently in a hide-and-seek game or the like. Not exactly the situation here. On a more positive note, Sonne has taken care with his translation also in cases of medieval references. Thus Chaucer's "Minstralcye", a reference to the minstrel performance tradition, is translated as "luthenspil" [lute play], which in Danish includes a reference to the main minstrel instrument, the lute, and covers the concept well. (Skeat, ed., H 251, Sonne 78). In passing let me also note that Chaucer's "swyve" (256), which correctly translated also in 1949 should be "kneppe" [fuck], understandably becomes "besove" [literally "be-sleep"] (79). Sonne uses "besove" again and also "ligge med" [lie with] for "swyve" in his *Reeve's Tale* translations, and in this respect he is on a par with most translators included in this study.

Turning to "En ung piges hoved", this is abbreviated to a degree where one would have expected the *Cavalcade* editor or Sonne himself to have added this information at the end, as was the case with Thorbjørnsen's

"Konen fra Bath". With only 286 lines this is a short Canterbury Tale already, but Sonne's three pages of prose skip past several lines, including some allusions near the beginning to the classical sculptors Pygmalion, Apelles and Zeuxis (14-16), the ensuing discussion of beauty and virtue, and some descriptive passages. This certainly affects the rhetoric of Chaucer's narrative voice and turns the reader's attention to the plot. From line 118 in *The Physician's Tale*, when the main plot starts, Sonne translates more or less everything, and he does so quite accurately, with a few exceptions. This is the cruel story from Livy of a traitorous judge, Apius, who provides false evidence to get possession as slave of the innocent and beautiful daughter of a noble knight, Virginius, and sentence is passed in Apius's favour. In an unbearable scene Virginius then agrees with his daughter that death is to be preferred to shame, and he chops off her head himself and hands it over to the judge, after which the latter gets his punishment. This is where Sonne is inaccurate, as he not only lets Apius lose his men by hanging and be turned in exile (Skeat, ed., C 270-3), he also makes him "fredløs" [outlawed] (Sonne 1949a, 48). Sonne may have been affected by the stories of Robin Hood, because there is no mention of outlawed people in *The Phycisian's Tale,* nor in Livy's story, nor in *The Romant de la Rose,* where the story also appears, (Langlois, ed., *The Romant de la Rose*: 5589-658).

Sonne has worked further with Chaucer by the time he publishes his de luxe edition of three further Canterbury tales. This is clear alone from the fact that he decided to revise his translations from *Cavalcade* of *The Reeve's Tale* and *The Franklin's Tale*. The title "De sorte klipper" [the black rocks] is changed to "Fribondens fortælling" ["The Franklin's tale", but could also mean "The Yeoman's tale"], and the portrait of the Franklin from *The General Prologue* is added in translation as an introduction, as are the portraits of respectively the Reeve and the Nun's Priest for the other two tales. Apart from that the changes are mainly small corrections, but a couple of revisions are more substantial. For instance Sonne has changed "aldrig" to "ingensinde" at the beginning of the tale, in the important promise from Arveragus to his beloved wife, "ingensinde i sit liv, dag og nat, skulle han tvinge hende" [never in his life, day and night, would he force her] (Sonne 1948: 10/ Sonne 1949-50: 23). "Aldrig" and "ingensinde" both mean "never", but the latter is a formal and slightly archaic word. The effect of using it here is a dramatic reinforcement of the promise, which fits the situation very well. Also a revision at the end of the tale is successful. Sonne first translated Chaucer's "Everich of yow dide gentilly til other" (Skeat, ed., F 1608) as "hver af jer handlede smukt" (Sonne 1948: 16), but sensibly changed this to the more idiomatic Danish expression "I handlede smukt begge to" (Sonne 1949-50: 32).

Whereas the second version of Sonne's translation of *The Franklin's Tale* can be characterized as improved in relation to the first version, there is still the question of abbreviating. For instance the scene just considered where Arveragus makes his promise does not contain a translation of 10 lines focused on his wife Dorigen (734-43), and no less than 50 lines (761-814) containing the narrator's reflections on the nature of love have been passed by. The omissions continue (e.g. 885-9 and 951-63), and again it seems that Sonne or his editor has wanted the plot only, with no narratorial side remarks. As some of the omitted passages contain references to classical legend, e.g. Ekko and Narcissus in lines 951-2, Sonne's abbreviated translation furthermore becomes a simplified version of the tale, losing the allusion and also the reflection and perspective that Chaucer wanted as part of his tale. With Erik Christensen's woodcuts illustrating the characters and the dominant image of the tale, the black rocks, with also a separate woodcut of the magician who calculates the disappearance of the rocks, the plot can be followed almost like a cartoon, but Chaucer's depth of perspective has been lost (Christensen in Sonne 1949-50: 21, 24, 27, 30). "Fribondens fortælling" becomes a poor reflection of Chaucer's advanced poetic composition.

In "Munkens fortælling om Hanen og Hønen, Chantecler og Pertelote" [The Monk's tale about the Cock and the Hen, Chantecler og Pertelote] Sonne stays far more loyal to *The Nun's Priest's Tale*. Less than 50 lines are missing, and mostly Sonne stays loyal to Chaucer's text. The omissions and abbreviations appear mainly in a passage with references to such authorities as St. Augustine and Boëthius (Skeat, ed., B2, 4416-4456) and in a few other allusions to classics later on. Whereas Sonne simply omits most allusions and references, Chaucer's mention of the medieval popular bestiary *Physiologus* (4461) is an exception. Here Sonne actually translates with a reference to another medieval work, the *Lucidarius*, a Danish theological handbook ca. 1350, based on a much earlier German handbook of the same name (Sonne 1949-50: 46, Kjær in Lund, gen. ed., 1998: 304). It appears that Sonne is not afraid of allusions to the medieval world, but that he has made a choice with preference for something more familiar to Danes. Whether his actual Danish readers knew of the *Lucidarius* is then another matter.

Sonne is clearly familiar with the genre of beast fable, and he makes a particular effort to draw up clear images of the animals. For example the fox, which in Chaucer is among other things "ful of sly iniquitee" (4405), becomes "fuld af underfundig træskhed" [full of cunning guile] (45). This must have sounded just right in 1950, although "træskhed" has since then lost ground as a common idiom. The cock Chantecler is characterized by the French loan word "grandiose" (46), which may be slightly off the mark as Chaucer has the adjective "free" [noble], but on the other hand the cock *is* grandiose in the eyes of the admiring hens in the passage. This image is further strengthened in Erik Christensen's woodcut of a full page proud cock (39).

A conclusion to this brief analysis of Sonne's *Nun's Priest's Tale* is that it is fairly successful compared to the severely abridged and transformed *Cavalcade* translations. Sonne certainly shows his translator's skills and takes well care not only of characters and plot. This evaluation includes also his neat translation of the famous proverbial guide to readings of fables expressed at the end of the tale, "Taketh the fruyt, and late the chaf be stille" (4633). Sonne writes "Tag kernen, og lad avnerne flyve" [Take the fruit/core and let the chaff fly], which is exactly the corresponding Danish proverb.

In the case of "Forvalterens fortælling", Sonne's translation of *The Reeve's Tale*, several proverbs are well translated, not least the proverb used as a narrator's moral comment at the end of the tale, "'Him thar nat wene wel that yvel dooth; A gylour shal him-self bigyled be'" (Skeat, ed., A 4321-2). Sonne translates this as "Den, der ikke ta'r sig i vare, når han vil narre, bli'r selv en nar" [He who is not careful when wanting to fool somebody will be fooled himself] (Sonne 1947/1949-50/1952/1967: 53/19/338/307). This is a slight transformation, but it covers the sense precisely and also sounds proverbial, with the rhyme "vare/narre" matching Chaucer's alliteration "wene wel", and with the same agent inversion, "narre"/bli'r en nar" as in Chaucer's "gylour/bigyled". "Forvalterens fortælling" is in my estimate Sonne's best *Canterbury Tales* translation exactly because he has taken so much care with details of this kind, and because he has not left out bits and pieces in this translation.

Sonne's revision of his 1947 translation for the 1949/50 edition is not successful in all respects, and he wisely decided to return to his first translation when contributing to a collection of humour published in 1952, very slightly revised again for a second edition in 1967 (Sonne in Knudsen & Lundbo, 1952/1967). The mistakes are not many but include the shape of Simkin the miller's nose, which in Chaucer is "camuse", a pug-nose (3934). Sonne first translated this as "buttet næse" [chubby nose] (Sonne 1947: 44) then changed it to "opstoppernæse" [snub-nose] (Sonne 1949-50: 9), before returning to "buttet næse" [chubby nose] in the revised editions (Sonne 1952/1967: 330/299). "Buttet næse" is not wrong and is at least better than the incorrect "opstoppernæse", but "braktud" would have been quite precise for pug-nose and is idiomatic Danish. Another correction involves a double mistake concerning the miller's wife's snoring, which can be heard "two furlong" away (4166), meaning 440 yards away or just a long distance away. Sonne first translates this incorrectly as "to favne væk" [two fathoms away] (Sonne 1947: 50), which is only 12 feet away, then changes it to the also incorrect "to minutter i træk" [two minutes non stop] (1949-50: 15), before returning to "to favne væk", (1952/1967: 334/304). Also in this scene there is another serious translation mistake, as all versions have "ungen" [the baby] accompanying the miller and his wife in the snoring concert. It is not very sensible to have a baby in a cradle snoring, and in Chaucer it is in fact their adult daughter who snores, after having taken a full meal with lots to drink. Finally, I have found an example where a correct revision is changed back to a mistake. This is Chaucer's reference in line 4055 of a mare speaking to a wolf, which Sonne rightly translates as "hoppen sagde til ulven" [the mare said to the wolf] in the 1949-50 edition (12). The first and the later editions have the wolf speaking to the mare (47/332/301).

These examples are exceptions to the, as a rule, very sensible translation. Sonne's idiomatic language generally brings about the liveliness of one of Chaucer's finest *fabliaux*. In some cases the idiomatic translations include giving up accuracy, such as the translation of "He was a market-beter atte fulle" (3936) about Simkin. Sonne first translated this as "Han var helt igennem en slagsbror" [he was a fighting man through and through] (1947/1952/1967: 44/330/299), which is a better idiomatic solution than the revision "Han yppede altid kiv på markederne" [He always started a quarrel at the market-places] (1949-50: 9), although the market-places have been left out. A similar strategy can be seen in the replacement of the more easily understandable paraphrase in Danish, "en stor præsteskole i Cambridge" [a big religious school in Cambridge] in the first version (45) with the place name "Soller Hall ved Cambridge" (11), directly translating Chaucer's "Soler-halle at Cantebregge", 3990. "Soler-halle" is present-day King's Hall, and the paraphrase avoids the possible name confusion and is a better communicative solution, as the name of the hall is not important in the context, and as Sonne does not operate with explanatory notes.

It may be regretted that Sonne has not translated the northern dialects of the two students into a Danish sociolect, but generally he has a successful hand with the dialogues. For instance the many exclamations are dealt with carefully, such as the colourful outcry "Æsch" from the miller's wife when realizing she might have gone to the wrong bed after taking a leak (1947,1949-50,1952/1967: 51/16/335/305). Chaucer's miller's wife says "ben'cite" (Skeat, ed., A 4220) or "benedicite" in other versions (e.g. Benson, gen. ed., *The Riverside Chaucer*: 1, 4220), but whereas Sonne's translation is not exactly accurate, it works rather well in the scene. "Æsch" in Danish is an outcry that belongs to a series of exclamation forms that can be varied endlessly and still recognized for an outcry of either surprise, relief or irritation with oneself. In the bedroom scene these are the exact mixed feelings that the miller's wife is meant to have.

It may be concluded that Sonne is generally a good, but not a flawless Chaucer translator. His revisions are not always successful, and in the case of "Forvalterens fortælling" the first translation is in many ways the best. However, the 1949-50 edition has by far the best illustrations with Christensen's woodcuts, including an openly erotic one of Allan and Malin (17). There is a far less exciting woodcut in the 1952 edition and nothing in the 1967 edition. Compared to Christensen, also Ib Spang Olsen's three illustrations from the 1947 translation are rather tame. The illustrations make up the most serious quality difference between the editions, but of course it also matters that the 1949-50 edition is a numbered ex libris edition in quality binding, paper and print. Moreover, the 1949-50 edition, as we have seen, includes translations of the portraits in *The General Prologue*, and this gives us at least some contextualisation. It would have been even better to translate the introductory passages in Chaucer's *Reeve's Tale*, *Franklin's Tale* and *Nun's Priest's Tale*, but the alternative, nothing at all, as in the revised translations, is of course a poor solution.

Chapter conclusion

In conclusion to this chapter the question could be asked whether prose translations of poetry should be avoided altogether? My answer is no, prose translations offer us something, if not everything. Chaucer's *Canterbury Tales* are full of intricate and enticing tales that may be rendered well in prose, as we have seen here and as we will also see in the next section. And many readers in the present day would probably give up on poetic versions of Chaucer. Ideally, there should be a choice, and even better, translations should be mainly used as support in reading the original, whenever that is possible for readers. When it is not possible, it is far better to read a prose translation of Chaucer than to read no Chaucer at all.

CHAPTER 9

THE 1950s. BOISEN AND JOHANSEN

The two complete or near-complete Danish translations of *The Canterbury Tales*, a prose translation by Mogens Boisen and a poetic translation by Børge Johansen, came about under very different circumstances and were published in 1952 and 1958, respectively, although they appear to have been begun around the same year, 1949 (Boisen 1952, Johansen 1958). This chapter is mainly devoted to an analysis of these translations, including comparisons with a number of other translations, both into Danish and into modern English. As we saw in the last chapter, a number of individual Canterbury tales appeared in Danish in the 1940s, and for that reason it is only natural that Danish publishers became interested in full translations. Another and probably more important reason was that Chaucer was getting more than usual attention in Britain and the United States, in Britain with Coghill's late 1940s BBC broadcasts and later published translation of *The Canterbury Tales* (Coghill 1951, Ellis 2000: 189, note 29), in the USA with Lumiansky's prose translation of the *Tales* from 1948 (Lumiansky 1948), and with Morrison's translation of Chaucer extracts, *The Portable Chaucer* (Morrison 1949). On both sides of the Atlantic there was clearly a renewed interest in seeking out the national cultural roots after the war, and Chaucer became part of this interest. This in turn led to publishing interest abroad, including Denmark. Also generally, the vast amount of translations from English into Danish continued throughout the 1950s and beyond. Having already in the last chapter established the major paradigm shift in linguistic, literary and cultural orientation in Denmark during and after the war, I will restrict myself here to a consideration of how some of these tendencies developed during the 1950s. I will also consider one more example of Chaucer reception, this time not an encyclopedia entry, but a similar presentation in a world history, *Grimbergs Verdenshistorie*.

English in Denmark in the 1950s

In previous chapters I have given indications of tendencies in translations from English and translations of classics, noting certain delays or occasional omissions as well as impressively comprehensive and immediate translations. After World War 2 this particular kind of contextualization of my main story of Chaucer translations becomes partly blurred, as there is an explosion both in the number of translations generally, and as we saw in the last chapter of translations from English in particular. This means that so much gets translated that it is hard to single out a publication strategy. However, it is possible to establish a canon of 20th century authors writing in English. For the purpose of a general picture of 20th century English literature translated by the 1950s, I will focus on an influential author encyclopedia in three large volumes, *Fremmede digtere i det 20. århundrede* [Foreign authors in Denmark in the 20th century], edited by professor of literature at the University of Copenhagen Sven Møller Kristensen, and published 1967-68 (Møller Kristensen, ed., 1967-8). Although published a few years later than the 1950s, this work contains portraits of 20th century authors that have become canonized through a substantial production and reputation in Denmark also before 1960. The portraits, which are very thorough, include the following English-language authors: Conrad, Shaw, Wells, Yeats, Waugh, Eliot, Joyce, Woolf, Hemingway, Faulkner, Sinclair Lewis, Anderson, Huxley, Forster, Lawrence, Lee Masters, Sandburg, Dreiser, Wolfe, Greene, Dylan Thomas, Miller, Steinbeck and Beckett. Although a number of further authors are mentioned in survey chapters such as "Amerikansk roman og novelle efter 1945" [American novel and short story after 1945], this can be considered the top part of the English 20th century canon in Denmark in the 1950s and 1960s. *Fremmede digtere i det 20. århundrede* includes a list of translations indicating that, with exceptions such as Woolf, most of these authors were nearly fully translated (Møller Kristensen, ed. 1967-68: vol. 3, 589 ff.), and with a high proportion of literary modernists it is easy to see what were the dominant interest of well educated readers and literary critics in Denmark. The Danish modernist movement in literature, inspired mainly by some of these writers, but also by French and German modernists, was chiefly a 1950s and 1960s phenomenon, and in fact two of these Danish modernists, Klaus Rifbjerg and Tage Skou-Hansen, are the authors of the portraits of respectively Hemingway and Faulkner in *Fremmede digtere i det 20. århundrede*.[60] Whether they also read Chaucer like their great early modernist predecessor, the author and critic Tom Kristensen, is unknown to me, but it is a fact that Chaucer's *Canterbury Tales* were made available in complete translation for the first time in Danish at a time when the canon of 20th century writers in English looked roughly like the list above. It should be emphasized again that also much else was translated from English, and I include for instance other classics translations elsewhere in this study.

Turning to a broader cultural orientation, we have already seen how especially American film and TV gained prominence in Denmark. As opposed to many other countries, Denmark has always had a tradition of subtitling rather than dubbing, which means that film and TV have been main educators and led to a relatively high standard of English oral proficiency in Denmark and the other Scandinavian countries. The first Danish TV programmes ran from 1951, and cinemas became an important part of youth culture even before the 1950s. Also jazz was, and is, a big thing in Denmark, though in popularity less prominent than rock and roll from the mid-1950s. As noted by Charlotte Rørdam Larsen, rock and roll really hit Denmark first as a dance phenomenon (Rørdam Larsen 2003: 499-500), but of course it was not long before Elvis Presley, and just as much his British counterpart Tommy Steele became heroes beyond the dance floor.

Whereas American mass culture made a clear mark on Denmark in the 1950s, British English remained the main pronunciation model in Danish schools, and the close link to Britain was made symbolically clear with Churchill's triumphant visit in 1950, as mentioned in chapter 8. A drawing by cartoonist Bo Bojesen from 1956 even represents Churchill as a Viking chief carried on a plate by Danish horned Vikings (reprinted in Hertel 2003: 462). Denmark had joined both the US and Britain in Nato in 1949, and there was a general effort to move foreign policy in the direction of the Western allies (Mariager 2003: 536-7), but culturally and politically the link to Britain was the stronger of the two. The Danish social democratic welfare state, modelled partly on the British welfare

---

60 Although Rifbjerg and Skou-Hansen both started out as modernists, both writers have developed and also written in different traditions, including realism.

state, developed further throughout the 1950s, and the import-export relations also gradually improved (Mariager 2003: 542-65). Sevaldsen notes that by the mid-1950s "West European nations were ... beginning to trade freely in a serious manner" (Sevaldsen 2003: 93). In this connection it was no coincidence that Denmark joined Britain in EFTA in 1960 rather than the EEC in 1957, and later that Britain and Denmark both joined the EEC on the same date, January 1st 1973. Emblematic of the improved trade relations in the mid-1950s is the British Industries Exhibition in Copenhagen, 1955, which among its notable features included a major tattoo in the gardens of Rosenborg Castle, Shakespeare guest performances and a real British pub erected in the Tivoli Gardens (Sevaldsen 2003: 93-7).

It will appear that the Danes in the 1950s were so sympathetic to and influenced by American and especially British culture that also the positive reception of something more classical like Chaucer's *Canterbury Tales* would be possible. The remainder of this chapter will be concerned with the two translations that actually appeared, except that I take a slight detour first to show how Chaucer was represented in a very popular work first published in Denmark in 1958-61 and reprinted several times, *Grimbergs Verdenshistorie* [Grimberg's World History] (Grimberg 1958-61).

Grimbergs Verdenshistorie

Grimbergs Verdenshistorie is one of the most popular publications in Scandinavia ever and can still be acquired in great numbers in antiquarian bookshops. The Danish version in 16 volumes was actually translated from the Norwegian version, which in turn was a translation of the Swedish original ("Grimberg", Anonymous *Danish Wikipedia* entry 2011). Carl Grimberg (1876-1941) died so early in the process of writing that his assistant Ragnar Svanström had taken over by the time they reached Chaucer, i.e., in the Danish volume 7. This volume was translated by Kai Petersen and edited by Sven Tito Achen, and quotes from Birkedal's translation of *The General Prologue* and from Bergsøe's translation of *The Wife of Bath's Prologue* are included. With also three unacknowledged manuscript illustrations and the *Regement of Princes* Chaucer portrait from 1412 reprinted, this eight pages long portrait is pieced together from several sources. The best part of the piece is clearly the page or so concerning the Wife of Bath, which has been written on the basis of a reading of Bergsøe's translation and represents it well. The translated and other edited parts, however, contain a few disasters, including some remarkable, unwarranted conclusions about Chaucer's view on life in general:

> "Chaucer var i høj grad et barn af denne verden. Han satte pris på et veldækket bord, en smuk kvinde, og en sikret tilværelse med gode indkomster… Chaucer var ingen reformator. Han fandt at livet stort set var godt som det var, og menneskene vakte ikke hans mismod." [Chaucer was very much a child of this world. He enjoyed a well laid table, a beautiful woman, and a secured life with a solid income… Chaucer was no reformer. He found that by and large life was good as it was, and human beings did not make him lose heart]
> (Grimberg 1959: 369 and 376)

How on earth anyone can draw a picture of Chaucer as a sort of philistine, complacent and not really up to any changes in society, is beyond my understanding, except that in this study we have seen other writers on Chaucer who use free imagination and no proper sources or personal readings of Chaucer.

A second disaster among several inaccurate details in the Grimberg Chaucer entry concerns the short account of the Reeve's reaction to *The Miller's Tale*:

> "Han føler sig stødt på fagets vegne, og hævner sig ved at fortælle om to præster, der voldtager en møllers kone og datter" [He feels offended on behalf of his trade and takes revenge by telling about two priests who rape a miller's wife and his daughter]
> (373).

Readers of Chaucer or of my chapter 8 will know that there are no priests, but students in *The Reeve's Tale,* and that they seduce the remarkably willing daughter and wife rather than rape them.

In conclusion to this short section it may reasonably be asked whether it matters that a massively popular world history contains grotesquely inaccurate information and evaluation of Chaucer and his works? The answer is clearly, yes! And now I quickly move on to the main part of this chapter.

Boisen and Johansen, an introduction

It is often claimed that Mogens Boisen (1910-1987) is one of the most formidable translators in Denmark from the 20th century, and despite what follows in this chapter, I agree up to a point.[61] His career included more than 800 translations from several languages, including three editions of *Ulysses,* translating and revising this translation during most of his lifetime. By 1949, when he began the Chaucer translation, Boisen had already made a name for himself, especially as the Danish *Ulysses* translator. He had worked on this translation late hours at night after finishing his duties as an officer in the Danish army (Boisen 1985). Boisen, when praised for his Joyce translations, used to joke about it by saying that someone really ought to translate *Ulysses* into English some day (Boisen lecture at Copenhagen University, personal attendance, 1980). He was put under pressure from publishers to have his name on the cover, in one known instance, a revised translation of *David Copperfield*, hardly having done any of the work (Nielsen 2009: 79). Such was his prestige and judgement that he was once responsible for removing a chapter he did not like in a novel, and he also admitted to "improving" certain writers' work, thus saving them from embarrassment.[62]

---

61 I attended a session at the bookfair in Forum, Copenhagen, in 2008, with another distinguished translator, Niels Brunse, who among his merits is on his way to becoming the latest of a handful of Danish translators over the last two hundred years to have translated the complete works of Shakespeare. Brunse said in the session interview that his ideal of a translator was Mogens Boisen.

62 Boisen records some of the working process behind his many translations in his autobiography, *Referat af et flerstrenget liv* (Boisen 1985). Needless to say this autobiography contains no information on the more dubious aspects of his translation practice considered here. I have with pleasure acquired knowledge of Boisen's translation practice and very lively personality through personal attendance at a short lecture series that Boisen gave at the University of Copenhagen in 1980. Further information in this presentation of Boisen's practice as a translator has been given to

Boisen's *Ulysses* translations were published in respectively 1949, 1970 and 1980. As pointed out by Hans Hertel, however, a translation had been undertaken already in 1941 by Børge Houmann, a communist and later editor-in-chief of the daily newspaper *Land og Folk*. As active in the resistance movement very early on, Houmann had to go underground already in 1941, and the manuscript was confiscated, according to Hertel by German or Danish police. Hertel also claims that the translation was complete and ready for printing (Hertel 2003: 464). Ida Klitgård has looked further into this matter with the help of the Danish James Joyce Society, and in her habilitation on the *Ulysses* translations she reports that Houmann had translated only "major parts" of *Ulysses* and that it was Danish police that "confiscated and destroyed" the manuscript, thus seeing "six years' work annihilated in a day." However, Klitgård allows for another possibility than this version of the mystery, which if true compromises Boisen even more than he will be compromised by my revelations in this study: "Evil tongues claim that Boisen secretly plagiarized all of the manuscript which explains the speed with which Boisen managed to finish his first translation of *Ulysses* in less than one year. But these of course remain speculations" (I. Klitgård 2007: 123-4). In my estimate this would not be beyond Boisen if somehow he managed to retrieve the confiscated Houmann manuscript. My estimate is based on evidence I provide below. However, the evidence about the connection to Houmann's *Ulysses* translation cannot be established for certain, and research librarian Morten Thing, who interviewed Houmann extensively shortly before Houmann's death in 1994, in connection with his study *Portrætter af 10 kommunister* [Portraits of 10 Communists] (Thing 1995), informs me that Houmann never referred to this possibility when talking about his lost *Ulysses* manuscript (personal correspondence, May 2011).

Like Boisen, our second main Chaucer translator, Børge Vigandt Johansen (1912-2002), had a civil career very different from the world of literature. He became a graduate in Economics in 1937 and had a long and flourishing career in the Danish finance ministry, starting before he graduated, in 1933. He ended his working life in 1982 in a high public

---

me in letters and conversation with the late J.E. Nielsen (cp. also Nielsen 2009 for a consideration of Boisen as Dickens translator). Finally, I have received information from members of the Danish James Joyce Society.

office, as chief of section in the ministry's mortgage bank *Kongeriget Danmarks Hypotekbank* [the mortgage bank of the kingdom of Denmark], from 1998 changed to the present *Finansstyrelsen* [the finance administration] (Balling in Lund, gen. ed., accessed 2011). It is remarkable that on top of this impressive career he managed to study for the degree of *mag. art.* in English and concurrently translate all of the *Canterbury Tales*, finishing the translation in 1958 and obtaining the degree in 1959. His degree was then a six-year master's degree. Johansen writes about his translation that it was begun nine years earlier, and that its publication was recommended by professor Bodelsen from the University of Copenhagen. The publication received support directly from the Danish Ministry of Education, so it must be considered quite a prestigious publication (Johansen 1958: preface).[63]

Johansen's later work included further publications on the late Middle Ages. His thorough introduction to the translation was later expanded to a broader study, *Fra Chaucers Tid* [From Chaucer's Time], published in 1965 (Johansen 1965). This study will be considered later in this chapter. Johansen published a new study in 1987, *Og rask igennem larm og spil: Middelalderens krønikeskrivere fortæller* [And briskly through noise and game: The chroniclers of the Middle Ages tell their stories], which looks at the period 1325-1400 in Europe through the eyes of chroniclers such as Froissart, translating their text with interlinking commentary from Johansen (Johansen 1987). *Kvinder, kirke, kættere: Mod middelalderens slutning* [Women, church, heretics: Towards the end of the Middle Ages] from 1996 is Johansen's final book-long study of late medieval England, yet another successful transmission of knowledge about the period to a general readership, with a focus on women (Johansen 1996). As this book contains a ten-page section on Chaucer, it will be considered separately as Chaucer reception in chapter 10, but it will not be included in

---

63 Besides the brief author information included in Johansen's translation, I received biographical information by J.E. Nielsen in 2007, cp. the previous note, and from Pia Sobieski at the Danish Agency for Libraries and Media, 2011. Finally I included some of the information about Johansen from the cover of Johansen 1987. Also in the case of Johansen, I had the pleasure of making personal acquaintance with this distinguished, now old gentleman in 1994, when he attended a guest lecture I gave at the University of Copenhagen, and his grandchild, a student of mine, kindly introduced him.

the translation analysis here, as the quotations Johansen uses from his translation of *The Canterbury Tales* have not been revised, except for modernised spelling.

Introduction to Mogens Boisen's translation from 1952

I will start this part by admitting that I have become wiser in relation to an earlier article surveying Danish reception and translation, including a brief analysis of Boisen's *Canterbury Tales* translation (Klitgård 2005). In that article I suggested in a note that "Boisen seems to have been using Skeat's edition of *The Canterbury Tales* as his base text, but may well have taken more direct influence from Lumiansky's translation. Further research would be needed to substantiate this point." (Klitgård 2005: 217, note 15). Now that this further research has been undertaken, let me say that it cannot be convincingly established whether Boisen has used Skeat or perhaps Robinson's first edition (Skeat 1897, Robinson 1933), because all he translates from these editions are a few lines in verse from his introduction. What I have now safely established, however, is that more or less the rest of Boisen's text is directly translated from R.M. Lumiansky's 1948 translation. As no mention of Lumiansky is made anywhere in Boisen's introduction or Christian Bernhardsen's afterword, I must draw the conclusion that I have revealed a case of plagiarism. Not even the editor's initial note that "CANTERBURY-FORTÆLLINGERNE er oversat af Mogens Boisen efter CANTERBURY TALES" [CANTERBURY-FORTÆLLINGERNE have been translated by Mogens Boisen from CANTERBURY TALES] reveals the source even with considerable goodwill, as Lumiansky's title is *Chaucer's Canterbury Tales*. Boisen will probably have consulted also either Skeat or Robinson, but his base text is Lumiansky's Chaucer, except 3-4 pages with a small part of *Melibee*, which Boisen includes and Lumiansky leaves out (Boisen 1952: 283-87).

I have decided not to dwell much further on Boisen's plagiarism here and simply state that a word for word comparison of Lumiansky's text to Boisen's will make this case plain to any reader. The analysis in this chapter of selected passages from Boisen compared to Lumiansky provides sufficient evidence. Furthermore, this is not the first time Boisen has been caught in using intermediate sources for his translations, although

Ida Klitgård's analysis of Boisen's *Ulysses* translations reveals plagiarism of a different kind. Here Boisen has occasionally used both a Swedish and a German translation as intermediary, which can be proved among other things on the grounds that he has reproduced a couple of their translator's errors. (I. Klitgård 2007: 128-31).

Boisen writes in his short introduction to his prose *Canterbury Tales* that he has left out a couple of tales that are longwinded and tedious. It turns out that they are not only *Melibee* and *The Parson's Tale*, which so many others exclude, but also *The Monk's Tale* and *The Prioress's Tale*, which can hardly be said to be longwinded. Lumiansky's translation provides a simple clue to this odd choice, because these are the exact tales Lumiansky also leaves out. Lumiansky's choice in the first edition of his translation to leave out *The Prioress's Tale* is known to be because of its Jewish antipathy, which, in Lumiansky's estimate, modern readers were unlikely to accept so shortly after the war. (Yager 2002: 10-11) He actually produced a translation of *The Prioress's Tale* in 1954 and included it in the second edition of his *Chaucer's Canterbury Tales*. This also meant that he had finished his work with translating Chaucer, including also a prose translation of *Troilus and Criseyde*, before writing the critical study of Chaucer that he has become best known for, *Of Sondry Folk* from 1955 (Lumiansky 1952 and 1955).

Lumiansky's translation has been substantially treated in an unpublished paper by Susan Yager, "'I speke in prose': Lumiansky's translation of Chaucer" (Yager 2002).[64] In this paper Yager takes a starting point in the fact that three Chaucer translations into modern English appeared in the postwar years: Coghill's British verse translation, *The Canterbury Tales*, first given as BBC readings in the late 1940s and subsequently published in 1951; Morrison's American verse translation published in *The Portable Chaucer* in 1949; and then Lumiansky's American prose translation from

---

64 Susan Yager and I were at the same session on "Chaucer and translation," chaired by Steve Ellis at the thirteenth biannual congress of the New Chaucer Society, Boulder, Colorado, 20 July 2002. Afterwards I have obtained a copy of the paper and a kind permission from Susan Yager to quote from it. My quotations from Lumiansky's translation in this chapter refer to the second edition published by Simon and Schuster in 1960 as a Washington Square Press Edition, *Chaucer's Canterbury Tales*, and several times reprinted. This edition includes the 1948 text with slight revisions and also *The Prioress's Tale* in a 1954 translation subsequently undertaken by Lumiansky.

1948, *Chaucer's Canterbury Tales,* preceding the other two.[65] Yager playfully suggests that Lumiansky's translation might be referred to "as a sort of G.I. Tales; created in and for the immediate postwar period, it was perfectly suited for the hurry-up, catch-up generation of U.S. veterans home from war." (Yager 2002: 5). I would add that the evidence of no less than three modern translations appearing in the postwar period signals an urging need for national awareness and celebration of authors seen as constituting part of the national identity.

Yager demonstrates convincingly that Lumiansky has adapted a strategy of focusing on Chaucer's narrative, "merely the stories... as clear as sunlight" as she quotes van Doren for remarking in his introduction to the translation (6). Secondly she proposes that Lumiansky's approach is essentially *modern,* "particularly insofar as *modern* meant "non-sentimental" ... [and] concerned with efficiency, a reader in a hurry." (5) This involves a dislike of archaism and adornment, even to a point where thirties-style language reminiscent of Al Capone finds its way into the translation as replacement for medieval English. Among Yager's examples of this is the choice to translate a line from the portrait of the Knight in the *General Prologue,* "everemoore he hadde a sovereyn prys (I, 67) as "he had always been given valuable loot" (Lumiansky: 2, Yager: 8). Yager sums up her general evaluation of Lumiansky's focus on narrative and his attempt to modernise by suggesting that the translation invites "a speedy novelistic reading of Chaucer" (12).

It is a pertinent question, also on the basis of the Danish prose translations considered in this study so far, whether all prose translations of poetic narrative are plain invitations to modern readers basically unfamiliar with all other narrative genres than the novel and the short story. Certainly Peter Ackroyd's 2009 translation of the *Canterbury Tales* shares the assumption that only appeal to the reader experienced with novels and short stories will do. This is seen in Ackroyd's general strategy of leaning on a novel-based narrative technique, and it can also be illustrated by the back cover's alluring description of the *Tales* in key terms: "Love ... sex ... infidelity ... villainy ... drunkenness ... murder" (Ackroyd 2009).

---

65 For further discussion of these translations see Ellis 2000, "Translated Chaucer", 98-120. Besides Lumiansky, I also use Coghill's, Wright's and Ackroyd's translations for comparison with Boisen and Johansen in my analyses below.

There is a parallel here to the outspoken ideal of Lumiansky to transform Chaucer into "natural, idiomatic, colloquial, modern English" (Lumiansky: "Introduction", xiv), especially, as we shall see in the analysis below, because this colloquial and modern idiom in Lumiansky's translation involves a relatively faithful representation of sex, if not exactly in the shape of the four-letter words so frequently used by Ackroyd.

In the analysis below I will return to Boisen's, and later to Johansen's translations of passages which will have appeared challenging for sensitive 1950s readers. However, let us first consider Boisen's own general attitude as expressed in his short introduction. Here he, unknowingly I'm sure, aligns himself with the tradition from Dryden that we considered in chapter 3:[66]

> "Selv om datidens stil var grov og plump og dette egentlig burde komme til udtryk også i en oversættelse, har jeg alligevel skønnet det rimeligt at afsvække nogle af de stærkeste sager en smule. Meningen er bibeholdt, men teksten er stedvis befriet for en ilde lugt." [Even though the style of that time was coarse and plump, and though this really ought to appear also in a translation, I have judged it reasonable all the same to weaken some of the most potent matters somewhat. The sense has been retained, but in places the text has been liberated from its bad odours.]
> (Boisen: 7)

Boisen shares the gross generalisation ironing out "the style of the time" with many translators, who have thus embarked on the task of smoothing out some of the rough verse. He has clearly made little effort to familiarise himself with knowledge from historical linguistics that could have cleared up this misunderstanding about Chaucer and medieval poetry. For instance a little acquaintance with the work of fellow Danes Jespersen or Brusendorff would have been sufficient.

Boisen's overall opinion about Chaucer's poetry is partly shared in the afterword to *Canterbury Fortællingerne* by Christian Bernhardsen

---

[66] I refer specifically to Dryden's description of Chaucer as a "rough diamond," who "must first be polish'd e'er he shines" in his preface to *Poems and Fables*. Cp. also the remarks about Chaucer's coarseness by C.L. Westergaard considered in chapter 4.

(1923-1989), a Norwegian-born cultural journalist, author and literary critic, from 1952 writing under the pseudonym of Bris in the Danish newspaper B.T. (Jensen, Niels, accessed November 2011, Stein Petersen 2005, Bernhardsen 1951: 315-18). The three pages long afterword about Chaucer's life and works does provide some basic knowledge for the general reader, and furthermore Bernhardsen must be praised for a focus on Chaucer's attitude to women, with a specific reference to *The Wife of Bath's Prologue* (317-18). This said it is hard to accept that no sources are given for other specific pieces of information, indeed for the whole afterword, which clearly draws on a couple of literary histories.[67] And an estimate like the following would be interesting to have substantiated:

> "For Geoffrey Chaucer var intet menneskeligt fremmed. Rent litterært tilhørte han Renæssancen, skønt Middelalderen ikke havde taget sig sammen til at holde op." [For Geoffrey Chaucer nothing human was unknown. From a literary perspective he belonged to the Renaissance, even though the Middle Ages had not pulled themselves together and managed to stop].
> (317)

Bernhardsen is of course not the only one to claim that Chaucer's *Canterbury Tales* are so fabulous that they cannot really belong to the dark Middle Ages, but that does not make this generalisation a true one. In fact Bernhardsen gives his limited knowledge of the age of Chaucer away in another passage, which clearly demonstrates that he is not familiar with any other works by Chaucer, although he mentions the existence of one of them, *Troilus and Criseyde*:

"Chaucer skrev flittigt hele sit voksne liv, i alt væsentligt efter franske og italienske forlæg, og ingen havde ondt af at ideerne som regel var hentet udefra. At det meste i dag er ulæseligt er så en sag for sig, for

---

67 It is striking that Bernhardsen seems unaware of any problems in using unacknowledged sources while at the same time explaining to his reader that Chaucer's practice of stealing his stories from others was normal: "Begreber som plagiat og litterært tyveri var ikke opfundet." [Terms such as plagiarism and literary theft had not been invented] (316).

det var klæg middelalderdigtning, der nu kun omtales som vedhæng til 'Canterbury-fortællingerne'. Disse er derimod geniale." [Chaucer wrote industriously all his life, in all essentials based on French and Italian sources, and nobody minded the fact that his ideas had mostly been imported from abroad. It is another matter that most of it is unreadable today, because this was sticky medieval poetry, now only mentioned as appendage to *The Canterbury Tales*. These are, contrary to his other works, the work of a genius]. (316)

Here is clearly someone who has not read anything by Chaucer outside *The Canterbury Tales*. To call medieval poetry apart from the *Tales* "sticky" is at best an amusing example of complete ignorance, but of course such notions about the medieval period belong to a long line of derogatory attitudes in Danish Chaucer reception, as we have seen in many examples already. And at least Bernhardsen is on a par with the translator, Boisen, and his remark about the style of the time being coarse and plump.

Analysis of Boisen's translation

In this section the main focus will naturally be on Boisen's translation of Lumiansky's translation of *The Canterbury Tales*. However, I draw on other translations for comparison, both Danish and modern English ones, which means mainly those by Coghill, Wright, Ackroyd and Johansen, returning in the next section to a focus on Johansen's Chaucer. My analysis starts with a famous passage from the end of the *Miller's Prologue*, which is given here first in Robinson's 1933 edition of *The Complete Works of Geoffrey Chaucer*, quoted by Boisen in his introduction without acknowledgement of the source. Then follows Boisen's poetic translation of these 9 lines, which he includes as an example of what he would have done, had he chosen not to translate into prose. After that follows Coghill's translation of the same passage and finally Lumiansky's and Boisen's prose translations.

> Demeth noght that I seye
> Of yuel entente, but for I mote reherse
> Hir tales alle, be they bet or werse,
> Or elles falsen som of my matere.

And therefore who so list it noght yhere,
Turne over the leef, and chese another tale,
For he shal fynde ynowe grete and smale,
Of storial thing that toucheth gentillesse,
And eek moralitee, and holynesse.
(F.N. Robinson, ed. 1933, I 3172-80, Boisen 7)

(- for Guds skyld ikke tro, at i min tale
Er skummel hensigt. Jeg må blot berette
Alt, had de sagde, det gode som det slette;
Thi ellers ville jeg med falske farver male.

Hvis derfor en fortælling ej behager,
Så blad blot om og vælg en af de mange,
Thi både i de korte og de lange
Der findes mangt om tugt og fromme glæder,
Om dyd og ædelhed og gode sæder.)
(Boisen: 8)

And so I beg of all who are refined
For God's love not to think me ill-inclined
Or evil in my purpose. I rehearse
Their tales as told, for better and for worse,
For else I should be false to what occurred.
So if this tale had better not be heard,
Just turn the page and choose another sort;
You'll find them there in plenty, long and short;
Many historical, that will profess
Morality, good breeding, saintliness.
Do not blame me if you should choose amiss.
(Coghill 104)

And therefore, I ask every well-brought-up person, for God's love, not to consider that I speke with evil intention, but that I must recount all their tales, good and bad, or else falsify my material. Whoever doesn't want to hear it, therefore, can turn over the page and choose another. For he will find plenty of

stories, long and short, which deal with courtesy, morality, and holiness. Don't blame me if you choose poorly.
(Lumiansky 60)

Og jeg beder derfor enhver veldannet person om for Guds skyld ikke at tro, at jeg taler med ond hensigt, men at jeg må genfortælle alle deres fortællinger, gode som slette, da jeg jo ellers ville forfalske mit materiale. Hvem der ikke ønsker at høre den, kan vende bladet og vælge sig en anden. Thi han vil finde talrige historier, lange og korte, der handler om høviskhed, gode sæder og hellighed. Last ikke mig, hvis Eders valg bliver dårligt.
(Boisen 67)

The fact that Boisen singles out this passage for an extra translation in poetry bears witness to the fact that he has enjoyed Chaucer's suggestion that we skip a tale if it does not please us, which is the sort of attitude Boisen himself has often shown in his translation practice, also in his Chaucer translation, in which he follows Lumiansky in excluding four of the tales.[68] In the prose translation Boisen lets his disregard for what he sees as the crudeness of the *Miller's Tale* run away with him by translating "churles tale", just above the quoted passage by "platte historie", meaning "crude and simplistic story", the adjective "platte" in Danish normally referring to the kind of stories and jokes that will not be tolerated by decent people. This sharpens the connotations of coarseness also in the storytelling, i.e. the tale is coarse rather than being told by a coarse character, which appears to have been Chaucer's intended meaning. Johansen has the more neutral adjective "plump" which roughly translates as Wright's solution "vulgar". Or so it did in the 50s, because it would not be understood by most Danes today. This may also be the case for Coghill's solution, "churl's tale", in English.

Boisen's brief attempt to show his capacity in poetic translation is

---

68 Boisen's motivation is disguised neatly in his introduction, where he claims to be widely oriented in normal translation practice in the case of Chaucer: "Udeladelserne er sket med forbillede I en række nyere amerikanske og engelske udgaver." [The omissions have been made following the example of a series of recent American and English editions] (Boisen 7).

quite a successful one, although he has not, unlike Coghill, quite managed to stick to Chaucer's rhyming couplets in the first few lines, placing the rhyme words in different positions. Boisen, like Coghill, has taken special care with this inspiring passage, and although Boisen has not been as elegant and rhythmically fluent as Coghill, he has provided striking poetic idioms that cover Chaucer's sense well. For instance "Thi ellers ville jeg med falske farver male" [for otherwise I would be painting with false colours] is dynamically equivalent with "Or elsen falsen som of my matere", and it strikes idiomatic Danish usage well. Also "turne over the leef" finds an idiomatically precise Danish equivalent in "blade", a Danish verb covering the process of turning pages in a book.

Interestingly Boisen's prose translation of the same passage is less successful as far as idioms are concerned. Here I need no back-translation for readers unfamiliar with Danish, because Lumiansky's text is the clear base for Boisen's translation. That is so much the case that had it been a back-translation of Boisen's passage, I would have accepted it as better than Boisen's. Boisen's prose here is rather flat, and the idiom, "veldannet" for "well-brought-up" could have been improved by deleting the Danish rarer equivalent to "well-", "vel-" and leaving just "dannet". Alternatively it should have been "veluddannet". And finally the elegance of "med falske farver male" from the poetic translation is replaced with another too direct translation, "forfalske mit materiale", which in Danish carries connotations in the direction of forgery or faking. This may in some people's estimates be what Boisen is in fact performing in his translation, but hardly the associations he would want from the idiom.

Turning to the *Nun's Priest's Tale*, we will see that Boisen fortunately retains his ability for idiomatic and fluent translation in other cases. Perhaps his choice of calling the cock and the hen "Kykelily" and "Klukkeluk", onomatopoeia in Danish for the sounds made by cocks and hens, is a debatable one, but on the other hand Boisen may have considered Lumiansky's Chanticler and Partlet, or Chaucer's Chauntecleer and Pertilote unfamiliar names in Danish. A domestication strategy is also well motivated in the beast fable genre, which after all has a traditional appeal also to children. As we saw in the previous chapter, however, Sonne in his translation keeps the names as Chantecler and Pertelote.

In the first few lines of the tale Lumiansky marks his translation of the poor widow's lodging in inverted commas when he refers to her "drawing room" and her "boudoir" (Lumiansky 140), whereas Boisen very sensibly avoids both the foreignisation and the inverted commas by referring simply to her "stue" [living room] and "køkkenet" [her kitchen] (Boisen 291). And when Lumiansky says about the widow that "no tasty morsels passed her lips, for her fare matched her coat" (140-1), Boisen elegantly finds corresponding Danish idioms: "ingen lækkerbidsken gled gennem hendes hals; hun satte tæring efter næring" [literally "no titbit/delicacy passed through her throat; she let her consumption be determined by her means"] (291). A final example from the beginning of this tale is also one where Boisen deserves praise. When Lumiansky says about the widow, "nor did apoplexy harm her head" (141), Boisen translates by "og intet bommesislag skadede hendes hoved" (291). The normal first choice of idiom would have been the corresponding Danish "apopleksi", but "bommesislag" is in fact far better in this context. "Bommesislag" no longer exists in most modern dictionaries of Danish, where the medical term "apopleksi" has completely replaced it, but the word was used especially in the countryside when Boisen wrote his translation, as illustrated by the fact that the expression was recently included in the jargon of a fictional 98-year-old woman from Jutland, who was the main character of a serial story in the satirical column of a leading Danish newspaper.[69] Boisen is quite right in letting the old, poor widow in *The Nun's Priest's Tale* know of a "bommesislag" rather than of "apopleksi".

The Wife of Bath's Prologue and Tale is, as will appear from other parts of this book, the most often translated tale in Danish. Boisen starts off his translation by following Luminansky's transformed sentence structure in the famous first lines from Chaucer, "Experience, though noon auctoritee/Were in this world, were right y-nough to me" (Skeat, ed., D 1-2), and he once again uses Luminansky's translation as his base text, even following his paragraph division most of the time. In cases where Lumiansky has been creative, Boisen follows suit, such as in the case of Lumiansky's invention of the names of abuse such as "You rascally old idiot" and "Sir Bad Temper" for Chaucer's "olde dotard shrewe" and "sir

---

[69] The collected stories of Elvira Mortensen, written over a couple of years by satirical columnists Ole Rasmussen and Gorm Vølver in the daily *Politiken*, have been published as *Elvira – forkortet af red.* [Elvira – shortened by the editor] (Rasmussen and Vølver, 2004).

shrewe". Boisen lets the Wife call her husband "Din gamle ærketåbe" [You old arch fool] and "hr. Arrigtrold" (literally Mr. Bad-tempered Troll], fine Danish idioms (Skeat 291 and 355, Lumiansky 158-9, Boisen 123-4).

In this tale translation, however, there are a few indications of Boisen occasionally having consulted other sources. The first of these is the detail of the Wife marrying at the church door, which is not found in Lumiansky, neither in *The Wife of Bath's Prologue*, nor in the portrait of the Wife in *The General Prologue*. (Boisen 119, Lumiansky 9-10, 153). Boisen could of course have had an edition such as Robinson's at hand here, but as will appear below, I have reason to believe that he has looked through Bergsøe's translation and spotted the first of his footnotes, which explains that the first part of the marriage ceremony in medieval England took place at the church door (Bergsøe 1943: 19, 6). Other examples indicating that Boisen has found the need to use other sources, probably Bergsøe, involve his translation of biblical names and place names. They include "St. Jodocus" for Lumiansky's "St. Joce", where Bergsøe has "St. Joce", but also a footnote explaining that he is identical with "Sankt Jodocus, en bretagnisk Eremit fra det 7. århundrede." [St. Jodocus, a Breton hermit from the 7th century] (Lumiansky 162, Boisen 126, Bergsøe 35/483). Secondly "Oxenford", which is the archaic form also found in Bergsøe, and Chaucer, but Lumiansky, following his general modernisation principle, has "Oxford" (Boisen 127, Bergsøe 37/527, Skeat 527, Lumiansky 163). In most cases, however, Boisen has used the same name forms as Lumiansky, or slightly adjusted Danish forms.

There is no doubt that Boisen has taken a genuine interest in being precise in his translation of names generally. One of the most challenging passages in *The Canterbury Tales* is the portrait of the Knight in *The General Prologue*, which is full of references to the Knight's presence on specific battlegrounds. This will have been of special interest to a translator such as Boisen with his background as an army officer, and it is clear that he has taken care. Some of the place names, such as "Granada" and "Algeciras" appear in identical form in Lumiansky's and Boisen's translations, or are translated as in their modern equivalents, e.g. "Prøjsen" for "Prussia" and "Lithauen" for "Lithuania". Others, however, are remarkably different: Lumiansky's "Benmarin" becomes "Belmaria" in Boisen's version, "Ayas" becomes "Layas" and "the Mediterranian" becomes "Levanten". It should be noted that Chaucer has "Belmarye", "Lyeys" and "the

Grete See" (Skeat, A 58-60), which would not have made it much clearer to Boisen. It appears that again he will have consulted other sources, and one obvious possibility is Birkedal's 1911 translation of *The General Prologue*. This translation, treated more substantially in chapter 6, does in fact provide most of the answers in the edition's footnotes. Although Birkedal uses "Algezir" for "Algeciras", he explains in the note that the present form is "Algeciras". Birkedal then uses the forms "Belmary" and states that it was a Moorish land in Africa. Also in the case of "Leyes" Birkedal spells the name slightly differently from Boisen, but he explains in the note that the form is now "Ayas", which means that Boisen may have chosen a mixed form between the two. In the case of "Levanten", which covers the geographical area correctly in Danish, Boisen has either chosen not to follow Birkedal's simpler "det store Hav" [the Great Sea] (Birkedal 1911: 9), or he has ignored it and found his solution elsewhere, perhaps in his general knowledge. Although Boisen, as we have seen, has a tendency to cut corners if he can, we should not forget that he also possesses impressive general knowledge and sound judgement.

Sound judgement is also displayed by Boisen in a number of additions and explications he has made as a service to his Danish readers. Additions include links or end markers such as "Her slutter prologen til denne bog" [Here ends the prologue to this book] at the end of the *General Prologue*, where Lumiansky has nothing (Boisen 27, Lumiansky 17). Also at the end of *The Knight's Tale* Boisen has added a bit by stating "Således slutter beretningen om Palamon og Emilie" [Thus ends the tale of Palamon and Emilie], where Lumiansky has the simpler phrased and more dramatic "Thus end Palamon and Emily" (Boisen 65, Lumiansky 58). Well-chosen explications include "Vilhelm Erobreren" [William the Conqueror] instead of a straight translation of Lumiansky's "King William", which would have been less easily understood by Danish readers (Boisen 17, Lumiansky 7). Lumiansky's "friendly Manciple of an Inn of Court" becomes "en venlig *proviantforhandler* fra et juristkollegium" [a friendly provisions dealer from a law college], which is less precise and specific than the source text, but on the other hand makes a virtue of communicating a cultural difference through a domestication strategy (Lumiansky 11, Boisen 21). Some of the changes Boisen has felt it necessary to make include rather free interpretations, as when cake in the next example from the portrait of the Summoner in the *General Prologue* becomes bread, but on the other hand Boisen's image is more readily understood than Lumiansky's: "He had made himself a shield of a cake." (Lumiansky, 13). "Han medførte et rundt brød så stort som et skjold." [He carried with him a loaf of bread as big as a shield] (Boisen 24).

Euphemism, avoidance, over-explicitness: Boisen compared to Johansen

If we look at the bawdy passages in *The Canterbury Tales* generally, Boisen's strategy turns out to be less conspicuous than promised in his introductory remarks about liberating the text from bad odours. Euphemisms are used by both Boisen and Johansen, but only in the case of Johansen getting the front and the behind of Alisoun wrong have I found reason to complain seriously about accuracy.[70] Generally there are no more euphemisms than must be expected in a Danish 1950s context, yet Johansen tends to go a bit further than Boisen in protecting sensitive readers. Thus at the end of *The Merchant's Tale* Johansen records only a remark by January that "Hvad I bestilte, saa jeg med det samme" [What you were doing, I saw at once] (Johansen II, 122, 2378), to cover the rather more explicit terms "in it wente" and "swyved" (Benson gen. ed., IV, 2376 and 2378). Boisen on his part avoids the visualization of Lumiansky, who follows Chaucer in saying that "It certainly went in all the way" (Lumiansky 245), but at least he makes it explicit, with an archaic term, that Damian "besov" [literally "beslept"] May (Boisen 202). Chaucer's "coillons" in *The Pardoner's Tale,* VI, 952, which Lumiansky modernises as "testicles" (299) are translated by Boisen as "pung" (Boisen 276), a popular but unmistaken term for testicles. Johansen only ventures the imprecise euphemism "det, du har imellem For og Bag" [what you have between front and back] (I, 291, 952). The host's evocation of a "hogges toord" in the same passage (VI, 955) is also avoided by Johansen, who simply writes "svinesti" (I, 291, 955, "pigsty"), where again Boisen's "svinegødning" ("pig dung") comes closer to the actual turd. Lumiansky has "hog's dung" (Lumiansky 299).

---

70 Steve Ellis has traced the strategies concerning these "bawdy" passages in the English translations before 2000. See Ellis, 102 ff.

Johansen provides the most faithful translation in a passage from *The Wife of Bath's Prologue*, Skeat D 115-34, where genitals and urine are also mentioned (Johansen II, 8, 115-34, Boisen 121). Johansen talks of the genitals as "lemmer" [members] and uses the Danish correspondent "Urin" directly (Johansen 116 and 120), whereas Boisen talks of "forplantningslemmerne" [the members used for procreation] and, worse, avoids the urine and uses a euphemism, "vandets udsondring" [the secretion of water]. By comparison this is one of several places where Peter Ackroyd allows himself to use the word "cunt" as well as mentioning the urine (Ackroyd 2009: 149). Other examples of this are found in his *Miller's Tale*, where this four-letter word is used twice, alongside its sibling "fuck" in Nicholas' seduction of Alison (Ackroyd: 84). It should be said that one other translator, David Wright, also uses cunt, but not fuck (83). Elisabeth Scala regrets this vulgar idiom in Wright's translation and prefers a 1964 translation by Kent and Constance Hieatt, where they translate by 'privily grabbed her where he shouldn't" (Scala 2005: 482 and notes 2-3). As I've indicated many times in this study, I respect culturally and historically bound euphemisms, but appreciate brave attempts like Bergsøe's to be as accurate as possible. The Hieatts are not accurate, but on the contrary insert a modern day morality which is not found in Chaucer's *Miller's Tale*. Perhaps in the present day and age we can try to be precise without being consistently vulgar like Ackroyd.

Whereas the bawdy passages provide examples of euphemism or direct avoidance strategies particularly in Johansen's translation, examples of the opposite can also be found, i.e. over-explicitness and pin-pointing. For both translators an element of interpretation and explication is unavoidable, since they are communicating to an audience far removed in history as well as geography, but in some cases I have found an unnecessary free hand employed by both Johansen and Boisen. One clear example is line 395 in the *General Prologue*, where Chaucer-the-pilgrim says about the Shipman, "And certainly, he was a good felawe." Lumiansky, who calls him the Sailor, follows Chaucer's ironic expression "a good fellow" (8). The irony is made clear in the surrounding lines, where the Shipman is described as stealing wine from the merchants while they sleep and as generally unscrupulous. Neither Johansen nor Boisen will allow the full verbal irony. Johansen translates the line by "og han var visselig en ærlig synder" [And certainly he was an honest sinner] (Johansen 395), whereas

Boisen simply changes the adjective to make it straight and logical: "Han var en hård fyr" [He was a hard fellow] (Boisen 18).

A similar suggestiveness in Chaucer's portrait of the Pardoner is turned to outspoken scorn when Johansen translates "And thus, with feyned flaterye and japes/He made the person and the peple has apes" (Skeat, A 705-6) by "Saaledes ved sit hykleriske Væsen/ tog Præst og Folk han med sit Pjat ved Næsen." [Thus with his hypocritical being/ and with his tomfoolery, he duped the priest and the people] (Johansen, I,705-6). This is a directly moralising translation, since Chaucer nowhere *tells* us, but only *shows* that the Pardoner is a hypocrite. Boisen's "Og således narrede han med forstilt smiger og listige kneb bade præsten og folkene" (Boisen 25), is much to be preferred as a both precise and idiomatic translation of Lumiansky's "And thus, with feigned flattery and tricks, he made monkeys of the parson and the people" (Lumiansky 14).

Johansen's translation from 1958 and his monograph Fra Chaucers tid [From Chaucer's time] from 1965

The general style of the introduction as well as of the monograph is that of a distinguished gentleman, whose language must even in the 1950s have appeared slightly old-fashioned. Although a Danish spelling reform in 1948 had officially done away with capital letters in nouns and invented the Danish 'å' for the sound formerly spelled 'aa' as in 'maaneden', Johansen makes the conservative choice of retaining the old spelling system, which is well in line with the generally somewhat archaic tone of his language. Johansen has undertaken his task with the utmost care, according to his acknowledgements taking nine years to complete his translation (Johansen 1958, vol. I, 5). He has made a real effort to represent Chaucer faithfully, and remarkably he includes all tales including *Melibee* and *The Parson's Tale*, thus providing the only complete translation of *The Canterbury Tales* in Danish. Johansen's 1958 edition is in two volumes, comprising a 20-page introduction to Chaucer and his time, a translation of William Skeat's Chaucer edition, and 25 pages of explanatory endnotes in each volume. Unlike Boisen, Johansen acknowledges his sources, first of all Skeat's edition from 1894-97, consulting also A.W. Pollard et al.'s 1899 edition. It appears that F.N. Robinson's 1933 edition was either not known by Johansen, or not preferred at Copenhagen University, where Johansen studied under among others professor C.A. Bodelsen, who as mentioned is acknowledged for recommending the translation for publication. That Skeat was preferred seems quite plausible, and I know from personal experience of studying and teaching at Copenhagen University that some of my older colleagues in literary studies even in the 1980s only had Skeat, and perhaps Coghill's translation, on their office shelves.

In order to draw a picture of the typical sources available for someone undertaking to translate *The Canterbury Tales* in Copenhagen between 1949 and 1958, let us briefly consider Johansen's bibliography, which is not particularly comprehensive. Besides Skeat and Pollard's editions, Johansen, not surprisingly from a Danish 1950s perspective, also acknowledges some German sources, including the edition by Adolf von Düring from 1883-86, John Koch's *Geoffrey Chaucer's Canterbury-Erzählungen* from 1925 and for historical background I.M. Lappenberg & R. Pauli's *Geschichte von England I-V*, published 1834-58. Besides a few further English sources, Hinckley's *Notes on Chaucer* from 1907 and Ward's *Chaucer* from 1893, there is also a reference to Jean Jules Jusserand's translated *English Wayfaring Life in the Middle Ages* from 1905 and to a Danish history of the Middle Ages, Kristian Erslev's *Oversigt over Middelalderens historie*, published 1933-35. The last three works in the bibliography are all Danish, namely Theodor Bierfreund's *Kulturbærere* from 1892, Otto Jespersen's *Chaucer's liv og digtning* from 1893 and Aage Brusendorff's *The Chaucer Tradition* from 1925. As the latter three works were considered in chapters 5 and 7, let me restrict my comments here to saying that Johansen has selected a useful, short bibliography for his purpose, which is after all to provide an apparatus of introduction and notes for the general reader, not an academic treatise. The only major regret is that he has not used Robinson's 1933 edition, or checked the final manuscript with the second Robinson edition in 1957 (Robinson 1933/1957).

With one major reservation, Johansen's introduction is generally very sensible and based on thorough reading and reliable representation of material from his sources, including the works of Chaucer himself. Johansen demonstrates thorough knowledge of not only the *Canterbury Tales*, but also other works by Chaucer, or at least some of them. This means that the introduction contains brief paragraphs about Chaucer's translation of *The Roman de la Rose* and his own *The*

Book of the Duchess, The Parliament of Fowls, The House of Fame and *The Legend of Good Women*, translated by Johansen as respectively, "Roseromanen", "Hertugindebogen", "Fugleparlamentet", "Berømmelsens Hus" and "Legenden om de gode kvinder" (Johansen 1958: vol. I, 19-21). However, what is striking is of course that a work that most modern Chaucerians estimate as Chaucer's most complete masterpiece, *Troilus and Criseyde*, goes completely unmentioned by Johansen, who may have followed Bierfreund's ill advice and hardly or never bothered to look at it. That this is the case appears more likely if we consider Johansen's revised introduction to Chaucer in *Fra Chaucers tid*, where there is the following brief mention: "'Troilus og Cressida' er for en moderne læser en noget udpenslet og trættende kærlighedshistorie, men den er en mesterlig omarbejdelse af et emne fra Trojanerkrigen, der er benyttet både i Roseromanen og hos Dante og Boccaccio." [For a modern reader *Troilus and Cressida* is an unnecessarily detailed and somewhat tiresome love story, but it is a masterful adaptation of a topic from the Trojan war, used both in the *Roman de la Rose* and by Dante and Boccaccio] (Johansen 1965: 138). It is indicative of this superficial and poor judgment that Johansen has not even got the title right, but uses Shakespeare's title. As I've regretted elsewhere in this study, this great poem has still never been translated into Danish, and even worse, it has been fairly consistently condemned by people who have not bothered to read it or have not been able to understand it.

Fortunately Johansen has a much safer hand with his introduction to the *Canterbury Tales*, undoubtedly because he has spent so many years familiarising himself with them in great detail. In the introduction he is frequently able to draw in examples from Chaucer's text, although his main purpose seems to be to draw a picture of the society the tales represented. Johansen draws a picture of "et Samfund i stærk indre Brydning" [a society in a strong inner upheaval] (Johansen 1958: vol. I, 23), and he goes on to place the members of the three estates that we meet as characters in the *Tales* in the broader context of crisis in government and church. A relatively large proportion of the introduction provides an even broader historical context from the Norman Conquest onwards, giving also the story of St. Thomas a Beckett. Although Johansen does not state his sources precisely by using notes, he does as indicated acknowledge them generally, and he has made a fairly good job of selecting relevant historical background material. Furthermore, he makes many historical events come alive as dramatic events, such as the murder of Beckett. The stabbing of Wat Tyler is another dramatisation in Johansen's also quite detailed account of the peasants' revolt. (Johansen 1958, vol. I, 8 and 12-13). These and other dramatic episodes form a contrast to the figure of Chaucer himself, who Johansen draws up in his biographical section as a genius of a poet, who lives a relatively undramatic personal life. Or at least not an unusual life, as indicated by Johansen's summary: "Dette var de ydre Rammer om Chaucers Liv, og de adskiller sig ikke synderligt fra dem, der var andre af Tidens Hofmænd beskaaret." [These were the outer frames around Chaucer's life, and they are not particularly different from those of other contemporary courtiers] (I, 19). Johansen is of course guessing a little bit, even though elsewhere he does refer to the many lacunae in our knowledge.

I have referred to Johansen's *Fra Chaucers tid* from 1965 as partly a revision of his introduction published 7 years earlier. This is true especially of the 15-page chapter specifically on Chaucer himself, but this book-length study is of course also much more than that. Whereas a writer like Langland was only briefly mentioned in the introduction, there is now a short separate chapter on him, and further parts on Gower, the Gawain poet and a few other contemporary poets.[71] Most of this book, however, focuses on historical events during the rules of Edward III and Richard II, and as very few lines are drawn to Chaucer in the main chapters, this material falls mainly outside the scope of this book.

The note apparatus of the 1958 translation is of great help to the general reader and demonstrates Johansen's fine sense of judgment concerning what needs an extra explanation. I will occasionally draw the notes into consideration of Johansen's translation practice in the analysis

---

71 In the 1958 introduction Johansen refers to Langland's Piers Plowman as the rather funny sounding Danish "Peter Pløjemand", whereas Birkedal (1913) called him Peder Plovmand. Both are correct, domesticated translations, but neither of them would be very fortunate in a translation today, cp. Birkedal's Gotfred Chaucer mentioned earlier. Johansen interestingly uses only one adjective to describe Langland's poem: "ejendommelig" [curious/strange] (Johansen 1958, 25). Seven years later he has managed to read more of it and gives a sober five-page presentation, even translating small bits of text from Skeat's 1886 edition. Here Langland is no longer "ejendommelig" (Johansen 1965, 48-56).

below, but let us first consider a few examples to illustrate Johansen's thoroughness, which deserves much praise. First of all there is the explanation of place-names such as those from the portrait of the Knight in the *General Prologue* considered above. Here Johansen provides far more information than Birkedal, giving not only the variants in spelling and other linguistic changes, but also full historical contextualization. One example will suffice:

> "Preussen var paa denne Tid de tyske Ridderordeners Ejendom og maatte stadig forsvares mod de hedenske Litauere og Russere. I disse kampe, der gav Lejlighed til at vinde Ære og Bytte, deltog mange engelske Riddere, saaledes den senere Kong Henry d. 4., der blandt andre er blevet udpeget som forbilledet for Chaucers Ridder – hvis Chaucer da overhovedet har tænkt på nogen bestemt."[At this time Prussia was the property of the German orders of chivalry and had to be defended against the Lithuanians and Russians. In these battles, which gave the knights the opportunity to win honour and loot, many English knights participated, such as the later King Henry 4th, who among others has been mentioned as a role model for Chaucer's knight – i.e. if Chaucer has thought of anyone in particular.]
> (Johansen's note to I, 53, Johansen 1958, vol. I, 292)

This is one of the many places in the notes where you can hear Johansen's enthusiasm for the historical context, and also a positive attitude to the Knight shared by many commentators and readers especially in the 19th and better part of the 20th centuries. The historically well analysed, but probably also too modern reading of the Knight as a cruel mercenary captain is a far cry from the tradition Johansen writes himself into in this and other notes, seeing the Knight as a role model hero.[72]

One more example of Johansen's notes is the portrait of the Prioress, where the longest note contains a 10-line explanation of the Stratford

---

72 See Terry Jones, *Chaucer's Knight: The Portrait of a Medieval Mercenary* from 1980, revised 1994. I have elsewhere discussed Jones's view and the dominant opposition to it in Chaucer studies. See Klitgård 1995, chapter 2, "*The Knight's Tale*: Narrator and Narration."

school with a sensible focus on French and the contemporary educational system. We also learn that grey eyes are beautiful eyes in the medieval tradition, that dogs and personal ornaments should not be kept by nuns, and that *Amor vincit omnia* is a quotation from Vergil. Perhaps Johansen could have made it clearer here that the Vergil motto is also out of proper context for a prioress, but the information in the other notes does help the reader to understand Chaucer's satirical portrait.[73]

A final example will serve to illustrate that Johansen is not afraid of including personal judgement based on his own reading of the *Tales*. In his long explanatory note to *The Monk's Tale* about Hugelino (Johansen, vol. I, 311) it is as if Johansen wakes up from the boring task of having to translate all the many tedious and anecdotal stories in that tale. After rendering the Ugolino inspiration from Dante's *Inferno*, he writes, "Ogsaa Munkens Fortælling hæver sig her til større Poesi end hans øvrige tørre Fortællinger."[Also *The Monk's Tale* is here elevated to greater Poetry than his other dry stories.] Johansen shares this opinion about Hugelino and *The Monk's Tale* with many others, among them Lumiansky, who includes this story as the only one from the tale. Boisen, in a rare example, chooses not to follow Lumiansky, although he translates most of his short summary of the other stories. There is thus no Hugelino and no *Monk's Tale* in Boisen, only *The Monk's Prologue*. (Lumiansky 136-8, Boisen 289).

Further analysis of Johansen's translation

Comparing Boisen's and Johansen's work in a general perspective, the two translations appear substantially different, as we have already seen. Boisen can be praised for his jocularity of style in tales that invite such, for instance the fabliaux, but of course Boisen borrows much from Lumiansky's modern approach. Compared to another post-war poetic translator, Coghill, Johansen is also far from having success in striking a modern note of popular idiom, which on the other hand

---

73 The most substantial treatment of the *General Prologue*, including the portrait of the Prioress as satire, is Jill Mann's seminal study *Chaucer and Medieval Estates Satire* from 1973 (Mann 1973).

may not have been what Johansen wanted. One notable exception is *Sir Thopas,* which in Lumiansky's and Boisen's prose translations, as in all the prose translations, falls to the ground because it misses the whole point of Chaucer's poetic pastiche. Johansen elegantly transfers Chaucer's parodic rhyming to Danish folk poetry of the worst kind, including the popular idiom of occasional verse, a genre still known in Denmark, where silver anniversaries, birthday celebrations and similar parties often include privately written songs to the person or persons celebrated, often of a dubious quality and with its own equally dubious syntax, rhymes and idiom.[74] A few examples from Johansen's *Sir Thopas* will illustrate this point.

Starting with the frame of *Sir Thopas,* where the Host first encourages Chaucer as one of the pilgrims to tell his tale, then interrupts him in order to stop his bad poetry and have him tell a tale in prose, Johansen strikes a merry note that elegantly meets the demands of Chaucer's self-parody:

> "Fortæl du nu, som før de andre har, ["Now
> you tell a tale, as before the others]
> og lad os faa en med lidt Lystighed." [And let
> us have one with a bit of merriment"]
> "Tag ej det ilde op," gav jeg til Svar, ["Take
> it in good part," I gave as answer]
> "jeg har en Vise kun at komme med, ["I only have a song to offer]
> Som jeg har lært et eller andet Sted." [which
> I have learned some place or other."]
> "Ja, det er godt," han svared, "lad os høre. ["That's
> all very well," he answered, "let us hear]
> Han ser da ud til Spas at kunne gøre." [He looks as if he can jest"]
> […]
> "Hold op, hold op, for Guds Barmhjertighed,"
> ["Stop, stop, for the mercy of God"]

---

74 In a newspaper column in the Danish newspaper *Politiken* language professor Jørn Lund discusses this tradition as unique to Danish culture, drawing also on a recent study of the history of occasional songs in Denmark (Lund 2011b and E. Preisler 2011).

skreg Værten, "for jeg er saa led og ked [Cried
the Host, "for I am so sick and tired]
af det fordømte Vaas, du har at byde, [Of all the
damned Nonsense you have to offer]
at jeg – saa sandt Guds Naade jeg maa nyde –
[That – as true as God's grace I enjoy -]
har ondt i Ørerne af dine Brokker. [it hurts
my ears to hear your scrapheap]
I Vers af denne Slags jeg giver Pokker! [I do not
give a damn about this kind of verse]
Det er jo bare Knyttelvers, det der." [What
you say here is only *Knüttelvers*."]
(Johansen 1895-1901 and 2109-15)

"Sey now somwhat, sin other folk han sayd;
Tel us a tale of mirthe, and that anoon;"
"Hoste," quod I,"ne beth nat yvel apayd,
For other tale certes can I noon,
But of a ryme I lerned longe agoon."
"Ye, that is good," quod he; "now shul we here
Som deyntee thing, me thinketh by his chere."

"No more of this for goddes dignitee,"
Quod oure hoste, "for thou makest me
So wery of thy verray lewednesse
That, also wisly god my soule blesse,
Myn eres aken of thy drasty speche;
Now swich a rym the devel I biteche!
This may wel be rym dogerel," quod he.
(Skeat, B 1894-1900 and 2109-15)

As explained by Johansen in his introduction (vol. I, 26) he has tried to obey Chaucer's metre as far as possible, but in some cases he has found it necessary to change the rhyme pattern. This is not surprising, and certainly as we see here, he has been able to come up with rhyming, but also sufficiently dubious poetry in *Sir Thopas*, sensibly assuring his readers in an explanatory note that this is supposed to be a romance parody

(307). Among the fine details of poor style in the first of the stanzas is a subject-verb inversion in the *inquit* "han svared", and the inversion of object and infinitive in "Spas at kunne gøre." The short and precise Danish idiom "spas" covers Chaucer's "Som deyntee thyng" well, as does the equally short, derogatory "vås" for Chaucer's "verray lewednesse" in the latter of the two quotations. The most ingenious idiom in this part, however, is "knyttelvers" in the last line, translating Chaucer's "Rym doggerel". Johansen has resorted to a term known especially from medieval German verse, hence my German back-translation. According to *Ordbog over det Danske Sprog* [*ODS*, Dictionary of the Danish Language] "Knyttelvers" or "Knittelvers" was also in Danish a "nedsættende betegnelse for tarvelige, knudrede vers af folkelig art" [a derogatory term for primitive, rugged verse of a popular kind] (*ODS*, vol. 10, 926-7). Johansen relies on a well-educated readership by selecting this exquisite term, or he simply allows himself the pleasure of a precise implicit reference and a wonderful, now lost idiom.

One more example from *Sir Thopas* will suffice:

> "Jeg give [I shall]
> Dig skal et hul i Maven svær, [admit you a hole in your fat belly]
> Før primen er os rykket nær, [before the
> prime of day has moved in on us]
> For her du dræbt skal blive!" [for here you shall be killed]
> (Johansen 2013-16)

> "Thy mawe
> Shal I percen, if I may,
> Er it be fully pryme of day,
> For heer thou shalt be slawe."
> (Skeat, B 2012-15).

Readers familiar with Danish will appreciate the hopelessness of both syntax and poetic diction, again with inversion, this time of subject and adjective ("Maven svær") and of infinitive and participle ("dræbt skal blive"). Idiomatically "Maven svær" is also another brilliant Danish archaism associated with low style romance. The choice of "primen" rather than the neutral "den tidlige morgen" [early morning] is similarly archaic and poetically too solemn, lofty and thus pathetic in connection with this knightly encounter.

I now turn to the most famous lines from Chaucer and consider Johansen's version of the first lines of the *General Prologue*, here with Chaucer's lines first:

> Whan that Aprille with his shoures sote
> The droghte of Marche hath perced to the rote,
> And bathed every veyne in swich licour
> Of which vertu engendred is the flour;
> Whan Zephirus eek with his swete breeth
> Inspired hath in every holt and heeth
> The tendre croppes, and the yonge sonne
> Hath in the Ram his halfe cours y-ronne,
> And smale fowles maken melodye,
> That slepen al the night with open yë
> (So priketh hem nature in hir corages);
> Than longen folk to goon on pilgrimages,
> (Skeat, A 1-12)

> Naar maaneden April med søde Byger [When
> the month of April with sweet showers]
> den tørre Martsjord overalt bestryger, [coats
> the dry March earth everywhere]
> og Væden i hver Sprække siver ned, [and the
> moisture seeps into every crack]
> saa der et Blomsterflor opstaar derved; [so that
> a profusion of flowers is created by it]
> imedens Zephyr med sin milde Vind [whilst
> Zephyr with his mild wind]
> i spæde Skud ny Livskraft blæser ind [blows
> new vitality into tender shoots]
> i Mark og Skov, og nu af Væddertegnet [in field
> and forest, and now by the sign of the Ram]
> paa Himlen Solen er kun halvt omhegnet, [the
> sun in the sky is only half fenced in]
> og Fugle smaa med Sang sig maa fornøje [and small

birds with song must please themselves]
og sover Natten lang med aabent Øje [and
sleep all night with an open eye]
(Naturen dem i Sindet saadan plager), [(Nature
does so their minds torment)]
Folks længsler da paa Pilgrimsfærd dem drager [That is when
people's longings make them want to go on a pilgrimage]
(Johansen, *General Prologue*, 1-12)

Johansen's translation works rather well as poetry and also covers Chaucer's meaning without pedantic formal equivalence and a strictly corresponding metre. Johansen expects of his reader that he or she understands names like "Zephyrus" (5), but occasionally, as in "Væddertegnet" (7), which in Danish specifies that it is the *sign* of the Ram, makes the reference clearer. David Wright in his 1985 translation, by comparison, skips "Zephyrus" altogether and simply writes "the west wind", and when he gets to the Ram makes aid of the specification "Aries". This is indicative of Wright's general strategy of reader pedagogy, or perhaps more precisely considering his intended primary readership, student pedagogy. Lumiansky, Coghill, Boisen and Johansen, translating in the 1940s and 50s did not have students as their main target group, and perhaps for that reason have all come up with a translation of this first part of the prologue that demands more implicit knowledge on the part of the reader. Boisen, following Lumiansky, has made the choice of leaving out explanatory notes altogether, and this means that he is even more dependent on his idioms to be immediately understood. This explains his solution in line 6 where he writes Moder Natur (mother Nature), which is the standard Danish idiom, whereas Johansen's "Naturen" in line 11 is a solution closer to Chaucer, if less idiomatic in Danish. Johansen again sounds a bit archaic in his choice of idiom, such as the two verbs in rhyme position, "bestryger" (2) and "drager" (12), but a certain poetic licence must be allowed him in recreating the prologue's spring atmosphere, which he is generally successful in doing.

Let us now consider how Johansen handles a very different kind of atmosphere than the pleasant one in the opening of *The General Prologue*. One of the most sinister pieces of poetry in all of Chaucer is undoubtedly the horror vision conveyed in the third part of *The Knight's Tale*, as

Arcite goes to pray for victory in the temple of Mars.[75] The following is only a small extract from this powerful scene:

> Ther saugh I first the derke imagining
> Of felonye, and al the compassyng;
> The cruel ire, reed as any glede;
> The pykepurs, and eek the pale drede;
> The smyler with the knyf under the cloke;
> The shepne brenning with the blake smoke;
> The treson of the mordring in the bedde;
> The open werre, with woundes al bibledde;
> Contek, with blody knyf and sharp manace.
> Al ful of chirking was that sory place.
> The sleere of him-self yet saugh I ther,
> His herte-blood hath bathed al his heer;
> [...]
> Yet saugh I brent the shippes hoppesteres;
> The hunte strangled with the wilde beres;
> The sowe freten the child right in the cradel;
> The cook y-scalded, for al his longe ladel.
> (Skeat A,1995-2007 & 2017-2020)

> Der saa jeg Udaads mørke Kontrafej [There saw I the dark portrait of Misdeed]
> og alle Ting, der findes paa dens Vej. [and all the things that are found on its way]
> Den grumme Vrede, rød som nogen Lue, [The cruel Anger, red as any flame]
> den blege Frygt og Ran der var at skue. [the pale Fear and Theft were there to behold]
> Med Kniven skjult den fule Stimand smilte, [with his knife hidden the foul robber smiled]
> den sorte Brandrøg over Stalde hvilte. [The black fire-smoke rested over the stables]

---

75 I have analysed this passage in my book *Chaucer's Narrative Voice in* The Knight's Tale (Klitgård 1995, 80-86).

Forrædderi i Sengen Ofret myrded. [Treachery
in bed murdered the victim]
Den aabne Krig helt blodtilsølet styrted. [The
open War fell over, quite soaked in blood]
Med blodig Kniv og Trusler praled Klammer. [With
bloody knife and threats Quarrel boasted]
Det fæle Sted var fuldt af Skrig og Jammer. [The
foul place was full of screams and whining]
Der saa jeg ham, der gav sig Banesaar; [There saw
I he who gave himself a mortal wound]
hans Hjerteblod trak gennem alt hans Haar. [his
life blood ran through all of his hair]
[…]
Jeg ogsaa saa de springske Skibe brænde [I
also saw the jumping ships burn]
og vilde Bjørne Jægersmanden skænde.
[and wild bears tear at the hunter]
Der saa jeg Soen, der et Spædbarn slugte, [There
saw I the sow that swallowed an infant child]
og Kokken skolded sig, skønt Slev han brugte. [and the
cook scalded himself, although he used a ladle]
(Johansen 1995-2007 & 2017-20)

Generally Johansen must be praised for not only getting rhyme and rhythm right, once again, but moreover he has succesfully re-created Chaucer's poetic *tour de force* of a dream vision, ostensibly simple with its repeated formula "saugh I", but full of horrific, unforgettable images. Chaucer's allegorical figures are by and large translated well, except the somewhat unfortunate example of line 2001, where Johansen creates an extra allegorical figure, "Forræderi" [Treachery], which actively murders its victim, whereas Chaucer in the corresponding line talks simply about the treason of people being murdered in bed. A parallel example is line 2002, where the personification of "Krig" [War] becomes problematic in Johansen's sentence construction. Chaucer's probable misreading of his partial source for this passage, Boccaccio, in line 2017 is explained by Johansen in a note based on Skeat (Johansen, I, 300). Lumiansky has "dancing ships" and Boisen accordingly "dansende skibe" (Lumiansky 39,

Boisen 48) for Chaucer's "shippes hoppesteres," whereas Johansen besides the note uses the somewhat rare Danish adjective "springske", normally only used in connection with frisky animals. Whether a ship dances or jumps like a foal is a matter of choosing between half-absurdities, but on the other hand Chaucer, not Johansen, first made the mistake.

The general praise for Johansen's effort in my estimate must be mixed with a kind of regret, which I have already hinted at, but which can be more clearly illustrated as a problem in this passage. The problem is that Johansen's preference for idioms with an archaic ring to them will have created difficulties already for his first 1950s readers, and that these difficulties are of course much more apparent for a later Danish readership. In my research into Johansen's translation I have found several words and idioms that I have never heard or seen before and that dictionaries of contemporary Danish no longer include. One example is the noun "klammer" [quarrel] (Johansen 2004) which ODS explains with mainly 18th and 19th century uses as examples (ODS, vol. 10, 439-40). Today only the derivative "klammeri" is in use, and even that is archaic and used mainly by older speakers of Danish or in formal police reports. Other examples of archaisms in the quoted passage above are "Kontrafej" [portrait], "Lue" [fire], "Ran" [theft], "fule Stimand" [foul robber], "smilte" [smiled], "hvilte" [rested], "Banesaar" [mortal wound] and "Slev" [ladle], which I would translate into modern Danish as "portræt", "ild", "tyveri", "grimme røver", "smilede", "hvilede", "en dødeligt såret" og "grydeske". These modern words, I grant, are not half as poetic as Johansen's, but still if the point of a translation is that it should be used for making an author in an unfamiliar language understood, I must point out that Johansen no longer fulfills that purpose fully. The pre-1948 spelling system alone would frighten away some readers, and readers may think of Chaucer as terribly old-fashioned and difficult to read, whereas really this image is one created by Johansen's translation practice. Johansen is not as extreme in his archaisms as Birkedal, who deliberately inserted obsolete idioms in his translation (see chapter 6), but with respect to the archaic tone I can understand that fellow Chaucer translator Jørgen Sonne in 2007 refers to Johansen's translation as "tør" [dry] (Sonne 2007: 23).

It is a great pity that Johansen's Chaucer has had the effect on readers such as the one who first owned my own second-hand copy of his translation that they gave up. This can be seen from the fact that I had to cut up the pages of this old-fashioned edition after roughly 100 pages of the first volume, the second volume having been read even more sporadically. It is even more of a pity, because Johansen is generally a highly competent and skilful translator, who has been extremely diligent in performing his task. Let me give a few more examples of his creative powers. In *The Franklin's Tale* Aurelius' brother makes an effort to help him in his predicament by looking into alternative sciences. He says to himself, "For I am siker that ther be sciences,/By whiche men make diverse apparences,/ Swiche as thise subtile tregetoures pleye (Skeat, F 1139-41). In Johansen's translation this becomes, "for der må sikkert Videnskaber være,/ der kan os den slags Koglesyner lære,/hvori saa mangen Gøgler er en Mester" [for I am sure there must be sciences/that can teach us this kind of sorcerers' visions,/wherein so many a jester is a master](Johansen, 1139-41). It is especially the word "Koglesyner" for "tregetoures" that impresses me here, because it comprises the essence of the kind of magic vision wanted to save the day for Aurelius. The word cannot be found in *ODS*, but "Kogle" and "Kogleri" refers to magic and sorcerers, whereas "syner" are magic visions or sights, and for that reason this new compound is quite appropriate.

Near the end of *The Shipman's Tale* the false monk is referred to with a *pars pro toto* as "Den Munkesnude" [literally that Monk's Snout] (Johansen, 1595), whereas in Chaucer the snout is not as such identified with the Monk in the line "What! yvel thedom on his monkes snoute!" (Skeat, B 1595). Johansen's solution is well in keeping with Danish practice in derogatory idioms, where you can for instance also refer to a "Københavnersnude [literally a Copenhagener-snout], if you want to express your disregard for a person from Copenhagen. In the same scene the wife says, "I am your wyf; score it upon my taille,/And I shal paye as sone as ever I may" (Skeat, B1606-7). Here Johansen operates with accounts being kept on "Konens Karvestok" [the wife's carving stick] (1606), which *ODS* (vol. 10: 185) explains was a stick kept to cut marks for keeping accounts in previous centuries. Again it is impressive how Johansen has taken care to find a Danish historical equivalent, but the question remains whether many readers today would follow him, despite the domestication strategy employed. A final example of Johansen's diligent work to find creative solutions is the scene in *The Miller's Tale* where the ridiculous

Absolon first tries in vain to win the heart of Alison. His efforts include, "He singeth, brokkinge as a nightingale;/He sente hir piment, meeth, and spyced ale, (Skeat, A 3377-8), which Johansen translates in accurate mock-poetic language as "Hans Røst i Sang som Nattergalen's dirred,/ med Sødvin, Mjød og krydret Øl han pirred," [His voice in song like that of the Nightingale quivered, with sweet wine, mead and spiced beer he titillated] (3377-8). Not least the rhyme words "dirred" and "pirred" help to paint a picture of the ridiculous erotic endeavours of Absolon.

Johansen is of course also a prose translator in the cases where that is required. In one instance, in fact the only one except the opening of *The General Prologue*, he reprints Chaucer's original in Skeat's edition. This is the *Retraction* at the end of the last fragment, following the *Parson's Tale*. I will take this important text as my only example of analysing Johansen's prose, although I have found no reason to complain about his translation of the long religious prose texts *Melibee* and *The Parson's Tale*. Only I doubt that many besides hard-core Chaucerians will read them. Johansen is of the same opinion, as he opens his explanatory notes to *Melibee* by saying, "Ved ingen af Chaucers Fortællinger føler man mere Lyst til at følge hans egen Anvisning i Møllerens Prolog paa at "blade om til nogle andre" end ved denne Fortælling," [In the case of no other Chaucer tales does one feel more of an urge to follow his own advice in *The Miller's Prologue* to "turn the page and choose another"] (Johansen, vol. II. 308). We should of course respect that Chaucer's first readers disagreed, as witnessed by the fact that the two religious tales in prose were among the ones most frequently copied by scribes, but since Johansen and I myself agree that they are hard to get through today, this translation analysis will also skip them and use only the *Retraction* as an example of Johansen's prose translation:

> Now preye I to hem alle that herkne this litel tretis or rede, that if ther be anything in it that lyketh them, that ther-of they thanken oure lord Jesu Christ, of whom procedeth al wit and al goodnesse./ And if ther is any thing that displese hem, I preye hem also that they arrette it to the defaute of myn unconninge, and nat to my wil, that wolde ful fayn have seyd bettre if I hadde had conninge./ [...] – and namely, of my translacions and endytinges of worldly vanitees, the whiche I revoke in my retracciouns:/

as is the book of Troilus; The book also of Fame; The book of
the nynetene Ladies; The book of the Duchesse; The book of
seint Valentynes day of the Parlement of Briddes; The tales af
Canterbury, thilke that sounen in-to sinne; The book of the Leoun;
and many another book, if they were in my remembrance; and
many a song and many a lecherous lay; that Christ for his grete
mercy foryeve me the sinne./ But of the translacioun of Boece de
Consolacione, and other bokes of Legendes of seintes, and omelies,
and moralitee, and devocioun,/that thanke I oure lord Jesu Christ
and his blisful moder, and alle the seintes of hevene;/ bisekinge
hem that they from hennesforth, un-to my lyves ende, sende
me grace to biwayle my giltes, and to studie to the salvacioun
of my soule: – and graunte me grace of verray penitence,
confessioun and satisfaccioun to doon in this present lyf; […]
(*Retraction,* Skeat I, 1081-92, reprinted in Johansen, vol. II, 271)

Nu beder jeg alle dem, der lytter til denne lille Afhandling
eller læser den, at hvis der er noget I den, som de synes om, at
de da siger Tak derfor til Vor Herre Jesus Kristus, fra hvem al
Kløgt og Godhed stammer. Og hvis der er noget, der mishager
dem, saa beder jeg dem ogsaa, at de ikke tilskriver det min
Uvidenheds Mangel og heller ikke ond Vilje hos mig, der meget
gerne vilde have talt bedre, hvis jeg havde haft Kundskab dertil./
[…] og navnlig mine Oversættelser og Digte om verdslig Tant,
som jeg frasiger mig i mine Tilbagekaldelser,/ hvilket er bogen
om Troilus, endvidere Berømmelsens bog, Bogen om de nitten
Damer, Bogen om Hertuginden, Bogen om Sankt Valentins
Dag for Fugleparlamentet, Canterbury-Fortællingerne, de
af dem, der handler om Synd,/ Bogen om Løven og mangen
anden bog, hvis de var i min Erindring, og mangen en Sang
og mangen en liderlig Vise, for at Kristus for sin store Naades
Skyld vil tilgive mig min Synd./ Men for Oversættelsen af
Boetius' De Consolatione og andre Bøger om Helgenlegender
og Homilier og Moral og Fromhed/ derfor takker jeg Vor
Herre Jesus Kristus og hans velsignede Moder og alle Helgene
i Himlen,/ idet jeg bønfalder dem om, at de fra nu af og til
mit Livs Ende vil sende mig Naade til at begræde mine Synder

og stræbe efter min Sjæls Frelse og skænke mig Naade til
ægte Anger og Skrifte til at gøre Bod i dette Jordeliv / [...]
(Johansen II, 270)

In this case I have decided that a back-translation is superfluous, since Johansen in his prose translations does not need to be as free as in his poetic translations. Generally speaking Johansen is also in the passage rendered here very loyal to his source text and does not omit anything. His prose is eloquent, and Johansen is able to write in the solemn language register belonging to devout religious writing. For that reason there is also less reason to complain about a certain archaic touch in this passage; it belongs to the genre of Christian writing. Expressions like "mishager" (for "displese"), "mangen en" (for "many a" or "many another") and "verdslig Tant" (for "worldly vanitees") are examples of such archaic expressions, and generally the passage in Danish is full of Danish biblical stock phrases such as "Vor Herre Jesus Kristus" [Our Lord Jesus Christ] and "min Sjæls Frelse og skænke mig Naade" [my soul's salvation and grant me mercy]. Clearly Johansen has performed well in this passage, perhaps taking extra care because of the tell-tale effect of the original being included in print.

The passage is of course particularly interesting for two reasons. First of all it shows the author taking back (retracting) every one of those works that modern readers tend to prefer. And secondly Chaucer's works, or most of them, are named, so as to form an author's testament. As Johansen explains in his notes (Johansen vol. II, 290-91) many critics over the centuries have wondered about the retraction and even doubted the authenticity of the passage. I offer here what I hope is a plausible explanation. First of all it is important that the author's testament is there, a list of works whose titles Johansen translates well into Danish, although regrettably hardly any of them have been translated in full. This includes, as also explained in his notes, the lost book of the lion and a title about 19 ladies that probably covers *The Legend of Good Women*. Also among others Chaucer's translation of Boethius, which Johansen perhaps could have given its full Latin title, *De Consolatione Philosophiae*. My point is that Chaucer has wanted two things with the *Retraction*. The first is to make sure his *oeuvres* are acknowledged in their full versatility, including the for Chaucer probably most inspiring work of all, the *Consola-*

tion. Secondly, that he also, as the deeply devout Christian he no doubt was, wanted to pray for his soul, probably in a situation where he knew that his death might be imminent. Why blame Chaucer for wanting to be on the safe side as far as his salvation is concerned? Written works, including funny or possibly non-doctrinal texts, will find their afterlife anyway, especially in the case of such world literature as Chaucer's, so why not let Chaucer in peace when he asks for the rescue of his soul?

Chapter conclusion

It may be concluded that whereas the two main Danish Chaucer translators have both produced useful translations that served diverse audiences in their time, both have taken liberties that would not be allowed by any sensible modern editor. Some of these liberties, as with the bawdy passages, may well be excused in hindsight, whereas many simplifications and explications are harder to accept if one wants to appreciate Chaucer's subtlety and poetic forcefulness. Much of the narrative subtlety is also completely lost in Boisen's translation of Lumiansky's adaptation in prose, and it is undeserved that his translation sold far more copies than Johansen's, including a book club edition. It is clear that Børge Johansen is the most important Danish translator of Chaucer so far, but also that his translation suffers from his now old-fashioned Danish.

CHAPTER 10

THE PERIOD 1960-2012

There is no recent Danish translation of *The Canterbury Tales* or any other of Chaucer's major works. After two relatively long chapters on respectively the 1940s and 1950s, long because of the prominence of the material analysed, it must be concluded that so far these two decades are the peak points of Chaucer translation in Denmark. This chapter covers some 50 years in about the same space as the previous chapters, because far less substantial material has been published since the 1950s. There are some brief translated pieces, which will be duly treated here, and encyclopedia entries and other texts falling within the category of Chaucer reception are also published, but this chapter is a record of a period where Chaucer has gradually become a poet that even well educated Danes may not have heard of, except if their education is in English studies. In the course of this chapter and in the general conclusion I will attempt to explain some reasons for this. First, however, it is time to provide a context in extension of previous chapters by considering the position of English in Denmark broadly, again with a focus on language and literature. Secondly, in this chapter I draw a picture of how Chaucer is read and used in the academic world and generally, including a brief comparison with other classics. Finally I turn to an analysis of Chaucer publications in the last 50 years by a number of translators and authors that will be introduced in connection with analysis of their work.

Danes and the English language

Bent Preisler's *Danskerne og det engelske sprog* [The Danes and the English language] from 1999 is a thorough study of a subject that few have treated in academic form, although opinions are many about the influence of English, not least American English, in postwar Denmark (Preisler 1999a). As we have seen in the last two chapters, both British and American culture, including literature, gained ground in Denmark as a direct result of the war, and by the end of the last millennium the Danish language itself had been further affected by this dominant influence from English culture. The influence of English on the Danish vocabulary is recorded in Knud Sørensen's dictionary of more than 400 pages on Anglicisms in Danish, published in 1992. In his introduction Sørensen categorizes the Anglicisms as e.g. direct loans, translation loans, hybrids, adaptations, pseudo-Anglicisms and indirect Anglicisms, and in his thorough explanations in the entries he provides examples of usage and translates his examples into English (Sørensen 1992: 4-6 and main dictionary part). Preisler provides a brief supplement to Sørensen's dictionary by recording a number of English loan-words from the 1990s, using one of them to characterize a new *trend* (Preisler 1999a: 12-13). A major part of Preisler's empirical investigation in the study shows how the use of English terminology and conceptualizations is particularly widespread in subcultures such as computer or hiphop communities, and that subculture uses of English affect general English usage in Denmark (Preisler 1999a: 133-224). Furthermore, as Preisler points out in a supplementary study from the same year, commercials and advertisements, especially those directed at young people, constitute a domain where English in some cases completely replaces Danish (Preisler 1999b). I will add that so-called domain loss of Danish to English also includes areas such as university education, where courses and in some cases whole programmes are now taught only in English. Corporate communication, where English takes over as the company's common language of communication, is another significant example of domain loss, although a recent study has shown that in practice communication involving Danes tends to take place in Danish despite company policies (Lønsmann 2011). There is generally no reason to believe that Danish is a dying language, which will be suffocated by English linguistic imperialism, although some linguists have voiced concerns for the situation. A sound academic debate on the topic can be found in *Engelsk eller ikke engelsk: That is the question* [English or not English: That is the question], the proceedings of a conference under the auspices of *Dansk Sprognævn*, the Danish Board for Language (Davidsen-Nielsen, Hansen and Jarvad, eds., 1999).

One reason for believing that Danish will survive well is the fact that quite a number of Danes do not master the English language or any other language besides Danish. One of the most often quoted findings of Preisler's investigation is that in 1999 20 per cent of the population, according to the questions answered about own assessment of proficiency, were not able to understand English or take part in even banal, everyday communication in English (Preisler 1999a: 109 and 236). With many more than 20 per cent far from fluent in English, it goes without saying that translation is still needed in all areas of cultural life, although the generations now growing up are better educated in English than earlier generations. A slightly earlier and less substantial study than Preisler's on Danes and foreign languages, including besides English a perspective on German and French, supports Preisler's general findings on the lack of foreign language competence of a high percentage of Danes. This empirical study concludes that as many as 1.6 million, or approximately 30 per cent of the Danes, are unable to embark on a simple everyday conversation in any foreign language, whereas 2.2 million or approximately 40 per cent are unable to read fiction in any other language than Danish (Bacher, Clemmensen, Jacobsen & Wandall 1992: 107, my percentage estimate). With many more than the 40 per cent able to read only in Danish preferring to read fiction in Danish translation, it is no surprise that the market spurts out so many book translations from English and other languages, including the Scandinavian neighbour languages. In a forthcoming study of Danish anglicisms Henrik Gottlieb quotes figures from *Dansk Bibliotekscenter* [Danish Library Centre] showing that since the mid-1990s more than 60 per cent of the fiction titles translated into Danish have been translated from English (Gottlieb, forthcoming), and in effect there is no longer any need for me to register developments in what quality literature gets translated from English. More or less all important English literature in prose is translated within a year of publication, and both drama and to a lesser extent poetry is sometimes translated as well.

With these strong indications that the English language and culture, including literature, is now more influential than ever in Danish history, whether in translation or not, let us now consider how far our case story, Chaucer, has been part of this picture in Denmark since 1960.

Chaucer in higher education and in general public use

I will begin explaining the present state of Chaucer reception and translation in Denmark by looking at the situation in the academic world, where my experience as teacher and external examiner has given me personal knowledge of all the English departments in Danish universities. Here Chaucer is most often taught with a selection of one or two tales from *The Canterbury Tales*, with a few extracts from *The General Prologue* in Middle English and typically in an anthology such as *The Norton Anthology of English Literature*. Modern English translations, mainly Coghill's or Wright's, are sometimes used instead of an edited medieval text (Coghill 1951, Wright 1985). For the well-educated reading public there are the same two preferred options, and in fact most of the few Danes now concerned with Chaucer would pick an English translation. This is probably because the two full Danish translations of the *Canterbury Tales* by Boisen and Johansen are out of print, though both can still be borrowed from public libraries or acquired second hand. But it also has to do with the general high standard of English in the Scandinavian countries discussed above. In Denmark there have been recent re-translations of Homer, Dante and Petrarca (Due 1999 and 2002, Meyer 2006, Sørensen 2011), but English classics other than Shakespeare and Dickens are rarely re-translated. In a small country like Denmark, some classics, needless to say, have never been translated at all. Chaucer's *Troilus and Criseyde* is a case in point, as we have seen, and generally English literature from the Middle Ages is poorly represented on the Danish book market, one remarkable exception being the critically highly appraised *Beowulf* translation by Andreas Haarder, which was reissued to compete with Seamus Heaney's modern English translation (Haarder, 1984/2001, Heaney, 1999). In fact Beowulf has been translated into Danish no less than five times, as recorded in a brief translation analysis by Viggo Hjørnager Pedersen (Hjørnager Pedersen 1986: 13-17). Like *Hamlet*, this classic has the advantage of being located in Denmark, whereas Chaucer by comparison has only one reference, "as any wyf from Denmark unto Ynde," at the end of the *Wife of Bath's Prologue* (Benson, gen. ed., III 824).

Many Scandinavian English departments today hardly include anything medieval at all in their English literature syllabi. In Sweden even big universities like Lund simply start their literature courses with Shakespeare and the Renaissance. The picture in Norway is similar, although an exception is The University of Oslo, which offers a Chaucer course as part of the English master programme. The tradition in Danish English departments, as carried by the two oldest universities, Copenhagen and Aarhus, has always included Chaucer, but up until the 1970s more or less only as part of a historical linguistics programme, as we have seen in earlier chapters. Danish students of medieval literature as late as the mid-1970s wrote their final theses on Chaucer's language only, with indicative titles such as *Chaucers verber. Deres bøjninger og endelser* [Chaucer's Verb Tenses and Verb Usage] and *Anvendelsen af konjunktiv i "The Parson's Tale" og "The Tale of Melibee"* [The Use of the Subjunctive in *The Parson's Tale* and *The Tale of Melibee*] (Johansen, H.B. 1972, Sørensen, L. G., 1975). Major curriculum changes in the Danish English departments occurred in the 1970s, unfortunately doing away with most of Old English, Middle English, and historical linguistics altogether, but at the same time Chaucer and other medieval writers anthologized in the Oxford and Norton Anthologies of English literature, in use in Denmark from the early 1970s, found their way into literature classes.

In extension of earlier chapters, notably chapter 8, let me also add a further perspective on Chaucer at Danish universities, now drawing on personal experience from being connected to the University of Copenhagen since 1979. There was and is still very little Chaucer at the English Departments in Aarhus and Aalborg, and until 1994 when I joined staff also Roskilde. At the University of Copenhagen it was very much the arrival from Scotland of a new associate professor in 1972, Dr. Graham Caie, which helped change the agenda. Caie's 17 years in Denmark gave Chaucer and medieval literature such a boost that the field was completely changed for the better when he returned to Scotland as professor. Not only was there a marked increase of new students of medieval literature, from 1980 including the present writer, but Caie's dynamic working methods and charismatic teaching gradually involved a number of colleagues both at Copenhagen and elsewhere, and a new centre for medieval studies saw a very fruitful exchange of interdisciplinary research and teaching. The present study focuses mainly on translation and reception in Danish, and most of Caie's students and colleagues have published chiefly in English as part of an international medievalist community, so I will only mention in passing that some of the substantial international Chaucer publications by Danish scholars all owe something to Graham Caie, e.g. Specht 1981, Børch 1993a, and may I add Klitgård 1995.[76] Perhaps even more importantly, Caie supervised a great number of theses on medieval literature, assisted by his colleague Dorrit Einersen, who because of severe budget cuts in English Studies from the early 1990s ended up as the only permanent member of staff teaching medieval literature at the University of Copenhagen, where she is still active. Einersen has supervised even more final theses in late medieval studies than her former colleague Caie.

The present situation in Danish Universities is that besides Einersen, only a couple of literary medievalists, Børch at the University of Southern Denmark and the present writer at Roskilde, are employed as permanent members of staff. Yet it is positive that so many Danes today have actually been educated with knowledge of Chaucer. I will conclude tentatively by suggesting that Chaucer taught as literature is a firm part of English Studies in most Danish universities, whereas the general public has been less well served since 1960. I will now turn to the publications that have after all appeared.

Chaucer translations in the 1960s and 1970s

This section will register all the Chaucer publications I have been able to locate from the period. Reprints of parts of Johansen's and Boisen's translations have been published in new contexts since the 1950s, and I will start by briefly mentioning two such publications. In 1961 Boisen's

---

76 Børch also published a summary in Danish of *Chaucer's Poetics: Seeing and Asking*, her doctoral dissertation (Børch 1993a and 1993b). I have chosen not to include any discussion of this summary in the present study, as it would be unfair to Børch not to consider the whole dissertation, which on the other hand falls outside the scope of my study, as explained in chapter one. Instead I refer the interested reader to my review of Børch's thesis (Klitgård 1993). In note form I will also mention one of the rare literary studies of Chaucer in Denmark before Caie's time, Jens Kr. Andersen's article "An analysis of the Framework Structure of Chaucer's 'Canterbury Tales'" (Andersen 1972). This is a stimulating discussion of its topic, but written in English and published in the Copenhagen based international journal *Orbis Litterarum* it also falls outside the central scope of the present study.

translation of *The Miller's Tale* appears in a collection where Chaucer's name is in the title, *Engelske fortællere fra Chaucer til Somerset Maugham* [English narrators from Chaucer to Somerset Maugham]. Relatively speaking this must be considered an honour, since there are extracts also from such diverse classic writers as Swift, Smollett, Fielding, Scott, Dickens, Kipling and Hardy. There is also a very brief introduction to Chaucer, which regrettably does not mention that *The Canterbury Tales* are verse tales. They are even called *noveller*, the Danish word for short stories written in prose (Grosen and Knudsen, eds., 1961: 303). Selections from Johansen's translation of *The General Prologue* are reprinted in the collection *Verdenslitteratur* [World Literature] from 1967, edited by Hans Mølbjerg. Chaucer is here printed in the good company of Dante, Petrarca, Boccaccio and Villon, also in reprint, in some of the cases from 19th century translations. Again there is an extremely brief introduction to Chaucer, repeating the probably incorrect claim that Chaucer met Petrarca and possibly Boccaccio (Mølbjerg, ed., 1967: 66-70).

Among the often rather odd pieces of Chaucer translation that appear after the two full translations of *The Canterbury Tales* in the 1950s had blocked the way for further enterprise for a while, we find the inclusion of one single portrait, that of the Prioress in the *General Prologue*, in translations of various short bits by librarian and author Martin N. Hansen (1893-1976) in 1963 (Hansen 1963, Anonymous entry from *Det alsiske dialektselskab*, accessed 2011). Hansen's short book is a piece of home publishing with brief translations of mainly German poets such as Goethe, Heine and Storm, but also a couple of English poets and a Swede, gathered together under the title *Fremmede klange* [Rings of foreign voices].

Although Hansen frankly admits that this is a "tilfældig samling" [random collection] of matters gathered over the years, his poetic translation of the portrait of the Prioress in *The General Prologue* (Benson, ed., I 118-639) is not bad at all. Rhyme and rhythm follow Chaucer's, and Hansen has also taken care to get the delicate details of this portrait right. Except for the Prioress giving her dogs "kage" [cake], which is neither the correct translation of "wastel-breed" (fine bread, 147), nor good for dogs, I have found no major inaccuracy. In one case, however, Hansen has cheated a little bit by inserting an extra couplet to explain the amusing details of the Prioress's French:

> At høre hendes franske var en lyst, [To hear her French was a joy,]
> Hun talte nemlig fransk, som det bliver lært
> [For she spoke French as it was taught]
> i Strattford nær ved Bow, det lød lidt sært [in
> Stratford near Bow, it sounded a bit strange]
> og var et andet fransk naturligvis [and was
> a different French naturally]
> end det der tales nede i Paris [than that spoken down in Paris]
> (Hansen 1963: 9)

> And Frenssh she spak ful faire and fetisly,
> After the scole of Stratford ate Bowe,
> For Frenssh of Parys was to hire unknowe.
> (Benson, gen. ed., *The General Prologue*, I 124-6)

Chaucer is clearly a better satirical writer than Hansen, but Hansen should be excused for inserting the extra couplet, because his Danish readers in the 1960s do not know what the school of Stratford near Bow refers to, and thus Hansen explicates with a bit of extra information. As we have seen in earlier chapters, the alternative would have been to offer notes, but since Hansen generally in his collection has wanted his poetic translations to speak for themselves, explication of this kind becomes necessary. It is of course a mistake, however, that Stratford is spelled with an extra "t".

Another somewhat odd place to find Chaucer is in a schoolbook for religious education from 1965 edited by Aage Nørfelt (1905-2007), who was principal of a teacher training college and a pioneer within religious education (Anonymous entry in *Dansk Biografisk Leksikon*, accessed November 2011, Nørfelt 1965: 134-8). This book provides a translation, presumably by Nørfelt himself, of Otto Jespersen's English prose summary of the *Pardoner's Tale*. This prose summary appeared in a schoolbook series that Jespersen began in 1895, and which he revised many times. After his death in 1943 the series in five short volumes was revised by several editors, including Svend Brüel, who is the editor of the 20th imprint published 1957-60, which Nørfelt probably used (Jespersen in Brüel, ed., 1957-60: 70-3). It is remarkable that the series, which contains beginners' grammar and phonetics as well as text pieces to read, was used in Danish schools for more than 70 years, but as we saw in chapters 5-7, Jespersen's role in English education in Denmark as well as in Chaucer studies is generally impressive.

It is not stated explicitly that Jespersen is the author of the summary, but it is a fair guess that he is. The title "The Three Drunkards" detaches the story from the Pardoner, who is not mentioned at all, although a reference is given to Chaucer's *Canterbury Tales*. The four-page summary turns Chaucer's poetic narrative into a short story much like Lumiansky and Boisen's prose tales (see chapter 9), but Jespersen has furthermore adapted the story for young readers learning English, e.g. by avoiding complicated language. The summary is very loyal to Chaucer's plot, and there is lively dialogue, which to a certain extent is also loyal to Chaucer with its dramatic content.

Nørfelt's translation is in turn very loyal to Jespersen and follows his text without abbreviations or changes of content. The translation is introduced by a brief presentation of Chaucer and the framework idea of *The Canterbury Tales*, but no mention is made of the Pardoner here either. On the contrary, "De tre svirebrødre" [The three topers], as Nørfelt names the story, is presented as illustrating two points from the Bible, "Du må ikke begære" [you must not covet] and "Penge er en afgud for mange mennesker" [Money is a false god for many people]. This is perhaps true enough, but it is also a simplification of Chaucer's complicated composition, including the haunting figure of the old man, who cannot find his death. Thus Nørfelt, unlike Chaucer and Jespersen, wants to hammer home a religious point, and many young readers will have believed that the Bible quotations were used by Chaucer.

A book of ghost stories edited by Tage la Cour from 1966 contains a two-page Danish prose version of the murder story rendered in *The Nun's Priest's Tale* (Benson, gen. ed., VII 2984-3062). Tage la Cour (1915-93) was a well-known editor, critic and translator, who specialised in suspense fiction (Lund, gen. ed., *Den Store Danske Encyklopædi*, accessed 2011). In Chaucer's version the murder story is a long digression that is part of a general consideration of the nature of dreams, and it records how a man dreams in cruel detail about the murder of his friend, after which he is able to locate the body and cry murder in public. The often quoted punchline or moral of the story is "Mordre wol out" ([Murder will out], VII 3057), which la Cour translates somewhat freely by a line he also uses as title for his version, "Mord råber til himlen" [Murder shouts to the sky] (la Cour 1966: 313 and 314). Idiomatically this is not a bad solution in Danish, and for a short suspense story it provides la Cour with a catchy title.

In comparison with Boisen's prose translation 14 years earlier (Boisen 1952: 293-4) la Cour also generally provides good idiomatic solutions, as in the first piece of dialogue, where one of the unnamed characters predicts his own murder and calls to his friend "In alle hast come to me!" (Benson, gen. ed.: VII 3007), which Boisen (with Lumiansky as an intermediary, see chapter 9) translates directly to "kom til mig i al hast!" [come to me in all haste] (Boisen: 293). La Cour seems to know better that this direct translation would not be used in Danish for somebody crying out in agony, so he translates by the correct idiomatic expression "Skynd dig og kom!" [Hurry up and get here] (la Cour: 313). In a later piece of direct speech la Cour is again more successful than Boisen when he translates "And in this carte he lith gapyng upright" (Benson, gen. ed.: VII 3042) by "og hans lig ligger med åben mund i denne vogn" [and his body lies with an open mouth in this cart] (la Cour: 314). Boisen has "og han ligger på sin ryg i denne vogn og gaber" [and he lies on his back in this cart yawning] (Boisen: 294), which is very unfortunate, since it sounds like the poor fellow is half-awake rather than dead.

On the other hand there are also a couple of places where Boisen finds a better translation. When the innkeeper addresses the murdered person's friend, he uses the common medieval form "Sire" (Benson, gen. ed.: 3030), which Boisen correctly translates by "Herre" (Boisen: 294), a slightly archaic form of address, but well in place in this situation. La Cour uses the English address "Sir" (la Cour: 314), which might have been permitted if he was translating a contemporary suspense story, where the form would signal an English setting, but here in an old legend the form is out of place. Another example is la Cour's translation of "woundes" (Benson, gen. ed., 3015), where he uses the etymologically related Danish word "vunder" (la Cour: 313). However, where "Sir" was too modern, "vunder" is not only too archaic, it is a term almost completely out of use in Danish. Boisen sensibly chooses the neutral translation of wounds, "sår" (Boisen: 294). In sum, la Cour is fairly successful with his short translation, and it is remarkable that we see Chaucer translated in the context of suspense fiction. However, la Cour has a few problems deciding what language register to apply.

In 1967 Chaucer is included in volume 40 of the series *Gyldendals Bibliotek: Verdenslitteratur* [Gyldendal's library: world literature], and this is not surprising since the editor of this volume on lyrics is Jørgen Sonne, whose early translations were discussed in chapter 8 (Sonne in Nielsen, gen. ed., 1967). Five translated medieval English lyrics by anonymous poets appear in this selection, among these "Adam Lay Ybounden" and a couple of other well-known lyrics translated by Sonne himself and by Kai Friis Møller and Elsa Gress, whom we have also met as knowledgeable of late medieval literature in earlier chapters. Sonne has also included three brief extracts from Johansen's 1958 translation, from respectively *The Knight's Tale*, Arcite's temple visit, Benson, gen. ed., I, 1975-2021, *The Miller's Tale*, the first description of Alison, I, 3233-70, and *The Nun's Priest's Tale*, Chauntecleer wooing Pertelote, VII, 3157-85 (Sonne in Nielsen, gen. ed., 1967: 159-65). There are a couple of translator's revisions in these pieces, presumably by Johansen, but besides a change from the old to the modern Danish spelling system, they are fairly insubstantial, and I will only mention an improvement in an episode we have already considered in chapter 9. This is the horror vision of Arcite's visit to Mars's temple, where line 2019 has been changed from "Der saa jeg Soen, der et Spædbarn slugte," [There saw I the sow that swallowed an infant child] to "så soen, der et barn i vuggen slugte" [Saw the sow that swallowed a child in the cradle]. This change is slightly more horrible in detail and follows Chaucer's "The sowe freten the child right in the cradle" more accurately (Skeat, ed., A 2019, identical line in Benson, gen.ed., I 2019).

Another two short pieces by Chaucer are translated by Sonne himself. The titles, like also the titles of the extracts from Johansen's translations, are constructed for the extracts given and are not provided with references. The first one, "Min dame" [My Lady] is the first stanza of Chaucer's short ballad known as "To Rosemounde", whereas the second extract, "Den døde elskede" [The dead loved one] is from Chaucer's first significant long poem, the elegiac dream vision *The Book of the Duchess,* more precisely lines 475-86, where the poem's man in black laments the death of his wife. Sonne's reason for choosing these precise extracts turns out to be their inclusion in Ezra Pound's *ABC of Reading* from 1951, a work Sonne translated as *ABC for læsere* and published in 1960 (Pound 1951,

Sonne 1960). Here, however, they are untitled both in Pound's original and Sonne's translation, which he prints alongside Pound's edited Chaucer text. Pound includes a couple of other brief examples from Chaucer's poetry, which he also cites without reference. These include "Lenvoy to King Richard" from the ballad "Lak of Stedfastnesse." Sonne translates these few lines well, but he misses out the important line 27, "Dred God, do law, love trouthe and worthinesse" (Benson, gen. ed., "Lak of Stedfastnesse": 27). In an article in Politiken from December 3rd 1960, published in his collection of articles *I min tid* [In my time] (Kristensen 1963: 142-153), critic and author Tom Kristensen reviews Sonne's translation. He includes a brief comparison with a Swedish translation and says that Sonne's translation is far better, since he has also translated poetry from various European languages, including Chaucer (144). I agree that the effort is impressive, but unlike Kristensen I find the translations in many cases flawed. The example of a missing line is one of several mistakes in these poorly edited translations. However, Sonne is quite right in pointing out in a translator's note that an included medieval poem on Absolon from *The Miller's Tale* is "slet ikke af Chaucer" [not at all by Chaucer] (Sonne 1960: 96-9).

As neither the 1960 publication, nor the 1967 reprints with new titles represent Sonne's main efforts in Chaucer translation, I will restrict myself here to a comment on his translation of the first five lines of Pound's extract from *The Book of the Duchess*:

> Jeg har af sorg så stor en kvide, [I have
> from sorrow so much agony]
> at glæde får jeg ingen tide, [that I will never more get joy]
> nu da jeg ser, min frue skær, [now that I see, my lady bright]
> som jeg af alt min magt holdt kær, [that
> I with all my might held dear]
> er død og borte fra min side. [has died and vanished from my side]
> (Sonne 1960: 94 and Sonne in Nielsen, gen. ed., 1967: 161-62)

> "I have of sorwe so grete woon
> That joye gete I never noon,
> Now that I see my lady bright,
> Which I have loved with al my myght,

Is fro me deed and ys a-goon."
(Pound 1951: 106)[77]

Sonne follows both rhyme and rhythm very well, creating also in Danish a fine and simple elegy. Moreover he is quite accurate in content, excepting perhaps the small freedom he has allowed himself by including the archaic poetical word for agony, "kvide", in the first line, where Chaucer's "woon" really refers to the abundance of sorrow that the speaker is suffering. The word "woon" is glossed in Pound's edition, and either Sonne has overlooked this or made a deliberate choice of making the in Danish common idiomatic match "sorg" and "kvide". Whatever the reason, I note in passing that we have at least 10 lines in Danish of Chaucer's first truly great work of literature.

The next publication including Chaucer translation to appear in Denmark makes use of *The Nun's Priest's Tale* like la Cour's translation, but for very good reasons not the murder story. This is a children's book for the age group 4-8, and it is a translation by well-known Danish writer Cecil Bødker (born 1927) of an American children's book, *Chanticleer and the Fox,* written and illustrated by Barbara Cooney, who in turn acknowledges the use of Lumiansky's Chaucer translation for her text. Cooney's book was published in 1958, whereas Bødker's Danish translation, *Hanen og ræven* [The cock and the fox] appeared in 1968 (Lumiansky 1948/1954, Cooney 1958, Bødker 1968). A book like Cooney's should be taken entirely seriously, and Bødker's translation is flawless, but it makes little sense to analyse a children's book on the premises and with the methods used elsewhere in this study, e.g. concerning loyalty to Chaucer's poetry or translation accuracy. I have decided to offer a general reflection on how Chaucer is transformed through several filters into a story for young children, and to give a few examples from Bødker's book.[78]

Chaucer's *Nun's Priest's Tale* is of course in its basic plot a typical

---

77 Pound himself appears to have edited the extract quoted here. I have checked both Skeat's and Robinson's edition, and there are several spelling variants compared to Pound's text.
78 Bødker's *Hanen og ræven* is now very difficult to get hold of, and I would hope for a reprint. The only copy I have located is available for reading room use only in the Royal Library of Copenhagen.

beast's fable of a fox and a hen who both get duped. With for instance the murder story side plot, it is also something more complicated, and it is first of all a very elegant poetic narrative. Taking the basic plot only and making sure to emphasize that the animals all survive safely although they get frightened, Cooney and Bødker come up with something different, and not least with the wonderful and rather dominant illustrations they communicate really well with young children. One example is the last drawing in the book, which portrays the widow with her cock safe in her arms, accompanied by two pretty young girls (Bødker 1968: 38). The girls offer identification, and both illustrations and language make the book recognizable for children as belonging to a genre, stories about animals who can speak, or fables. There is also an added moral at the end, which is an explication for children of Chaucer's point about false flattery (Bødker: 37-8, Benson, gen. ed.: VII 3436-7).

Apart from such changes a surprisingly high number of descriptions, plot and dialogue go back to Chaucer, whereas most of the narrator's comments on the plot have been deleted or changed. We hear for instance that "En sortspidset ræv, der var fuld af snu ondskab, havde boet i lunden i 3 år" [A black-tipped fox, full of sly malignity, had lived in the grove for 3 years] (Bødker 22). This is very close to the details in Chaucer's lines 3215-16, "A col-fox, ful of sly iniquitee,/That in the grove hadde woned yeres three", which Lumiansky translated as "A fox, tipped with black, full of sly wickedness, who had lived in the grove three years" (Benson, gen. ed.: 3215-16, Lumiansky: 147). Also the dramatic episode of the fox abducting Chanticleer echoes Chaucer, who describes how various other animals on the farm react by making noises (Benson, gen. ed., VII 3375-3401). Cooney/Bødker refer to exactly the same, if not as many animals as Chaucer and use the episode for big illustrations of respectively cows, sheep, pigs, bees and geese in uproar (Bødker: 30-33). Finally, even Bødker's naming of the cock as "Gladensang" [happy singer] is a translation of Chaucer's Chauntecleer. I will forgive that the name of his sweetheart, the hen Pertelote, whom Lumiansky calls Partlet, is named "fru Putte" [lady Chuck-Chuck], but I am a bit surprised that a quality author, including children's author, like Bødker should find this name change necessary. On the other hand it will have been a familiar name to young Danish children.

In 1971 another well-known Danish writer, Frank Jæger (1926-1977), translated a Swedish audioplay by Allan Edwall, which he claims in a brief introduction is inspired by *The Wife of Bath's Prologue and Tale* (Jæger 1971: i). The play script is available only in two typed copies, one of which belonged to *Dramatisk Bibliotek* [library for drama] and is now in the possession of the Royal Library, whereas the other is in *Hørespilsarkivet* [the archive for audioplays] in *Danmarks Radio*. The former is a photocopy of the latter, and I have used that. It is full of typos, which I assume are Jæger's own. Some of them are so gross that they must have created difficulties for the actors on the play's first broadcast on May 7th 1971 as *Den underskønne Lina eller konerne derhjemme* [The divinely beautiful Lina or the wives back home]. Edwall had called his play from 1967 *Snus er snus* [Snuff is snuff] with an allusion to Swedish poet Gustaf Fröding, but this title, which would be identical in Danish translation, is crossed over twice in the manuscript, Jæger apparently wanting both to avoid the for Danes difficult allusion and come up with a title that signals the actual content of the play. Apart from the poor quality of the typing, Jæger's text works well as drama, but my problem in this context is that I do not recognize it as Chaucer at all. Edwall, a brilliant Swedish actor and dramatist, whom Jæger rightly praises very highly in the introduction, said that his play was "en moralitet a la Chaucer" [a morality play like Chaucer's], so of course Jæger has good reason to go one step further and refer to the Wife of Bath (Jæger 1971: i). However, the play's main plot of Olaus, a man, who is tempted by the beauty of the young woman, Lina, but in the end decides to settle for the more mature beauties of his own wife, has nothing to do with the Wife of Bath. Only in one respect is there an echo of Chaucer, since the play is composed in rhyming couplets, mostly iambic pentameters. It is an unusual experiment in the late 1960s and early 1970s, but it does not make it Chaucerian to any real extent. I shall thus refrain from any further treatment of it, registering only that the name Chaucer has found its way into a place where it does not belong.

The last entry in this section also appeared on the national Danish radio channel *Danmarks Radio*, in 1979, when Danish actor Jørgen Reenberg read Boisen's translation of *The Shipman's Tale*, "Skipperens fortælling", in a series of classics readings (Reenberg 1979). In the series Chaucer was placed among 30 other Danish and world classics, e.g.

Blicher, Wied, Skjoldborg, Swift, Pusjkin, Dostojevskij, Tjekhov and Kipling. Good company for Chaucer, but since Boisen's *Canterbury Tales* translation was discussed in chapter 9, enough about it here.

The Danish reception of Chaucer in the 1960s and 1970s

Apart from Johansen's book *Fra Chaucer's tid* from 1965, discussed in chapter 9, most Danish Chaucer publications in these two decades were short. This certainly goes for the anonymous entry in *Hirschsprungs Konversationsleksikon*, which in 15 lines characterizes Chaucer superficially (Budtz-Jørgensen, Rode and Thomassen, eds., 1962, vol. 1: 748). The unsigned author claims that *The Canterbury Tales* were started around 1372, which even if we count possible early versions of a tale or two is far too early. For instance Derek Pearsall in a thorough dating discussion settles on in or around 1387 (Langer, ed., 1982: 112-13, Pearsall 1992: 226-7). We are also told that Chaucer's poetry expresses "adelens tolerante, humane, skeptiske livssyn" [the nobility's tolerant, humane and skeptical view of life] (Langer, ed., 1982: 112). Whereas the three adjectives tolerant, humane and skeptical might indeed be used of Chaucer, he is certainly not a spokesman for the nobility. Both Danish *Canterbury Tales* translations from the 1950s are mentioned, but no further sources are given.

B. Østergaard Pedersen's *Litteraturleksikon* [Literary encyclopedia] from 1968 (Østergaard Pedersen: 62) has an even shorter and more superficial entry with its 12 lines and no sources, and I have also come across encyclopediae of various kinds that do not have an entry on Chaucer at all. They will not be mentioned further here.

There is another anonymous entry consisting of 30 lines and a picture portrait in *Nordisk Konversationsleksikon* (Møller and Nielsen, eds., 1973: 126). Here unfortunately only Boisen's translation is referred to, and although a praiseworthy effort is made to list several works by Chaucer, one of the most important of them is misspelled as *Troylus and Criseyde*. Apart from these reservations, this is a fairly competent short portrait.

A Chaucer entry from 1974 in *Gyldendals litteraturleksikon* by Viggo Hjørnager Pedersen (Hjørnager Pedersen 1974) is also competent. Hjørnager Pedersen sensibly presents Chaucer's works by dividing them into three periods, the early period with French influence, the period 1372-85 with mainly influence from the Italian renaissance, and finally the last period that includes Chaucer's two main works, *Troilus and Criseyde* and *The Canterbury Tales*. Hjørnager Pedersen mentions all Chaucer's major poems and correctly says that Chaucer had "umådelig stor indflydelse" [immense influence], not least on Scottish literature and on the English renaissance and romanticism (Hjørnager Pedersen 1974: 158). As I have demonstrated in earlier chapters, it would have been reasonable to mention also the influence on the neoclassicists Dryden and Pope, but this is a minor complaint. Hjørnager Pedersen does well in referring his reader to F.N. Robinson's edition and Brusendorff's treatise for further reading, and his choice of mentioning one critical work, Speirs' *Chaucer the Maker* from 1951, is quite acceptable since the editors have generally only allowed room for one or two critical works.

There is a second entry in *Gyldendals litteraturleksikon* on *The Canterbury Tales*, also by Viggo Hjørnager Pedersen (Hjørnager Pedersen 1974: 150-1). This registers the two main Danish translations by Boisen and Johansen and mentions that parts of the tales have also been translated elsewhere. There is a general presentation of the frame narrative, followed by very brief summaries of most of the tales. Hjørnager Pedersen also points out that the theme of marriage is discussed in several tales. He is generally hesitant as regards suggesting the quality of individual tales, with a few exceptions such as calling *The Nun's Priest's Tale* "morsom" [funny] (150). However, this is generally a sober and informative encyclopedia article.

I will finish my discussion of short encyclopedia entries in the 1960s and 1970s by considering Henning Fonsmark's *Verdenslitteraturen før 1914* [World Literature before 1914] from 1979 (Fonsmark 1979: 26). This consists of nearly 60 lines and a picture, and there is a reference to the standard edition in 1979, Robinson's 2nd edition from 1957. Strangely, however, there is only mention of one translation, Birkedal's, and only his 1913 translation. Fonsmark does a little better in his reference to further literature, but the references are to the fairly old studies by Brusendorff, Ward, Jespersen and Spurgeon. Only one study published after 1925 is mentioned, and somewhat surprisingly this is a monograph by Finnish linguist Niels Erik Enkvist (Enkvist 1964). The article itself is balanced more in the direction of life than works, and Fonsmark seems to have gathered his very general information from other sources rather than from reading Chaucer.

There is a more substantial entry in the Norwegian literary historian Francis Bull's (1887-1974) history of world literature, *Verdens litteraturhistorie*, which was originally published in Norwegian in 1940, but was translated into Danish as *Verdenslitteraturens historie* by Karl Hornelund and published in 1963 (Bull 1963). The one and a half pages are full of the expected basic information about life and works, and there is very little remarkable in the portrait, in fact so little that Bull can well have written it without having read Chaucer himself.[79] Bull says that Chaucer is "den største digter i det 14. århundrede i landene nord for Alperne" [the greatest poet of the 14th century in the countries north of the Alps] (Bull 1963: 75), which is true, but also, with this particular geographic delimitation, Bull is playing it rather safe. The only really noteworthy statement in the piece is the claim that Chaucer like the Norwegian folklorist Asbjørnsen became as interested in the framework around as in the content of his *Canterbury Tales*. This to my mind may be truer of Asbjørnsen than of Chaucer, who admittedly constructs an interesting framework, but first of all tells a variety of poetic narratives of the highest calibre.

A *kronik* [feature article] entitled "På selskabsrejse i middelalderen" [Joining a travel party in the Middle Ages], published in *Aarhus Stiftstidende*, August 21st 1969, and written by Anders Iversen, provides a general introduction to Chaucer (Iversen 1969). Anders Iversen (born 1928) was then employed as *amanuensis* at the English Department of the University of Aarhus, but later he became an associate professor until his retirement in 1998. The feature article was written for a special occasion, the opening of a musical at Aarhus Theatre two days later with the title "Canterbury Fortællinger". This was an English language production of Chaucer translator Nevill Coghill's and composer Martin Starkie's musical based on *The Canterbury Tales*. The show had opened in London in March 1968, where it ran for five years and was adapted for a BBC television production in 1969. Steve Ellis includes a discussion of it in

---

79 My own experience working with a writers' encyclopedia in the late 1990s (Michelsen, ed. 1999) tells me that this sometimes happens, and at least it can safely be assumed that a single author like Bull, however well read he was, could not possibly have read even the main works of all the authors covered in a work of this kind.

his study of Chaucer in modern English versions, *Chaucer at Large*. He establishes that "the pilgrimage theme remains important in the musical", but that the compression and the selection of especially the fabliaux gives the production an emphasis on "good-hearted" and "good-humoured" joy and love with an edge of bawdiness, apparently welcome at a time when "the Beatles were recording songs with titles like 'All You Need is Love'" (Ellis 2000: 128-9). It is interesting that the musical also reached Danish shores, but since Iversen when writing his article has not yet seen the musical, he does not write about it, except a brief mention of what may be expected. Instead he provides an introduction to Chaucer that is generally praiseworthy for his serious attempt to make the reading of Chaucer attractive.

As opposed to the case of Bull, the reader is left in no doubt that Iversen himself has carefully read *The Canterbury Tales*, and he adds spice to his presentation by quoting and translating a couple of passages, from *The Wife of Bath's Prologue*. Besides the opening, Iversen quotes lines 149-153, where the Wife says that her husband shall have access to her "instrument" as often as he pleases. Although Iversen translates these few lines well, and by picking them shows that he is not afraid of quoting some of Chaucer's juiciest passages, he acknowledges that there are other Danish translators by mentioning Boisen, Johansen, Bergsøe and Birkedal, as we have seen in this study a selection of the most important Danish translators, except perhaps for Sonne. However, he challenges his reader to try and read Chaucer in the original, and he spends a substantial part of the article introducing the reader to Chaucer's English, which, as he rightly asserts, is in many ways easier for a Dane to learn than for a modern English person. Taking Chaucer's poetry seriously by talking about "klangfarven og rytmen" [the sonority and rhythm] of his poetic language, Iversen, probably unknowingly, distances himself from the many Danish writers on Chaucer who talk about it as crude poetry, as we have seen. He very sensibly goes on to give his reader a short introduction to the pronunciation of Middle English, then jokingly interrupts this introduction by saying, "Hvis det utrolige skulle ske at læseren vil afbryde kurset i middelengelsk og springe over hvor gærdet er lavest, kan vi henvise ham til Nevill Coghills gengivelse af *Canterbury Tales*" [If, incredibly, the reader should want to interrupt this course in Middle English and follow the line of least resistance, we can refer him to Nevill Coghill's rendering of *The Canterbury Tales*], or, as Iversen adds, to the mentioned Danish translations. This gently joking tone is characteristic of Iversen's witty writing style. Since he also manages to cover life and works in a respectful way and say more or less everything that could be reasonably expected from an introduction to Chaucer, I can only regret that Iversen has not published anything else on Chaucer.[80] His article, which is available from *Statsbiblioteket* in Aarhus, deserves more readers than those that happened to read it in August 1969, and although this is not a review but a record of Chaucer reception, I will, as an exception among the many sources discussed here, recommend it strongly for educational purposes as well as to the generally interested reader.

There is a five-page presentation of Chaucer in Politiken's *Verdenslitteraturhistorie* from 1971, in a part called "England: Langland, Wyclif og Chaucer." This world literary history was edited by F.J. Billeskov Jansen, Hakon Stangerup and P.H. Traustedt, and it is the first work of its kind in Denmark since Niels Møller's world literary history from 1928, which was discussed in chapter 7. A couple of hundred pages concerning the European late Middle Ages were written by Knud Togeby, including the part in question here. Knud Togeby (1918-74) is first of all known for his internationally renowned publications in linguistics, mainly in the French-speaking world. He was a professor of French literature and language at the University of Copenhagen from 1955, and he published widely in many fields (unsigned entry in Lund, gen. ed. 2001). As we saw in chapter 7, Hakon Stangerup, who wrote so well about Chaucer in an encyclopedia article in 1934 (Stangerup 1934), would certainly be capable of assisting Togeby in the editing of the text, but there is no specific record of him doing so. Whereas this can easily be forgiven, it is not very fortunate that Johansen's translation of the *Canterbury Tales* is used for quotations without acknowledgement. Here of course the editors and publishers are to blame, rather than Togeby, and it does not help them much that Johansen's translation is among the books cited in a "litteraturvejledning" [Guide to further reading], as the other references include the translators Birkedal and Boisen (Billeskov Jansen, Stangerup and Traustedt, eds., vol. 2: 662)

---

80 I thank Iversen's son Poul Tornøe for clarifications concerning Iversen's publications.

Togeby's Chaucer portrait is unusual compared to many other portraits analysed in this study, because he spends only seven lines depicting Chaucer's life, focusing on his life at court, besides a brief mention of his travels to Italy in 1372-3. The rest of the piece is devoted to Chaucer's works, and it is a pleasure to see that all major works, i.e. *The Book of the Duchess*, *The House of Fame*, *The Parliament of Fowls*, *Troilus and Criseyde*, *The Legend of Good Women* and *The Canterbury Tales* are introduced, in a short space but competently. He even manages to include mention of some of Chaucer's lost works, as he ends his portrait by quoting from Chaucer's *Retraction* at the end of *The Canterbury Tales*, where a certain "book of the Leoun" is also mentioned (Benson, gen. ed., X 1086).

Togeby leaves an impression of having read through most of Chaucer's works, and he refrains from any derogatory remarks. *Troilus and Criseyde* is even lauded as "et psykologisk mesterstykke af en trekantsroman" [a psychological masterpiece in the shape of a triangular novel] (Togeby 1971: 509), which apart from calling it a novel is quite true. *The Canterbury Tales* are also presented in an enthusiastic manner, as they should be. Togeby has enjoyed the jokes that Chaucer pulls on himself and quotes the humorous remarks of the Host about Chaucer before *Sir Thopas* (Benson, ed., VII 695-706), which I also considered in Johansen's translation in chapter 9. He has also enjoyed the portraits in *The General Prologue* and some of the tales so much that his text begins to sound like mere plot summary. However, Togeby ends his generally praiseworthy discussion of Chaucer by emphasising the poet's "frodige blanding af realisme og fantasi" [vigorous mixture of realism and imagination], which is a fair generalization.

Chaucer translations 1980-2012. Jørgen Sonne

In this period there are a few publications that include earlier translations, whereas only Jørgen Sonne, to my knowledge, has published new translations. The re-publication of translations include a reading by Sonja Bentzen of Boisen's *Canterbury Tales* translation, published on ten cassette audiotapes in 1985 (Bentzen 1985). Johansen reprints bits of his own 1958 translation in his last Chaucer publication *Kvinder, Kirke, Kættere* from 1996 (Johansen 1996). His section on Chaucer will be discussed in the next section on reception.

Jørgen Sonne's Chaucer selection in his ambitious book of poetic translations *Europæisk lyrik fra 1100tallet til 1700 i England, Frankrig og Italien med biografier og essays* [European lyric poetry 1100-1700 in England, France and Italy] includes a series of translated Chaucer poems (Sonne 2007). The collection contains a great variety of medieval and renaissance poetry from the three countries. In the middle English section there are, besides Chaucer and a number of anonymous poems, brief translations of Dunbar and Lydgate. Two of the Chaucer poems are reprints of Sonne's earlier translations from *The Book of the Duchess* and "To Rosemounde", treated above, but to the latter has been added a new translation of the poem's other two stanzas. The main piece from Chaucer is a new abbreviated translation of *Sir Thopas*, and there are also translations of the roundel from the end of *The Parliament of Fowls*, the first and the third roundel from "Merciles Beaute" and finally "The Complaint of Chaucer to His Purse" (Benson, gen. ed., 1987/2008). Regrettably Sonne and his publisher have not mentioned these sources and the edition used. Again I quote the present standard edition, Benson's *The Riverside Chaucer*.

"To Rosemounde" now gets the Danish title "Oh, Rosamund" and the subtitle "Ballade (og drilleri)" [ballade – and teasing], and furthermore Sonne has written a note to explain the significance of the poem's reference to Tristan and Isolde. It is a general strategy in this edition to take the reader by the hand, and many of Sonne's comments explain and interpret the poems in his characteristic far from objective voice. Thus in his comment here he says, "For Isolde hun lå lynende snild med sin elsker" [For Isolde – she was lying with her lover, tremendously ingenious] (Sonne 2007: 64). The translation itself is successful, obeying rhyme and rhythm well, and Sonne has taken care to preserve Chaucer's playful and unusual imagery. For instance lines 17-18, "Nas never pyk walwed in galauntyne/As I in love am walwed and ywounde" are translated by "Aldrig i kryddersovs en gedde flød/som jeg I elskov boltrer mig for to" [Never was there a pike floating in a spicy sauce/As I in love float about as much as two people] (Sonne: 64, "To Rosemounde": 17-18). Although Sonne has not been able to find a Danish pun like Chaucer's on "walwed", he has certainly with this relatively free translation represented the comparison between the pike in a sauce and the rejected lover well. It is also acceptable, although perhaps not the most obvious solution, that Sonne in the poem's repeated last line in each stanza "Thogh ye to me ne do no daliaunce" ("To Rosamounde": 8, 16 and 24) chooses three different translations of "daliaunce": "pjanken", "ganten" and "elskovsleg" (Sonne: 64, lines 8, 16 and 24). These are all possible translations of the word, but they carry different connotations. "Ganten" is now outdated, but could once be used more or less like "pjanken" and suggest foolish, playful behaviour, whereas "elskovsleg" more directly names the game as lovers' fun. Sonne may have wanted several nuances of "daliaunce", but in the context of the poem he might reasonably have chosen to stick to "elskovsleg" in all three stanzas.

The two stanzas from Chaucer's "Merciles Beaute", presented in *The Riverside Chaucer* as "A Triple Roundel" have not only been translated very differently by Sonne, they have also been printed apart with the extract from *The Book of the Duchess* between them. With also the separate titles "Sår og Syn" [Wound and Sight] and "Færdig med Kærlighed" [Through with Love] they consequently appear as different poems, which they are not (Benson, gen.ed. 1987/2000, Sonne 2007: 61 and 63). The rhyme scheme in Chaucer's connected roundels operates with only two end-rhymes, which are repeated respectively five and eight times out of 13 lines, e.g. "sustene, kene, grene, sustene, quene, sene, sustene, kene" in roundel 1 ("Merciles Beaute", 2-3, 5, 7, 9-10, 12-13). In this case Sonne has given up and used no rhymes at all, and frankly his "Sår og Syn" is a failure both as far as rhyme and rhythm are concerned. The content is more or less correctly rendered, but lines like the repeated "sådan sårer de indigennem mit hjerte" [thus they wound me through my heart] (Sonne 2007: 61, lines 3 and 13) are neither worthy of Chaucer, nor of the poet Sonne. Sonne has had a somewhat better hand in the case of the third roundel in "Merciles Beaute", which he translates obeying the intricate rhyme scheme as well as the rhythm. However, Chaucer's "Sin I fro Love escaped am so fat,/I never thenk to ben in his prison lene" becomes the rather prosaic and uneven Danish sentence "Siden jeg slap fra Kærlighed så fed, vil I Hans fængsel aldrig Jeg bli' mager –" [Since I got rid of Love so fat, I will never become thin in his prison] ("Merciless Beaute" 27-8, Sonne 2007: 63, lines 1-2). It is rarely a good solution to have to use inverted word order as in the second of these lines.

An exception to the rule of obeying correct syntax also in poetry was mentioned earlier in this study in connection with Johansen's brilliant translation of *Sir Thopas*, in which he makes use of deliberately poor Danish syntax and idiom to represent Chaucer's poetic pastiche of the popular romance tradition. Sonne's *Topas* is far from the standard set by Johansen. In fact it seems that he has completely misunderstood Chaucer's poetic satire, because he has translated it into neat rhythmical verse, well-rhymed and perfectly idiomatic in Danish. The genre of romance is recognized, but not the parody. In view of the fact that Sonne has also cut out about a hundred lines without indicating so, a single example will suffice to indicate his failure:

"I skal af denne lanse lære [You will learn from this lance]
Ej mer så dristig stå! [Not to stand so daringly]
Jer vom [Your belly]
Skal jeg jage huller i – [I will put holes into]
Så vidt jeg kan, – fø'r klokken 9 [As far as I can, – before 9 o'clock]
Skal her I falde om!" [you will fall down here]
(Sonne 2007: 70)

"… at jeg med denne Lanse her […that I with this Lance]
Skal dyrt dig lade bøde [shall make you pay dearly]
Jeg give [I shall]
dig skal et Hul i Maven svær, [admit you a hole in your fat belly]
Før Primen os er rykket nær,[Before the
prime of day has moved in on us]
For her du dræbt skal blive!" [For here you shall be killed]
(Johansen 1958: 190-1, lines 2011-16)

"That thou shalt with this launcegay
Abyen it ful sowre.
Thy mawe
Shal I percent, if I may,
Er it be fully pryme of day,
For here thow shalt be slawe."
(Benson, gen.ed., 1987/2008: VII 821-6)

I used part of the example in connection with the analysis of Johansen's translation in chapter 9, and I take up again in this new context because it well illustrates the problem with Sonne's translation. The threat in Sonne's translation sounds serious, not ridiculous as in Chaucer and Johansen. And Sonne's poetic language sounds like a romance at the highest point of suspense, whereas Johansen follows Chaucer in using inappropriate and insecure rhetoric. Chaucer lets his timid Sir Thopas ask "if I may", thus taking out the seriousness of his threat, whereas Johansen uses the equally feeble "Jeg give/dig skal et Hul i Maven svær", which is both pompous and in poor syntax. Sonne may be wise in translating "prime" by 9 o'clock in a 2007 context, where "primen" would not be understood by so many Danes as in 1958, but this only supports the impression of a rather prosaic translation that foregrounds plot rather than language as in Chaucer and Johansen.

In the case of the very funny short poem "The Complaint of Chaucer to His Purse", which Sonne translates as "Bøn til min pung" [Prayer to my purse] (65), I have found no serious reason to complain, although I would have preferred an attempt to translate the rhyme scheme. However, when a poet and translator of Sonne's calibre has such difficulties with parts of his Chaucer translations as we have seen, it must be concluded that it is absolutely necessary to be well acquainted with Chaucer's language and poetic universe to be able to translate him, and in this connection I remind my reader that Johansen took a degree in English and spent nine years on his *Canterbury Tales* translation. And even he can be criticized at points, as we have seen. It may well be that future Chaucer translations require both a skilled poetic translator and a Chaucer scholar for the translator to consult.

The Danish reception of Chaucer 1980-2012. Encyclopediae and literary histories

One of the most popular and best-selling encyclopediae in Danish ever is *Lademanns Leksikon* published in 30 volumes between 1982 and 1988 with Torben W. Langer as general editor. It is especially known for its many illustrations that soon earned it the nickname "Farvelademann" ["paint-box-man"] with a pun including the publisher's name. The Chaucer entry is among the illustrated articles, with a nice reproduction of the Ellesmere Chaucer portrait, although it is not stated that this is where the illustration is from. The text is only 60 words and like many other articles in *Lademanns Leksikon* of a dubious quality. In this case it is mainly because the text is effectively copied directly with a few abbreviations from *Hirschsprungs Konversationsleksikon* from 1962, which as I showed above includes two rather serious mistakes repeated verbatim here, about the year of composition and Chaucer being a spokesman for the nobility. Lademann to my knowledge got away with this and many other points of plagiarism, even though the editors were so incompetent that they also stole their material without checking other sources. Finally, Lademann's only original information, that the two translations from 1952 and 1958 are respectively in prose and verse, is characteristically incomplete, as neither of the translators are mentioned by name.

Two other Chaucer representations from the 1980s are fortunately of a completely different calibre. Two pages on Chaucer are included in F.J. Billeskov Jansen's *Verdenslitteratur* [World Literature] from 1982 (Billeskov Jansen 1982: 117-19). Billeskov Jansen (1907-2002) was a professor of Danish at the University of Copenhagen with a very broad field of competence in world literature (Hertel 1995/2011). His Chaucer portrait is very stimulating, and he uses a couple of lines from Bergsøe's Wife of Bath translation to illustrate Chaucer's humour. However, he also has a keen eye for the versatility of *The Canterbury Tales* and the diversity of storytellers and genres. Billeskov Jansen has very clearly read and enjoyed Chaucer himself, and his enthusiasm is shared with his readers. Sensibly most of his text is focused on work rather than life. The only regret is that no other works by Chaucer are discussed.

Gyldendal's *Verdenslitteraturhistorie* was published in 7 volumes between 1985 and 1993, edited by Hans Hertel and written by a team of Scandinavian literary scholars. This is an important and substantial contribution to world literary history in Denmark, and the second volume from 1985 includes a 4-page section written by the Swedish literary historian Lars Lönnroth (born 1935) as the main author and entitled "Chaucer – den høviske epiks fornyer" [Chaucer – the reviver of courtly poetry] (Lönnroth in Hertel, Hans, gen. ed., 1985: 318-22). Besides the Chaucer portrait from 1412 in a manuscript of Hoccleve's *De Regimine Principum*, the illustration of pilgrims from the also 15th century *Les Heures de la*

Duchesse de Bourgogne and the 1498 London woodcut of pilgrims, there is the less expected illustration of the Chaucer character performed by Pier Paolo Pasolini in his 1972 film of *The Canterbury Tales*. The less said about that film the better, but Lönnroth's text is very informative, and furthermore an extract from Johansen's translation of *The General Prologue* is quoted.

I have found no factual mistakes in Lönnroth's text, but the spelling and naming of poetic titles, such as *Boke of Blaunche the Duchesse*, go against accepted standards in modern medieval scholarship and most of the publishing world, and this title should be *The Book of the Duchess*. Lönnroth gives a concise introduction to Chaucer's life and proceeds to characterize his works briefly, including periods and influences. The most interesting part of this well written piece is a discussion near the end, where Lönnroth enters a discussion about Chaucer's often postulated realism, having talked about how each Canterbury tale fits the position in society of the teller:

> "Både dette fortællertekniske greb og de livlige samtaler mellem pilgrimmene bidrager til at skabe det indtryk af "realisme" man tit har ment er Chaucers største styrke som kunstner. Men spørgsmålet er om dette indtryk ikke er fejlagtigt. Chaucer er ikke realist i moderne forstand, men høvisk middelalderdigter der søger det for den pågældende samfundsklasse idealtypiske hvad angår gestus og attributter, for det meste for at opnå en ironisk kontrast til de høviske idealer… Han forbliver listigt skjult bag sine mange masker." [Both this narrative measure and the lively conversations between the pilgrims contribute to creating the impression of "realism" often said to be Chaucer's greatest strength as an author. However, it is a question whether this impression is not wrong. Chaucer is not a realist in the modern sense, but a courtly medieval poet in search for the typical gestures and attributes in each social estate, mostly in order to obtain an ironic contrast to the courtly ideals… He remains cunningly hidden behind his many masks] (Lönnroth 1985: 322)

This is certainly a statement that may be discussed, and the issue it raises of narrative technique and realism in *The Canterbury Tales* is in fact one of the most important discussions in modern Chaucer studies. I would agree that Chaucer wears many masks, but I am hesitant in reading too much irony into the tale-teller relations, although Lønnroth's point about realism is well taken (cp. Klitgård 2011).

Klitgård and Johansen

My article "Chaucer: Den engelske litteraturs far" [Chaucer: The Father of English Literature] appeared in *Humaniora* in 1995 (Klitgård 1995: 7-10). This is a magazine published by the Danish Research Council for the Humanities, and I was allowed to include a full page colour illustration reprinting the 15th century illumination of Chaucer performing for the court by permission of Corpus Christi College, Cambridge, where it is kept. Also the National Gallery Chaucer portrait of Chaucer is reprinted in black and white, and here the accompanying picture text includes an embarrassing misspelling of the poet's name as "Chauser". I will use this occasion to emphasize that I was not guilty of that, but otherwise refrain from commenting on my own Chaucer portrait and introduction.

In the following year, 1996, Børge Johansen ended his impressive life-long effort in the service of Chaucer and the Late Middle Ages by publishing *Kvinder, kirke, kættere: Mod middelalderens slutning* [Women, church, heretics: Towards the end of the Middle Ages]. Johansen shares his broad reading in medieval history and culture with his readers with a focus on the key words of his title. There are ten pages on Chaucer under the heading "En venlig samfundsrevser" [A kind castigator of society], and Johansen quite naturally cites several passages from his own *Canterbury Tales* translation, mainly *The General Prologue*. He adds summaries and commentary to his quotations and produces inviting introductions to four pilgrims and their tales: The Wife of Bath, The Pardoner, The Summoner and The Friar. Besides there is also a brief account of *The Clerk's Tale*, whose representation of women Johansen strongly disapproves of, and he believes he shares that opinion with Chaucer (Johansen 1996: 58). The emphasis is on Chaucer's humour, and Johansen interestingly calls Chaucer "den første humorist i ordets moderne betydning" [the first humorist in the modern sense of the word] (56), an estimate that I would tend to share.

One of the most humourous episodes in Chaucer's catalogue of funny stories is *The Summoner's Prologue* where The Summoner ridicules the Friar by telling the story of how friars' actual habitat in Hell is up the arse of the devil himself (Benson, gen. ed., III 1665-1708). This grotesque episode is rendered with great pleasure by Johansen, who apparently in the 1990s has become a little less careful about what he can write than we saw in his 1958 translation, and certainly compared to Vilhelm Møller's translation from 1901 (chapter 6). Still, Johansen ends his section on Chaucer by warning his reader that part of *The Summoner's Tale* is "så plat, at kun Chaucers mesterlige fortællekunst gør den acceptabel" [so coarse that only Chaucer's masterful narrative art makes it acceptable]. By this remark, his last in writing about Chaucer, he combines an appreciation of Chaucer's art with an invitation to his Danish readers to go and read for themselves. At least that is what I think many readers will do when told that there is a dirty story awaiting them.

Kaaber's dramatic adaptation Chaucers Canterbury-Fortællinger

In 1999 the Danish Shakespeare scholar, teacher and theatre director Lars Kaaber produced his own adaptation of *The Canterbury Tales* for performance at the old monastery Esrum Kloster, which is often used for exhibitions and public lectures. The play was also performed at the University of Copenhagen. A copy of the unpublished manuscript has kindly been given to me by the author, but since it is unpublished I will treat it only briefly here (Kaaber 1999). The play was performed by only three actors, and as a consequence involves a substantial transformation of Chaucer's text. Most strikingly *The Pardoner's Tale* has only two young rioters who meet an old woman rather than an old man. The main focus is understandably on drama and action, but the author has taken care to reproduce the tales in poetic form, and he is generally successful in doing so. Besides an opening giving the framework of the tale-telling contest, the audience is invited to choose the sequence of the tales, although not the grand finale, which consists of a highly condensed, yet brilliant piece of low comedy based on *The Miller's Tale*. The other tales included are *The Clerk's Tale, The Wife of Bath's Tale, The Nun's Priest's Tale* and very surprisingly also the rarely preferred *The Cook's Tale*.

Two further encyclopedia entries

The Chaucer entry in *Den Store Danske Encyclopædi* is substantial, with two full columns including a reproduction of the Chaucer miniature from Hoccleve's *De Regimine Principium* from 1411-12 (Børch in Lund, gen. ed, 1996: 144-5). As most often in articles from this brilliant encyclopedia, which I have already quoted so extensively in this study, we find the Chaucer article written by a leading expert in Denmark, Marianne Børch. Børch, who is the author of several scholarly publications on Chaucer (including Børch 1993a), writes well and engaging about the great poet. Needless to say the factual side of the portrait is impeccable, but moreover we get sound judgement based on thorough personal reading and research. I will just single out two interesting general observations, which deserve a translation into English: "Hele forfatterskabet kan ses som en søgen efter et personligt udtryk via en dialog mellem digteren og en tradition, han omfatter med lige dele skepsis og beundring" [The whole production can be viewed as a search for a personal expression through a dialogue between the poet and a tradition that he looks at with an equal portion of skepticism and admiration]. And secondly: "Chaucer fik afgørende indflydelse på engelsk sprog og litteratur. Gennem sammenføring af flere traditioner har han beriget den engelske ordskat; han eksperimenterede utrætteligt med litterære genrer, ligesom han udviklede og tillempede versemål, der senere slog rod i engelsk poesi." [Chaucer had a decisive influence on English language and literature. By bringing together several traditions, he has enriched the English treasure of words; he experimented indefatigably with literary genres, just as he developed and adapted verse forms that later became rooted in English poetry. (Børch in Lund, gen. ed, 1996: 144). I am happy to observe that such highly qualified statements about Chaucer are now the typical first reference point for Danes having been made curious about Chaucer or simply browsing the encyclopedia pages, which are now also web-based. I have nothing bad to say about the portrait at all, except perhaps that at least Johansen's translation should have been mentioned besides Boisen's.

The Chaucer article in *Forfatterleksikon: Udenlandske forfattere* [Author encyclopedia: Authors from abroad] from 1999 was written by Rigmor Bækholm, who writes well, although her conditions spelled out by the editor's policies were very different from Børch's (Bækholm in Michelsen, ed., 1999: I, 135). This is said without any regret, but as we have seen many times in this study, translators as well as encyclopedia writers often have to obey certain formats as well as other demands. In this case I myself provided the literary references of this article, but joined the project as an author of articles so late that Chaucer had already been dealt with. Bækholm covers life and works well, although the article is less than half the size of Børch's. She talks about Chaucer's "virtuose og træfsikre sprog" [linguistic virtuosity and accuracy] and briefly characterizes all Chaucer's main works with due respect. One mistake has found its way into the portrait, as it says that the Wife of Bath tells about her husband. A plural form is strongly needed, but let us assume that this is an unfortunate typo.

Mittet and Børch

Sidsel Sander Mittet (born 1986), a student of Danish, has used a webpage, *Litteratursiden* [the literature page] to give a presentation of Chaucer, which was last updated in September 2009 (Mittet 2009/2011). She has made a commendable effort and presents both Chaucer and his work with enthusiasm, while also giving advice to fellow students about where to start (and I thank her for referring to my *Humaniora* article mentioned above, Klitgård 1995), and where to proceed. This is a fairly thorough presentation, but there are a few mistakes, e.g. in spelling, and there are inaccuracies, such as guesses about Chaucer's life of the kind we have seen frequently in this study. Whereas it is certainly a good thing that students can find advice on Chaucer studies in Denmark on the internet, the article is also an example of the many web-pages that have not been edited by professional scholars.

One professional Chaucer scholar in Denmark whose work I have already discussed, Marianne Børch, published a web-based research article in Danish in 2010, which discusses the relationship between picture and text in two Chaucer portraits, the 1412 portrait mentioned above and Speed's Chaucer portrait from 1598 (Børch 2010). This is mainly a discussion and presentation of previous work by Salter and Pearsall, who presented it in a paper given at Odense University, published in 1980 (Pearsall 1980). There is also a brief discussion of Martha Driver's 2002 article on Speed's portrait (Driver 2002). Børch's main contribution is actually presented in what she refers to as a final footnote. Here she points out that nobody seems to have noticed how Chaucer's index finger in the 1412 portrait "ikke blot vender væk fra manden selv, men også peger direkte mod den sandhed, Hoccleves digt fremhæver: at Chaucer *var* noget særligt! Den mulighed er der" [not only points away from the man himself, but also points directly at the truth, Hoccleve's poem stresses: that Chaucer *was* someone special! That possibility is there] (Børch 2010, last of unnumbered article pages). I would add that this is a very plausible interpretation, and that Børch has made a precise observation.

Wikipedia Chaucer

Probably the most frequently used information on Chaucer in Denmark today is the Wikipedia entry (Anonymous at http://da.wikipedia.org/wiki/Geoffrey_Chaucer). However, this 5-6 pages long document is of limited interest, first because it appears to be a more or less direct translation of the corresponding English Wikipedia entry (Anonymous at http://en.wikipedia.org/wiki/Geoffrey_Chaucer), secondly because all contributors are anonymous, and the principle of open editing makes it hard to criticise an editorial line. The text is not full of mistakes, and there is an impressive amount of factual information about Chaucer's life and works, but in my estimate the attempt to list bare facts as objectively as possible, so characteristic of Wikipedia, makes the text dry and unappealing. Compared to such eminent encyclopedia entries as Børch's in *Den Store Danske Encyklopædi*, considered above, the Wikipedia text fails to engage its reader and does little to make anyone want to turn to Chaucer himself.

Some odd pieces

Other substantial treatments of Chaucer for the general public than this have not been noticed by the present writer, and since I've checked libraries and catalogues endlessly and am an ardent daily newspaper reader, let me venture the guess that there are none. I shall end this chapter by mentioning a few odd pieces that I have collected over the years and which deserve mention, although these references to Chaucer do not fit into the categories of Chaucer reception discussed so far.

In a long newspaper article by Jens J. Kjærgaard, "Computer på pilgrimsfærd" [computer on pilgrimage] in *Berlingske Tidende* from September 15th 1998 there is an interview with Chaucer scholar Peter Robinson about his and his colleague Christopher Howe's computer-based stemmatic analysis of *Canterbury Tales* manuscripts. Chaucer and stemmatic analysis are introduced at length and quite well, except that unfortunately Kjærgaard cites the Wife of Bath from *Grimbergs Verdenshistorie*, which as I demonstrated in chapter 9 is one of the most unreliable sources. However, Kjærgaard is lucky that the translated *Grimberg* quotation he uses is actually correctly cited from Bergsøe's translation. The article's focus on stemmatic analysis is clearly the main interest of Kjærgaard, and with the help of Peter Robinson the article becomes very informative about this technique. I would have liked Norman Blake's name mentioned in this connection, as he was one of the leading figures in Robinson and Howe's project before retirement, but his name seems to have slipped away.[81]

Student of literature Martin Laurberg published a two-page article on the webpage *Litteratursiden* in 2002 (Laurberg 2002/2009), which is far less substantial than Mittet's, but still introduces Chaucer alongside Andreas Cappelanus, Chrétien de Troyes, Dante, Boccaccio, Julian of Norwich and Margery Kempe. Also here there are several inaccuracies and mistakes, and the paragraph on Chaucer very strangely has an account of his life until 1367, before jumping to a brief mention of *The Canterbury Tales*. No sources are given.

---

81 I visited Blake and his graduate students at the University of Sheffield in 1997 and was introduced to *The Canterbury Tales Project*. Later I also reviewed a collection of articles based on the project for *English Studies* (Klitgård 1999).

In July 2007 journalist Ib Skovgaard reported from the Tour of France, which that year included a stage from London to Canterbury. Skovgaard has a single reference to Chaucer: "Chaucer spøgte for en stund med i kulissen som sufflør til dagens Canterbury-fortællinger på hjul." [For a while Chaucer acted behind the stage as prompter for this day's Canterbury tales on wheels]. I am sure Skovgaard was not the only journalist to get the idea of this Chaucer reference in connection with a cycling race through Chaucer's route, but I am still a little bit impressed. At least the reference is cleverer than the invariably repeated sports metaphor in the British press about Peter Schmeichel being "a great Dane".

Chapter conclusion

The odd pieces treated at the end of this chapter are signs of Chaucer still popping up in Danish reception from time to time, even though he is a rare guest. In one of the most recent English literary histories for secondary schools in Denmark he is mentioned briefly (Barkholt and Jepsen 2010: 8), but this chapter has also been the story of a development where one can no longer be sure that Chaucer at least gets to be mentioned in the right places. Since the two full translations in the 1950s, there have only been occasional new bits of translation, and excepting a few quite brilliant efforts mentioned in the course of this chapter, the Danish reception of Chaucer has been full of copyists who have not read Chaucer themselves. In the general conclusion I shall outline the Danish history of Chaucer translation and reception on the basis of my findings, and I will also discuss further perspectives for the future. Here let me conclude on a less optimistic note and regret that the development since 1960 in Denmark has not been much in the direction of knowledge about Chaucer.

GENERAL CONCLUSION

The story of Chaucer in Denmark from 1782 to the present day has now been told, and it is time to sum up the main findings and consider further perspectives in relation to the wider context of English in Denmark in the same period.

Until Westergaard's booklet *Engelske digtere: Chaucer* from 1853 Chaucer reception in Denmark is characterized by almost complete ignorance of him in a language culture that kept up a distance to English generally, although many English works were in fact translated. Both Wessel's *Feen Ursel* and Bruun's *Slagelse-Madamen* were found to be text transformations that depended on already adapted texts, going back to the very free translations by the neo-classicist Chaucer imitators and adaptors Dryden and Pope. Wessel's dramatic text was demonstrated to be so far removed from *The Wife of Bath's Tale* that Chaucer had almost disappeared, although *Feen Ursel* is not a bad play. My analysis of Bruun's text focused on his inspiration from Pope and his very creative reworking of *The Wife of Bath's Prologue*, including added passages and a clear domestication strategy involving transposition in time and place. The result is a humorous and in many ways brilliant poem that will have entertained contemporary readers. However, Chaucer's controversial discussion of theology seen from the point of view of an erotically very active middle-aged woman has been heavily edited and partly lost, and in the light of Bruun's personal experience with censorship, this is not a surprise.

Westergaard's Chaucer publication was presented as the first genuine effort to introduce Chaucer to a Danish audience. I portrayed Westergaard as a pioneer in English studies in Denmark in a strongly nationalist period. Her Chaucer booklet, which was discussed in the context of her other publications, was shown to be a personal mixture of editing, translation, summary and commentary, one highlight being her engaged representation of *The Clerk's Tale*. In my analysis I found numerous errors and I made it clear that Westergaard was not a scholar, but rather an engaged educator, who should be praised for her effort. Since the series in which the booklet of Chaucer was supposed to have appeared was abandoned after the first issue, it must, however, be concluded that her effort had a limited effect, as also witnessed by the lack of reference to her work in later Danish publications on Chaucer.

The recognition of Chaucer in Danish scholarship was begun in 1893 when Otto Jespersen published his short book on Chaucer. Theodor Bierfreund published a thesis as well as a book including studies of Chaucer in respectively 1891 and 1892, but these were discussed as serious misrepresentations of his work by an incompetent reader. Jespersen was the first Dane to make use of the results from the great German philological tradition, and he contributed with many original observations on Chaucer himself. This study has established that Jespersen was far more important than his modesty allowed him to think also in Chaucer studies, although it is still true to say that his pupil Aage Brusendorff is the single most influential Dane in the history of modern Chaucer scholarship. I have tried to demonstrate that Brusendorff not only built a bridge between German and English Chaucer scholarship, he also firmly established a Chaucer canon that still stands.

In this study Jespersen has been seen as the most important figure behind the development of English in the Danish educational system, especially with the *gymnasium* reform of 1903. His role in promoting the English language, literature and culture in Denmark can be measured against his specific role in promoting Chaucer, which is also exemplary. His many collaborators in the good cause included Niels Møller, who started translating Chaucer in the 1880s and wrote an important piece about him in his literary history from 1928. Also Uffe Birkedal, in 1911 the first translator of *The General Prologue*, acknowledged Jespersen's help, although his unfortunate love of obsolete archaisms cannot be blamed on Jespersen. Birkedal was still a very competent translator, and his two publications from the works of *Gotfred* Chaucer were in use for many years.

Also Vilhelm Møller was found to be a competent translator in his translation of half of *The Summoner's Tale*, but his apparently necessary decision to leave out the prolonged climax of that tale contributes to making his introduction to *The Canterbury Tales* a bizarre one. It is no less bizarre to write in all seriousness that Chaucer composed the tales after having been on an actual pilgrimage with the people Chaucer readers have learned to love as fictive characters. These two points alone give Møller's chapter in his *Verdenslitteraturens Perler* a unique position in the history of Danish Chaucer translation and reception. His other somewhat dubious practices, such as providing a very personal summary with textual borrowings from *The General Prologue*, are not as unique, but can in fact be compared with the practice of both Westergaard and Thunbo.

Margrethe Thunbo's Chaucer summaries for children and young readers from 1929 were compared to Westergaard's booklet for the same age group, and her representation of *The Clerk's Tale* was found to be less engaging, although she generally communicates well with young readers. The same can be said about Cecil Bødker, who has an even younger age group as her target in the 1968 translation of Cooney's version of *The Nun's Priest's Tale*. The only partly questionable attempt of transforming Chaucer for children was found to be Aage Nørfelt's use of an otherwise impeccable summary of *The Pardoner's Tale* in 1965, probably first written by Jespersen. Nørfelt was criticized for using the tale in a didactic religious context that involved unnecessary explications of Chaucer.

The 1940s and 1950s were clearly the two decades where the paradigm shift towards an anglophile culture in Denmark also involved a host of Chaucer translations. One of the best translations of Chaucer into Danish, Flemming Bergsøe's *Konen fra Bath* from 1943, was unfortunately the only translation he made, whereas Lis Thorbjørnsen and in particular Jørgen Sonne, who also made their debut in the 1940s, undertook several prose translations of various Canterbury tales. The 1940s translators were discussed as paving the way for the full *Canterbury Tales* translations from the 1950s, Mogens Boisen's prose translation and Børge Johansen's poetic translation. In chapters 8 and 9 I thus had a chance to offer extensive translation critique and compare revisions, translations and commentary, also involving English translations. The results of these analyses include a number of details that are difficult to render in a general conclusion, but on the other hand there are certain repeated patterns. First of all the prose translations by Thorbjørnsen, Sonne and Boisen tend to turn Chaucer's poetic tales into short stories, and there is a general tendency to foreground plot and omit narrative reflections or subplots found in Chaucer's texts. Abbreviations are not very often noted by translators and editors, and many translators have also in other ways shown insufficient respect for Chaucer's subtleties. The clearest case of this is Boisen, who displays his ignorance of medieval poetry in a preface before embarking on his plagiarized translation of Lumiansky's American prose version of the *Tales*. Although I also show how Boisen often demonstrates his great talent for translation, taking care with accuracy in many passages, my conclusion must be that he has transgressed all acceptable translation ethics. Let me stress again here that Johansen remains the most important figure in Danish Chaucer translation, deserving praise also for his several historical studies of Chaucer and the Late Middle Ages. The one translation that stands out as masterly is his version of *Sir Thopas*, which makes impressive use of a particularly Danish tradition for occasional verse. By comparison with Sonne's misconceived *Topas* from 2007, Johansen's *Herr Thopas* is so much better that it can be used as a model for literary translators. However, as I have also demonstrated, Johansen's language is often so old-fashioned that many young readers today would have difficulties reading it. Clearly a modern Danish translation of *The Canterbury Tales* would be highly welcomed, as would translations of Chaucer's other works.

The final chapter of this study discussed a great number of short translations and representations of Chaucer. First of all the study of encyclopedia entries, literary histories and similar texts were finished in this chapter, showing a high degree of difference in quality. There is a tradition for copying the work of earlier encyclopedia writers and literary historians, and in many cases this was demonstrated to be either plagiarism or something close to plagiarism. Unfortunately this has also led to mistakes being repeated and perhaps more importantly to the prolongation of certain unsubstantiated myths about Chaucer and his time, such as the image of him as a nature lover in old, merry England. The last chapter, however, also registered quite a few excellent contributions to Chaucer studies and to general knowledge about Chaucer and his time. It may be concluded that it is both possible to find good translations of and good introductions to Chaucer in Denmark, and that compared to the size of the country there is also much Chaucer scholarship. Hopefully this study has guided readers well in selecting the right Danish sources for further reading.

Let me also comment further on the purpose of a study like the present one. My idea has not simply been to review the Danish sources available, but to provide a connected analysis of translation and reception that will serve as an exemplary indication of how English in Denmark has developed since the late 18th century. I have in other words wanted to tell the particular story of how the most important medieval English poet has been translated, presented, analysed and discussed in one European country in the period from the Enlightenment to the present day. Although I have of course had to be selective especially as regards choosing passages for analysis and discussion in my sources, my approach is also characterized by an effort to include everything published for a Danish readership. This means that as opposed to many similar reception studies I have not been satisfied with what can be located in searches for my author in library catalogues. Moreover, I have found it important to work as carefully with the source text, Chaucer, as with the representations of him. At the beginning of this project this led to many frustrations, as I realized how poorly Chaucer had often been treated, but I soon decided that a long complaint in academic prose would miss the whole point of translation and reception, which is that the communication always takes place in a particular context which affects the outcome. One of the important lessons that I, and I hope the reader of this study, have learned in the process is that translators, encyclopedia and literary history writers, scholars and others work under conditions that are rarely ideal, and as we have also seen, classics translations and transmission of knowledge about a classic author are very demanding. As I have suggested earlier in this study, classics translators need help from not only editors, but also scholarly consultants, and literary historians and others writing for a general audience need to be carefully selected, and they need competent readers before publication. The most successful attempt to do that in Denmark so far is *Den Store Danske Encyklopædi*, but of course even that has not avoided some criticism.

I conclude this study by arguing that I have moved the discipline of translation and reception studies further by insisting on comprehensive inclusion of all substantial sources and exhaustive analysis of translations and representations, including comparative analysis across cultural and historical space. Cultural and historical context has been shown to be multifaceted and diverse, but the main contextual framework has been gathered under the headline English in Denmark. The dedication to always discussing text in context and the refusal to stop before every stone has been turned has enabled me to throw light on a subject not investigated before, Chaucer in Denmark, in the context of a field that has now become one further study richer, English in Denmark. The research within the framework of English in Denmark has included several habilitation theses and other substantial studies so far, as I established in my introduction and by continuous references to such studies in the opening sections of each chapter. My own contribution includes historical, cultural, educational and linguistic perspectives within this very diverse field of English in Denmark, but first of all my study has been a literary one, with an emphasis on literary translation and reception. Moreover it is the first study of translation and reception of a medieval writer in Denmark and by focusing on this exemplary case study I demonstrate that cultural transmission is historically bound by the changing cultural ties between the English-speaking world and Denmark. In other words my case study exemplifies the reception history of Anglophone culture in Denmark, reflecting the developments from 1782 to the present day. The main result of this study is thus the use of the story of Chaucer in Denmark as an illustrative and very complicated story of cultural change in Denmark.

BIBLIOGRAPHY

Ackroyd, Peter, transl. and adapted, *A Retelling of Geoffrey Chaucer's The Canterbury Tales*. London: Penguin, 2009.
Alexander, Michael, "Old English Poetry into Modern English Verse" in *Translation and Literature*, vol. 3, 1994, 70.
Alkjær, Niels, "Chaucer" in Raunkjær, Palle, ed., *Raunkjærs Konversationsleksikon*, vol. II. København: Det Danske forlag, 1948, 1031-2.
Allen, Valerie, *On Farting: Language and Laughter in the Middle Ages*. New York and Houndsmills, Basingstoke, Hampshire: Palgrave Macmillan, 2007.
Andersen, Jens Kr., "An Analysis of the Framework Structure of Chaucer's *Canterbury Tales*" in *Orbis Litterarum*, 27, 1972, 179-201.
Andersen, Victor, "Bergsøe, Svend" in Lund, Jørn, gen. ed., *Den Store Danske Encyklopædi*, vol. 2, 513. Copenhagen: Gyldendal, 1995.
Anderssen, Otto, "Chaucer" in Rørdam, E., ed., *Illustreret Konversationsleksikon*. Copenhagen: Hagerups Forlag, vol. 2, 1908, 344-5.
Anonymous, "Geoffrey Chaucer" at http://da.wikipedia.org/wiki/Geoffrey_Chaucer, accessed July 2012.
Anonymous, "Geoffrey Chaucer" at http://en.wikipedia.org/wiki/Geoffrey_Chaucer, accessed July 2012.
Anonymous, "Grimberg", http://da.wikipedia.org/wiki/Carl_Grimberg, accessed July 2011.
Anonymous entry in *Dansk Biografisk Leksikon*, "Aage Nørfelt" at http://www.denstoredanske.dk/Dansk_Biografisk_Leksikon/Uddannelse_og_undervisning/Skoledirekt%C3%B8r/Aage_N%C3%B8rfelt, accessed November 2011.
Anonymous entry from *Det alsiske dialektselskab*, "Martin N. Hansen" at http://alsingergildet.dk/martin-n-hansen, accessed November 2011.
Anonymous, http://en.wikipedia.org/wiki/Johannes_Scherr, accessed July 2012.
Anonymous, "Thorbjørnsen, Lis" at http://www.litteraturpriser.dk/aut/tl.htm#TLisThorbjoernsen, accessed May 2011.

Anonymous, "Bredsdorff, Kaj" at http://www.rostra.dk/fss/laerere/Bredsdorff-Kaj.html, copied from *Dansk Skole-Stat*, 1933-34. *Frederiksborg Statsskoles årsskrift* 1947-48, 1970-71, accessed November 2011.

Bacher, Peter, Clemmensen, Niels, Jacobsen, Kim Mørch & Wandall, Jakob, *Danskerne og fremmedsprog*. Copenhagen: Udviklingscenteret for folkeoplysning og voksenundervisning, 1992.

Balling, Morten, "Hypotekbank og Finansforvaltning, Kongeriget Danmarks" in Lund, Jørn, gen. ed., *Den store danske encyclopædi*, http://www.denstoredanske.dk, Copenhagen: Gyldendal, accessed June 2011.

Barkholt, Gitte Vest & Jepsen, Jørgen Døssing, *A Short History of Literature in English*. Aarhus: Systime, 2010.

Bassnett, Susan, *Translation Studies*. London and New York: Routledge, 1980, 2nd ed. 1988.

Bassnett, Susan, *Reflections on Translation*. Bristol, Buffalo and Toronto: Multilingual Matters, 2011.

Bayer, Gerd, and Klitgård, Ebbe, eds., *Narrative Developments from Chaucer to Defoe*. New York and London: Routledge, 2011.

Benson, Larry D., gen. ed., *The Riverside Chaucer*. Boston: Houghton Mifflin, 1987, 2nd edition 2008.

Bentzen, Sonja Bjørn, reading Boisen, Mogens, transl., *Geoffrey Chaucer: Canterburyfortællingerne*. 10 cassettes. Odense: Den grimme ælling, 1985.

Bergsøe, Flemming, "Chaucer bør oversættes" in *Aarstiderne*, No. 1, 1941, 12-16.

–, transl., Møller, Kai Friis, preface, Christensen, Poul, illustrations, *Geoffrey Chaucer, Konen fra Bath*. Copenhagen: Thaning & Appel, 1943, 7th imprint 1967.

–, *Det underlige år*. Copenhagen, Thaning & Appel, 1945.

Bernhardsen, Christian, "Efterord" in Boisen, Mogens, transl., *Geoffrey Chaucer: Canterburyfortællingerne*. Copenhagen: Martins Forlag, 1952.

Bierfreund, Theodor, *Palemon and Arcite: En literaturhistorisk Undersøgelse som Bidrag til Shakespearekritiken*. Copenhagen: Lehman & Stages Forlag, 1891.

–, *Kulturbærere*. Copenhagen: Andr. Fred. Høst & Søns Forlag, 1892.

Billeskov Jansen, F.J., Stangerup, Hakon and Traustedt, P.H., eds., "England: Langland, Wyclif og Chaucer" in *Verdenslitteraturhistorie*, vol. 2, "Middelalderen." Copenhagen: Politikens Forlag, 1971.

–, "Den sene middelalder," [Chaucer], in *Verdenslitteratur*. Copenhagen: Politikens Forlag, 1982, 117-19.

Birkedal, Uffe, transl., *Prologen til Kanterborg-historierne af Gotfred Chaucer. Studier fra Sprog- og Oldtidsforskning,* no. 83. Copenhagen: Tillge's Boghandel, 1911.
–, transl., *Af Chaucer og Langlands Digtning. Studier fra Sprog- og Oldtidsforskning,* no. 90. Copenhagen: Tillge's Boghandel, 1913.
–, transl., John Milton, *Det tabte paradis.* Copenhagen: Vangsgaards Forlag, 2006 (1905).
Birket Smith, S., *De tre ældste danske Skuespil, (Christiern Hansen's Komedier).* Copenhagen, 1874.
Blangstrup, Christian, "Lütken, George F. A.", in Blangstrup, Christian, ed., *Salmonsens Konversationsleksikon,* 2nd ed., vol. 16, Copenhagen: Schultz, 1924, 202.
Boisen, Mogens, transl., Balfour, Ludmilla, illustrations, Bernhardsen, Christian, afterword, *Geoffrey Chaucer: Canterburyfortællingerne.* Copenhagen: Martins Forlag, 1952.
–, *Referat af et flerstrenget liv.* Rødovre: Rolv Forlag, 1985.
Bostrup, Ole, "Bergsøe, Paul" in Lund, Jørn, gen. ed., *Den Store Danske Encyklopædi,* vol. 2, 513. Copenhagen: Gyldendal, 1995.
Bowden, Betsy, *The Wife of Bath in Afterlife 1660-1810.* Forthcoming.
Brandes, Georg, *Hovedstrømninger i det 19de Aarhundredes Litteratur,* 2nd edition. Copenhagen: Gyldendalske Boghandel, Nordisk Forlag 1872-1890.
–, *Main currents in nineteenth century literature.* London: William Heinemann 1901-1905, 6 volumes.
–, *Samlede skrifter. Danmark.* Copenhagen: Gyldendalske Boghandel, Nordisk Forlag, 3 volumes, 1919.
Bredal, Bjørn, *Forandring fryder: En bog om år 1900.* Copenhagen: Gyldendal, 1999.
Bredsdorff, Kaj, *From Beowulf to Kipling: A Survey of English Literature.* Copenhagen: H. Hagerup, 1943, 2nd ed. 1948, 3rd ed. 1956.
–, "Chaucer, Geoffrey" in Engelstoft, Povl, ed., *Hagerups Illustrerede Konversations Leksikon,* 4th ed., vol. 2, 392-3. Copenhagen, H. Hagerup, 1948.
Bredsdorff, Thomas, "Wessel, Johan Herman" in Lund, Jørn, ed., *Den Store Danske Encyklopædi.* Copenhagen: Gyldendal, 2001, vol. 20, 327.
Brink, Bernhard Ten, *Geschichte der englischen Literatur.* Strassburg: Karl J. Trübner, 1893.
Bruun, T.C., *Rimerier.* Copenhagen, 1788.
–, *Engelsk accentueret Læsebog.* Copenhagen: Frid. Brummers Forlag, 1802.
–, *Poetisk læsebog eller Samling af Fortrinlige Engelske Digte.* Copenhagen: A. & S. Soldin, 1804.

–, *Thomas Christopher Bruuns udvalgte Digte, samlede ved forfatteren.* København: Frid. Brummers Forlag, 1816-1927. Six volumes.

–, transl., *Slagelse-Madamen; efter Popes, Konen i Bath.* Copenhagen: P.E. Martin, 1823.

Brusendorff, Aage, *The Chaucer Tradition.* London and Copenhagen: Humphrey Milford & Oxford UP; V. Pio & Branner, 1925.

–, Untitled notes from 1928? and unknown year in Jespersen, Otto, et al., *Breve til og fra prof. Otto Jespersen, div. tryksager m.v., samt nogle optegnelser af Aage Brusendorff.* Unpublished letters and notes 1908-1943. The Royal Library of Copenhagen.

Budtz-Jørgensen, Inger, Rode, Mikal, and Thomassen, Ellen, eds., *Hirschsprungs Konversationsleksikon* 1962, vol. 1: 748.

Bull, Francis, transl. Hornelund, Karl, [Chaucer] in *Verdenslitteraturens historie.* Copenhagen: Gyldendals uglebøger, 1963, 75-7.

Butt, John, ed., *The Poems of Alexander Pope.* Frome and London: Butler and Tanner, 1963, repr. 1968.

Bækholm, Rigmor, "Chaucer, Geoffrey" in Michelsen, Knud, ed., *Forfatterleksikon: Udenlandske forfattere.* Copenhagen: Rosinante, 1999, vol. I, 135.

Bødker, Cecil, transl., *Barbara Cooney: Haren og ræven.* Copenhagen: Illustrationsforlaget, 1968.

Børch, Marianne Novrup, *Chaucer's Poetics: Seeing and Asking, I-II.* Bagsværd: Home publishing, 1993a.

–, *Chaucers poetik.* Odense: Odense Universitet, 1993b.

–, "Chaucer, Geoffrey" in Lund, Jørn, gen. ed, *Den Store Danske Encyclopædi*, vol. 4. Copenhagen: Gyldendal, 1996, 144-5.

–, "Historiografiske læsninger af et portræt: Forholdet mellem billede og tekst i portrætteringen af den engelske digter Geoffrey Chaucer." Odense: University of Southern Denmark, http://static.sdu.dk/mediafiles//Files/Om_SDU/Institutter/Ilkm/ILKM_files/InternetSkrift/TeksterInternetskrift/MarianneBorch_001.pdf, *Interstititel, Litteratur, Kultur og Medier,* 2010.

Caws, Mary Ann, and Lockhurst, Nicola, eds., Shaffer, Elinor, series ed., *The Reception of Virginia Woolf in Europe.* London and New York: Continuum, 2002.

Chaucer, Geoffrey, *The Canterbury Tales.* Ware, Hertfordshire: Wordsworth editions, *The Wordsworth Poetry Library*, 1995. [Other editions of Chaucer listed under editors and translators.]

Christiansen, Palle Ove, *De forsvundne: Hedens sidste fortællere.* Copenhagen: Gads forlag, 2011.

Clarke, Charles Cowden, ed., *The Riches of Chaucer: In Which His Impurities Have Been Expunged; His Spelling Modernised; His Rhythm Accentuated and His Obsolete Terms Explained; Also Have Been Added a Few Explanatory Notes and a New Memoir of the Poet.* London: Effingham Wilson, Royal Exchange, 1835.

Clausen, J., "Bierfreund, Theodor" in Chr. Blangstrup, ed., *Salmonsens Konversations Leksikon*, 2nd ed., III, 1915, 207. Also at http://runeberg.org/salmonsen/2/3/0225.html, accessed April 2011.

Coghill, Neville, transl., *Chaucer: The Canterbury Tales*. Harmondsworth: Penguin, 1951, repr. with revisions 1979.

Cooney, Barbara, *Chanticleer and the Fox*. New York: Thomas Y. Cromwell, 1958.

la Cour, Tage, ed., "Mord råber til himlen" in *Spøgelseshistorier fra hele verden*. Copenhagen: Carit Andersen, 1966, 313-15.

Crow, Martin M, and Olson, Clair C., eds., *Chaucer Life-Records*. Oxford: Clarendon Press, 1966.

Cummings, Hubertis M., *The Indebtedness of Chaucer's Works to the Italian Works of Boccaccio*. Cincinatti: University of Cincinatti, 1916.

Dahl, Per, "Drachmann, Holger" in Lund, Jørn, gen. ed., *Den Store Danske Encyklopædi*. Copenhagen: Gyldendal, 1996, vol. 5., 230.

Davidsen-Nielsen, Niels, Hansen, Erik and Jarvad, Pia, eds., *Engelsk eller ikke engelsk: That is the question. Dansk Sprognævns skrifter,* 28. Copenhagen: Gyldendal, 1999.

Disen, Jens, "Niels Alkjær" at http://www.schroeder.dk/slaegt/getperson.php?personID=I843&tree=schroeder, 2007, accessed November 2011.

Downs, Brian W.,"*Anglo-Danish Literary Relations 1867-1900: The Fortunes of English Literature in Denmark*". The Modern Language Review, vol. 43, No. 2, Apr., 1948, *145-174.*

–, *Modern Norwegian Literature, 1860-1918,* Cambridge University Press, 1966.

Drachmann, Holger, *Derovre fra Grænsen: Strejftog over det danske Termopylæ (Als-Dybbøl) i April Maaned 1877.* Copenhagen: Nyt Nordisk Forlag, repr. 1919 (1877).

–, transl., George Gordon Byron, *Don Juan*. Copenhagen, 1880-1902.

Driver, Martha W., "Mapping Chaucer: John Speed and the Later Portraits" in *The Chaucer Review*, vol. 36, 2002, 228-49.

Dryden, John, "Metaphrase, Paraphrase and Imitation." Extracts of "Preface to Ovid's Epistles" (1680) and "Dedication of the Aeneid" (1697) in R. Schulte and J. Biguenet, eds., *Theories of Translation*. Chicago and London: University of Chicago Press, 1992, 17-33.

Due, Otto Steen, transl., *Homers Iliade*. Hjørring: Klassikerforeningen, 1999.

–, transl., *Homers Odyssé*. Hjørring: Klassikerforeningen, 2002.

Elling, Christian, "Bierfreund, Theodor" in *Dansk biografisk leksikon*, 2nd ed., II, 1933: 596-7.
Ellis, Steve, *Chaucer at Large: The Poet in the Modern Imagination*. Minneapolis: University of Minnesota Press, 2000.
Enkvist, Niels Erik, *Chaucer*. Stockholm: Natur och Kultur, 1964.
Everett, Dorothy in *The Year's Work in English Studies*, 1925, VI (1): 83-107.
Fischer-Nielsen, Niels, "Danmarks Jernbaner" in Lund, Jørn, ed., *Den Store Danske Encyklopædi*. Copenhagen: Gyldendal, 1998, vol. 10, 80-2.
Fjord Jensen, Johan, *Turgenjev i dansk åndsliv: Studier i dansk romankunst 1870-1900*. Copenhagen: Gyldendal, 1961.
Foersom, Peter and Wulff, P.F., transl., Shakespeare, *Tragiske Værker* 1-9. Copenhagen, 1807-25.
Foersom, Peter and Lembcke, Edv., transl., Shakespeare, *Dramatiske Værker* 1-18. Copenhagen, 1861-73.
Fonsmark, Henning, ed., Zerlang, Poul, rev., "Chaucer, Geoffrey" in *Verdenslitteraturen før 1914*. Copenhagen: Politikens Forlag, 1979, 26.
Frandsen, Bent, "Forårshilsen til Høng-samfundet 2003, at http://www.hoeng-samfundet.dk/Foraarshilsen_2003_til_hjem.pdf, accessed 7 April 2011.
Gaarder, Jostein, *Sofies Verden*. Oslo: Aschehoug, 1991.
Glenthøj, Rasmus & Rahbek Rasmussen, Jens, eds., *"Det venskabelige bombardement": København 1807 som historisk begivenhed og national myte*. Copenhagen: Museum Tusculanum Press, 2007.
Gottlieb, Henrik, "Phraseology in Flux: Danish Anglicisms beneath the Surface." Forthcoming.
Gress, Elsa, "Geoffrey Chaucer" in *Cavalcade*, no. 1, 1947, 74.
–, *Fuglefri og fremmed*. Copenhagen: Gyldendal, 1972.
Greve, Jacob, and Klitgård Povlsen, Steen, "The Reception of James Joyce in Denmark" in Leernout, Geert, and Van Mierlo, Vim, eds., Shaffer, Elinor, series ed., *The Reception of James Joyce in Europe*. London and New York: Continuum, 2004.
Grimberg, Carl, *Verdenshistorien*. Copenhagen: Politikens Forlag, 1958-196, vol. 7, 1959, 368-76.
Grosen, Vagn, and Knudsen, Mogens, *Engelske fortællere fra Chaucer til Somerset Maugham*. Copenhagen: Carit Andersens Forlag, 1961.
Grundtvig, N.F.S., *Verdenskrønike* in *Udvalgte skrifter*, 2, 165-422. Copenhagen: *Arkiv for dansk litteratur* at http://www.adl.dk, accessed April 2011 (1812).
–, *Bjowulfs Drape, et Gothisk Helte-Digt fra forrige Aar-Tusinde*. Copenhagen: Andreas Seidelin, 1820.

–, *Beowulfes Beorh eller Bjovulfs-Drapen, det old-angelske Heltedigt, paa Grund-Sproget.* Copenhagen, 1961.

Haarder, Andreas, transl., *Sangen om Bjovulf.* Copenhagen: Gad, 1984, reissued 2001.

Haislund, Niels, "Brusendorff, Aage" in *Dansk Biografisk Leksikon,* IV, 1934: 222-3.

Hansen, Adolf, "Geoffrey Chaucer" in Clausen, Julius, ed., *Illustreret Verdenshistorie.* Copenhagen: Gyldendal, 1901. Vol. 3, 28-38.

–, *Engelsk litteraturhistorie med billeder.* 3rd ed., ed. Helweg-Møller, H. Copenhagen: Nordisk Forlag, 1929 (1907).

Hansen, Adolf, transl., *Bjovulf.* Copenhagen and Kristania: Oskar Hansen, 1910.

Hansen, Martin N., "Priorinden" in *Fremmede klange.* Odense: Home publishing (Odense Amts bogtrykkeri), 1963, 9-10.

Hartmann, Sys, et al., eds., *Weilbach dansk kunstnerleksikon.* Copenhagen: Munksgaard, 1994.

Heaney, Seamus, transl., *Beowulf.* London: faber and faber, 1999.

Henryson, Robert, *The Testament of Cresseid.* Ed. Bruce Dickins. Edinburgh: Porpoise Press, 1925.

Hertel, Hans, "Sydstatsromaner", caption in Hertel, Hans, ed., *Verdenslitteraturhistorie.* Copenhagen: Gyldendal, 1992. Vol. 6: 191.

Hertel, Hans, "Billeskov Jansen, F.J." in Lund, Jørn, gen. ed., *Den Store Danske Encyclopædi*, vol.2. Copenhagen: Gyldendal, 1995, 618. Updated at http://www.denstoredanske.dk/Kunst_og_kultur/Litteratur/Dansk_litteratur/Kritikere/Frederik_Julius_Billeskov_Jansen, accessed November 2011.

–, "Armstrong, Churchill… Penguin: the Danish Turn to Anglo-American Cultural Values from the 1920s to the 1950s" in Sevaldsen, Jørgen, ed., with Bjørke, Bo and Bjørn, Claus, *Britain and Denmark: Political, Economic and Cultural Relations in the 19th and 20th Centuries.* Copenhagen: Museum Tusculanum Press, 2003, 431-75.

Hilden, Adda in *Dansk kvindebiografisk leksikon*, at http://www.kvinfo.dk/side/597/bio/1494/origin/170/query/westergaard/. *Kvinfo* webpage, Copenhagen, last edited 2003, accessed January 2011.

Hilden, Adda, og Nørr, Erik, *Lærerindeuddannelse: Lokalsamfundenes kamp om seminariedriften.* Dansk læreruddannelse 1791-1991, bind 3: 40 og 259-60. Odense: Odense Universitetsforlag, 1993.

Hjørnager Pedersen, Viggo, "Chaucer, Geoffrey" and "Canterbury fortællinger" in Harmer, Henning & Jørgensen, Thomas, eds., *Gyldendals litteraturleksikon.* Copenhagen: Gyldendal, 1974, 158 and 150-1.

–, "Drape-lige Beowulf: Om den oldengelske litteraturs hovedværk i dansk gendigtning" in *Engelsk litteratur i Danmark*. Odense: Odense Universitetsforlag, 1986.

–, *Ugly Ducklings: Studies in the English Translations of Hans Christian Andersen's Tales and Stories*. Odense: University Press of Southern Denmark, 2004.

Hjørnager Pedersen, Viggo and Quale, Per, "Danish and Norwegian traditions" in Baker, Mona, ed., *Routledge Encyclopedia of Translation Studies*. London and New York: Routledge, 1998, 384-92.

Hutcheon, Linda, *A Theory of Adaptation*. London and New York: Routledge, 2006.

Idle, Eric et al., "Nudge, Nudge" in episode three of *Monty Python's Flying Circus*, broadcast by the BBC in 1969. Published in Wilmut, Roger, ed., *Monty Python's Flying Circus: Just the Words*. London: Methuen, 1989, vol. 1, 40-1.

Iversen, Anders, "På selskabsrejse i middelalderen." *Aarhus Stiftstidende*, 21 August 1969.

Jacobsen, Eric, "C.A. Bodelsen, 18. november 1894 – 24. november 1978" in *Universitets Årbog 1979*. Copenhagen: University of Copenhagen, 1979, 521-25, reprinted in Kabell, Inge and Lauridsen, Hanne, *Den belejrede humanisme*. Copenhagen: Department of English, University of Copenhagen, *Publications on English Themes*, vol. 21, 1995, 128-35.

Jacobsen, Eric, *Mine universiteter – et tilbageblik*. Copenhagen: Museum Tusculanum Press, 1990.

Jernström, Harald, transl., *"Ur Fåglarnas Ting"* Av *Geoffrey Chaucer*. Stockholm: Kungl. Hovboktryckeriet Iduns Tryckeri, 1932.

–, *Chaucer, Geoffrey, Canterburysägner I-II*. Helsingfors: Forumbiblioteket, 1956.

Jensen, Niels, "Bernhardsen, Christian" and "Birkedal, Uffe" at http://www.litteraturpriser.dk/aut/be.htm, accessed November 2011.

Jespersen, Knud J.V., "Verdensudstilling" in Lund, Jørn, gen. ed., *Den Store Danske Encyklopædi*, vol. 20. Copenhagen: Gyldendal, 2001: 105.

Jespersen, Otto, *Chaucers liv og digtning. Studier fra Sprog- og Oldtidsforskning*, no. 12. Copenhagen: Kleins forlag, 1893.

–, "Små randnoter til engelske texter" in *Nordisk Tidsskrift for Filologi*, vol. 3.1, 1893-4.

–, "Zu Chaucers Prolog der Canterbury Tales" in *Englische Studien*, vol. 26, 1899.

–, *The England and American Reader*. Copenhagen: Det Schubotheske Forlag, 1903.

–, "Chaucer" in Blangstrup, Christian, ed., *Salmonsens Konversationsleksikon*, 2nd ed., vol. IV. Copenhagen: Schultz, 1916: 802-4.
–, *Rasmus Rask: i hundredåret efter hans hovedværk*. Copenhagen: Gyldendal, 1918.
–, with Bodelsen, C.A. and Helweg-Møller, H., eds., *A British Reader*. Copenhagen: Gyldendalske Boghandel, 1928, 2nd edition 1931.
–, *En sprogmands levned*. Copenhagen: Gyldendal, 1938. Translated and edited as *Life of a Linguist* by Arne Juul, Hans Frede Nielsen and Jørgen Erik Nielsen. Odense: Odense University Press, 1995.
–, "The Three Drunkards" in Brüel, Svend, ed., Otto Jespersen, *Engelsk 4: Engelske læsestykker, 1. halvdel*. Copenhagen: Gyldendalske Boghandel, Nordisk Forlag, 20th imprint, 1953, 70-3.
Johansen, Børge V., transl., *Geoffrey Chaucer: Canterburyfortællingerne I-II*. Copenhagen: Nyt Nordisk Forlag Arnold Busck, 1958.
–, *Chaucer og hans tid,* Copenhagen: Nyt Nordisk Forlag Arnold Busck, 1965.
–, *Og rask igennem larm og spil: Middelalderens krønikeskrivere fortæller*. Lynge: Bogans forlag, 1987.
–, *Kvinder, kirke, kættere: Mod middelalderens slutning*. Lynge: Bogan, 1996.
Johansen, Heidi B., *Chaucers verber. Deres bøjninger og endelser*. Copenhagen: University of Copenhagen, unpublished MA thesis, 1972
Jones, Terry, *Chaucer's Knight: The Portrait of a Medieval Mercenary*. London: Eyre Methuen, 1980, revised 1994.
Jæger, Frank, transl., *Allan Edwall, Den underskønne Lina eller Konerne derhjemme: Moralitet a la Chaucer*. Danmarks Radio: Hørespilsarkivet, 1971.
Kaaber, Lars, transl., *Chaucers Canterbury-fortællingerne*. Unpublished play performed at Esrom Kloster and at the University of Copenhagen, 1999.
Kaalund, Kr., "Horn, Fr. Winkel" in *Dansk Biografisk Leksikon* at http://www.denstoredanske.dk/Dansk_Biografisk_Leksikon/Historie/Litteraturhistoriker/Fr._Winkel_Horn, accessed July 2012.
Kabell, Inge, *Thomas Cristopher Bruun, 1750-1834: The First Professor of English in Denmark*. Odense: *Prepublications of the English Department of Odense University*, No. 72, 1994.
–, "Et portræt af George Stephens – professor i engelsk ved Københavns Universitet og fremtrædende medlem af den engelske menighed i Danmark i en menneskealder" in *Magasin*, 11, no. 3, 21-42, 1996.
–, "Three University Teachers of Anglo-Saxon Extraction Teaching English Language and Literature at the University of Copenhagen in the Period app. 1850-1940" in (Addendum to) Sanna-Kaisa Tanskanen and Brita Wårvik, eds., *The Proceedings from the 7th Nordic Conference on English Studies*, 429-438. Turku: University of Turku, 1999.

–, "Bomber over København" in *Jyllands-posten*, 21 April 2007.
Kabell, Inge and Lauridsen, Hanne, *Den belejrede humanisme*. Copenhagen: Department of English, University of Copenhagen, Publications on English Themes, vol. 21, 1995.
–, "The Future Postponed: English at the University of Copenhagen during the 2nd World War" in Sevaldsen, Jørgen, ed., with Bjørke, Bo and Bjørn, Claus, *Britain and Denmark: Political, Economic and Cultural Relations in the 19th and 20th Centuries*. Copenhagen: Museum Tusculanum Press, 2003, 477-91.
Kaaring, Liza W., and Kühn-Nielsen, Peter, "Spang Olsen, Ib" in Lund, Jørn, gen. ed., *Den Store Danske Encyclopædi*, vol. 17, 540. Copenhagen: Gyldendal, 2000.
Kinsley, James, ed., *The Poems of John Dryden*, vol. IV. Oxford: At the Clarendon Press, 1958.
Kirchhoff, Hans, Poulsen, Henning and Trommer, Aage, *Den 2. verdenskrig 1939-45*. Copenhagen: Gyldendal, 1989, 3rd ed. 2002.
Kirkegaard, Lars, "Nyborg Gymnasiums Kostskoles historie" at http://www.nyborg-gym.dk/kostweb/da/historie/historie.htm, accessed 7 April 2011.
Kjær, Iver, "*Lucidarius*" in Lund, Jørn, gen. ed., *Den Store Danske Encyclopædi*, vol. 12, 304. Copenhagen: Gyldendal, 1998.
Kjærgaard, Jens J., "Computer på pilgrimsfærd" in *Berlingske Tidende*, 15 September, 1998.
Kissner, Alfons, *Chaucer in seinen Beziehungen zur italienischen Literatur*. Marburg, 1867.
Klassen, Norman, "To Seek to Distant Shrines: A Syntactical Problem in Chaucer's General Prologue 12-16" in *Modern Philology* (forthcoming).
Klitgård, Ebbe, Review of Børch, Marianne Novrup, *Chaucer's Poetics: Seeing and Asking, I-II* in *Angles on the English Speaking World*. Copenhagen: The English Department of the University of Copenhagen, vol. 7, 1993, 103-5.
–, *Chaucer's Narrative Voice in The Knight's Tale*. Copenhagen: Museum Tusculanum Press, 1995.
–, "Chaucer: Den engelske litteraturs far" in *Humaniora*, 3, 1995, 7-10.
–, review of Rand Schmidt, Kari Anne, *The Authorship of The Equatorie of the Planetis*. *English Studies*, Vol. 77, 1996.
–, "Chaucer's Narrative Voice in *The House of Fame*" in *The Chaucer Review*, vol. 32, 1998, 260-6.
–, articles on "Dryden, John", "John Milton", "Pope, Alexander", "William Shakespeare", "H.G.Wells" and "Oscar Wilde" in Michelsen, Knud, ed., *Forfatterleksikon: udenlandske forfattere*, Copenhagen: Rosinante, 1999, 179-80, 448, 591-3, 706-7, 713-4 and 522-3.

–, Review of Blake, Norman & Robinson, Peter, *The Canterbury Tales Project: Occasional Papers II*. *English Studies*.Vol. 80, 1999.

–, Review of Ellis, Steve, *Chaucer at Large: The Poet in the Modern Imagination* in *English Studies* vol. 84:5, 2003: 474-5.

–, "Chaucer i Danmark: reception og oversættelse" in *Danske Afhandlinger om Oversættelse*, 11, Copenhagen: University of Copenhagen, Centre for Translations Studies, 2004: 11-29.

–, "Chaucer Reception and Translation in Denmark" in *The Chaucer Review*, vol. 40, no. 2, 2005: 207-17.

–, "Translation as Transformation: Two Translators of Chaucer in 19th Century Denmark" in *Perspectives: Studies in Translatology*, vol. 16, 2008: 133-141.

–, Review of Allen, Valerie, *On Farting: Language and Laughter in the Middle Ages*. English Studies, vol. 90:3, 2009: 364-5.

–, "The Encoding of Subjectivity in Chaucer's *The Wife of Bath's Tale* and *The Pardoner's Tale*" in Bayer, Gerd & Klitgård, Ebbe, eds., *Narrative Developments from Chaucer to Defoe*. London & New York: Routledge, 2011.

Klitgård, Ida, "Waves of Influence: The Reception of Virginia Woolf in Denmark" in Caws, Mary Ann and Luckhurst, Nicola, eds., Shaffer, Elinor, series ed., *The Reception of Virginia Woolf in Europe*. London and New York: Continuum, 2004.

–, *Fictions of Hybridity: Translating Style in James Joyce's* Ulysses. Odense: University Press of Southern Denmark, 2007.

Koch, John A.H., *Ausgewählte Kleinere Dichtungen Chaucers*. Leipzig: Wilhelm Friedrich 1880, appendix.

–, "Textkritische Bemerkungen zu Chaucers Hous of Fame." *Anglia Beiblatt*, 27, 1916, 139-53.

Kolind, Lars, "Spejderbevægelsen" in Lund, Jørn, gen. ed., *Den Store Danske Encyclopædi*, vol. 17, 2000, 573-4.

Kondrup, Johnny & Kristensen, Niels Peder, "Bergsøe, Jørgen Vilhelm" in Lund, Jørn, gen. ed., *Den Store Danske Encycklopædi*, vol. 2.: 513. Copenhagen: Gyldendal, 1995.

Kristensen, Tom, "Pionéren, Ezra Pound: A.B.C. for læsere og Masker" in *I min tid*. Copenhagen: Gyldendal, 1963, 142-153.

Krogh, Torben, *Zur Geschichte des dänischen Singspiels im 18. Jahrhundert*. Berlin: Walter Hillger, 1923.

Langer, Torben W., gen. ed., *Lademann's Leksikon*, vol. 4. Tønder: Th. Laursen, 1982, 112.

Langlois, Ernest, ed., *Guillaume de Lorris & Jeun de Meun: Le roman de la rose*. Societé des Ancient Textes Francais, 1914-24, 5 vols.

Laugesen, Anker Theilgaard, *Middelalderdigtning. Gyldendals bibliotek*, vol. 6. Copenhagen: Gyldendal, 1967.

Laurberg, Martin, "Om forfattere i den europæiske middelalder" at http://www.litteratursiden.dk/artikler/forfattere-i-den-europaeiske-middelalder-hvad-med-chretien-de-troyes-andreas-cappelanus-ell, published 2002, updated 2009, accessed December 2011.

Lembcke, Edv., transl., Shakespeare, *Dramatiske Værker* 1-9, Copenhagen, 1897-1900 and 1-5, Copenhagen, 1910-1. Later revisions Henning Krabbe.

Lemberg, Kai, "London: Trafikanlæg" in Lund, Jørn, gen. ed., *Den Store Danske Encyklopædi*, vol. 12. Copenhagen: Gyldendal, 1998: 269-70.

Lidegaard, Bo, *Kampen om Danmark 1933-45*. Copenhagen: Gyldendal, 2006.

Lumiansky, R.M., transl., *Chaucer's Canterbury Tales*. New York: Simon and Schuster, 1948.

–, transl., *The Canterbury Tales of Geoffrey Chaucer*. New York: Simon and Schuster, 1948, 2nd ed., New York: Holt, Rinehart and Winston, 1954.

–, transl., *Geoffrey Chaucer's Troilus and Criseyde*. Columbia: University of South Carolina Press, 1952.

–, *Of Sondry Folk: The Dramatic Principle of the Canterbury Tales*. Austin: University of Texas Press, 1955.

Lund, Jørn, gen. ed, *Den Store Danske Encyclopædi*, Copenhagen: Gyldendal, 1995,1997 and 2001. "Bergsøe, Flemming", "Birkedal, Uffe", "Friis Møller, Kai", "Togeby, Knud", unsigned articles in *Den store danske encyclopædi*, vols. 2, 513, vol. 3, 44, vol. 7, 138, vol. 19, 151, and "la Cour, Tage", unsigned article in http://www.denstoredanske.dk, Copenhagen: Gyldendal, accessed August 2011.

Lund, Jørn, "Åreladning og spanske fluer" in *Politiken*, 1 August, 2011a.

–, "Hvad mente lille Karen" in *Politiken*, 24 October, 2011b.

Lönnroth, Lars, "Chaucer – den høviske epiks fornyer" in Hertel, Hans, ed., *Verdenslitteraturhistorie*, vol. 2, "Middelalderen:" Copenhagen: Gyldendal, 1985, 318-21.

Lütken, George, ed., *Allers Illustrerede Konversations Leksikon*. Copenhagen: Carl Allers Etablissement, vol. 1, 1906, 652.

Lyy, Toivo, transl., *Canterburyn tarinoita*. Porvoo: WSOY, 1975.

Lønsmann, Dorte, *English as a Corporate Language: Language choice and language ideologies in an international company in Denmark*. PhD thesis. Roskilde: Roskilde University Printers, 2011.

Mandel, Jerome, *Geoffrey Chaucer: Building the Fragments of* the Canterbury Tales. Cranbury, New Jersey: Associated University Presses, 1992.

Mann, Jill, *Chaucer and Medieval Estates Satire: The Literature of Social Classes and the General Prologue to the Canterbury Tales*. Cambridge: Cambridge University Press, 1973.

Mariager, Rasmus, "Political Ambitions and Economic Realities: Anglo-Danish Relations and the US in the Early Cold War" in Sevaldsen, Jørgen, ed., with Bjørke, Bo and Bjørn, Claus, *Britain and Denmark: Political, Economic and Cultural Relations in the 19th and 20th Centuries*. Copenhagen: Museum Tusculanum Press, 2003, 535-73.

Meyer, Ole, transl., *Dante Alighieri: Den guddommelige komedie*. Valby: LFL's bladfond, 2006.

Michelsen, Knud, ed., *Forfatterleksikon: udenlandske forfattere,* vol. 1-2. Copenhagen: Rosinante, 1999.

Milow, Cecilia, *Canterbury-berättelser efter Geoffrey Chaucer*. Stockholm: P.A. Nordstedt & Söners Förlag, 1900.

Minnis, Alistair, *Fallible Authors: Chaucer's Pardoner and Wife of Bath*. Philadelphia: University of Pennsylvania Press, 2007.

Mittet, Sidsel Sander, "Geoffrey Chaucer". http://www.litteratursiden.dk/analyser/chaucer-geoffrey, 2009, accessed December 2011.

Molbech, Chr. K.F., transl., *Dante Alighieris Guddommelige Komedie*. Copenhagen 1851-62, 5th edition 1908 with an introduction by Valdemar Vedel.

Moltke, L., transl., Charles Dickens, *Samtlige værker*. Copenhagen, 1852-59, rev., 29 vol., 1889-94.

Morrison, Theodore, transl. and ed., *The Portable Chaucer*. New York: Viking Press, 1949.

Mortensen, Peter, "'Forstand og Hjerte,' Or: How Nineteenth-Century Danes Learned to Stop Worrying and Love Jane Austen" in Klitgård, Ida, ed., *Literary Translation: World Literature or 'Worlding Literature'?* Copenhagen: University of Copenhagen, *Angles on the English-Speaking World*, 6, 2006: 53-67.

Moth, Fr., *Prøver af Petrarcas digtning*. Copenhagen 1924.

Munday, Jeremy, *Introducing Translation Studies: Theories and Applications*. London: Routledge, 2001.

Munk, Jens Peter, "Thorvaldsen, Bertel", "Thorvaldsen's medalje" and "Thorvaldsens museum" in Lund, Jørn, gen. ed., *Den Store Danske Encyklopædi*, vol. 19. Copenhagen: Gyldendal, 2001: 67-8.

Mølbjerg, Hans, *Verdenslitteratur*, vol. 2., "Fra middelalderen til det attende århundrede". Copenhagen: J.H. Schultz Forlag, 1967.

Møller, Harald W., and Nielsen, Henning, eds., *Nordisk Konversationsleksikon*, vol. 2. Copenhagen: Kolportage Forlag, 1973, 126.

Møller, Niels, *Efterår: digte*. Copenhagen: P.G. Philipsen's Forlag. Thieles bogtrykkeri, 1888.

-, "O, kvalfuld kvide!" http://www.archive.org/stream/efteraardigteoomlgoog/efteraardigteoomlgoog_djvu.txt, accessed May 2011)

-, *Verdenslitteraturen*. Vol. 2. Copenhagen: Gyldendalske Boghandel, Nordisk Forlag: 1928.

Møller, Paulette, transl., Jostein Gaarder, *Sophie's World*. New York: Berkley Books, 1995.

Møller, Vilhelm, transl. and editor, untitled translation of *The Summoner's Tale* (extracts) in "Chaucers Canterbury-Fortællinger" in *Verdenslitteraturens Perler*. Aarhus: Jydsk Forlags-Forretning, 1901. Vol. 3, 44-55.

Møller Kristensen, Sven, ed., *Fremmede digtere i det 20. århundrede*, 1-3. Copenhagen: Gad, 1967-68.

Nida, Eugene, "Principles of Correspondence" in Venuti, Lawrence, ed., *The Translation Studies Reader*. London and New York: Routledge, 1964/2000, 126-40.

Nielsen, Fr., in Blicka, C.F., ed., *Dansk Biografisk Leksikon*, XII, 1887-1905: 81-2.

Nielsen, Jørgen Erik, *Den samtidige engelske litteratur og Danmark 1800-1840*, I-II. Publications of the Department of English, vol. 4. Copenhagen: University of Copenhagen 1976-1977.

-, "English Literature in Denmark in the First Half of the 19th Century" in Sevaldsen, Jørgen, ed., with Bjørke, Bo and Bjørn, Claus, *Britain and Denmark: Political, Economic and Cultural Relations in the 19th and 20th Centuries*. Copenhagen: Museum Tusculanum Press, 2003: 357-72.

-, *Dickens i Danmark*. Copenhagen: Museum Tusculanum Press, 2009.

Nørfelt, Aage, ed., "De tre svirebrødre" in *Litteraturhæfte til den kristne troslære*. Copenhagen: Gjellerup, 1965, 134-38.

Olrik, Axel, ed., following Grundtvig, Svend, gen. ed., *Danske gamle Folkeviser*, 5th ed. Copenhagen, 1877-90.

Olsen, Per & Schou, Søren, eds., *Denne Sonne*. Copenhagen: Munksgaard/Rosinante, 1995.

Pakkala-Weckström, Mari, "Translating Chaucer's Power Play into Modern English and Finnish" in Fox, Bethany Hall, Alaric, Kiricsi, Agnes and Timofeeva, Olga, eds., *Interfaces between Language and Culture in Medieval England: A Festschrift for Matti Kilpiö*. Leiden: Brill, 2010, 307-327.

Pearsall, Derek, "Pictorial Illustration of Late Medieval Poetic Texts: the Role of the Frontispiece or Prefatory Picture" in Anderson, F.G., Nyholm, E., Powell, M., Stubkjær, F.T., eds., *Medieval Iconography and Narrative. A Symposium*. Odense: Odense University Press, 1980, 100-23.

–, *The Life of Geoffrey Chaucer: A Critical Biography*. Oxford and Cambridge, Massachusetts: Blackwell, 1992.

Politikens Oplysning in *Politiken*, 26 March, 2011, 20.

Poulsen, Ib, *Radiomontagen og dens rødder: Et studie i den danske radiomontage med vægt på dens radiofoniske genreforudsætninger*. Frederiksberg: Samfundslitteratur, 2006.

Prahl, Sophus, transl., Giovanni Boccaccio, *Dekameron 1-3*, Copenhagen: Forhen A. Christiansens Forlag, 1907.

Preisler, Bent, *Danskerne og det engelske sprog*. Frederiksberg: Roskilde Universitetsforlag, 1999a.

–, "Engelsk ovenfra og nedenfra: Sprogforandring og kulturel identitet" in Davidsen-Nielsen, Niels, Hansen, Erik and Jarvad, Pia, eds., *Engelsk eller ikke engelsk: That is the question. Dansk Sprognævns skrifter,* 28. Copenhagen: Gyldendal, 1999b.

Preisler, Ebbe, ill. Albrechtsen, Klaus and music Dal, Hans, *Om lidt er sangen klar*. Knebel: Vistoft, 2011.

Pound, Ezra, *ABC of Reading*. London: faber and faber, 1951.

Rahbek Rasmussen, Jens, *Modernitet eller åndsdannelse: Engelsk i skole og samfund 1800-1935*. Copenhagen: Museum Tusculanum Press, 2006. Also published as free open access.

Rand Schmidt, Kari Anne, *The Authorship of The Equatorie of the Planetis*. Oxford: D.S. Brewer, 1993.

Rasmussen, Ole and Vølver, Gorm, *Elvira – forkortet af red*. Copenhagen: Politiken, 2004.

Reenberg, Jørgen, a reading of Boisen, Mogens, transl., "Skipperens fortælling". Copenhagen: Danmarks Radio, 1979.

Robertson, D.W., Jr., *A Preface to Chaucer*. Princeton: Princeton University Press, 1962.

Robinson, F.N., ed., *The Complete Works of Geoffrey Chaucer*. Oxford: Oxford University Press, 1933, 2nd ed. 1957.

Rodenberg, J., *For Romantik og Historie*, xxi, 1878.

Rubow, Paul, *Dansk litterær Kritik i det nittende Aarhundrede indtil 1870*. Copenhagen: Levin & Munksgaard, 1921.

Rømhild, Lars Peter, "Rubow, Paul V." in Lund, Jørn, gen. ed., *Den Store Danske Encyklopædi*, vol. 16, 350. Copenhagen: Gyldendal, 2000.

Rørdam Larsen, Charlotte, "'Above all it's because he's English…': Tommy Steele and the Notion of 'Englishness' as Mediator of Wild Rock 'n' Roll" in Sevaldsen, Jørgen, ed., with Bjørke, Bo and Bjørn, Claus, *Britain and Denmark: Political, Economic and Cultural Relations in the 19th and 20th Centuries*. Copenhagen: Museum Tusculanum Press, 2003, 493-509.

Said, Edward, *Orientalism*. New York: Vintage, 1978.
Scala, Elisabeth, "Editing Chaucer" in Ellis, Steve, *Chaucer: An Oxford Guide*. Oxford: Oxford University Press, 2005.
Scherr, Johannes, transl. and ed. Horn, Fr. W., *Almindelig Literaturhistorie: En Haandbog*. Copenhagen: Philipsens Forlag, vol. 2, 1876, 13-17.
Shaffer, Elinor, series ed., *The Reception of British and Irish Authors in Europe*. London and New York: Continuum, 2002-.
Scholdager, Anne, with Gottlieb, Henrik and Klitgård, Ida, *Understanding Translation*. Aarhus: Academica, 2008, 2nd ed. 2010.
Scott, Sir Walter, *Ivanhoe*. Croydon: Penguin Popular Classics, 1994 (1819).
Sevaldsen, Jørgen, "Culture and Diplomacy: Anglo-Danish Relations 1945-49" in Sevaldsen, Jørgen, ed., *The Twain Shall Meet*. Copenhagen: Department of English, University of Copenhagen, *Publications on English Themes*, vol. 18, 1992, 9-46.
-, "Trade Fairs and Cultural Promotion c. 1930-1970: Visualising Anglo-Danish Relations" in Sevaldsen, Jørgen, ed., with Bjørke, Bo and Bjørn, Claus, *Britain and Denmark: Political, Economic and Cultural Relations in the 19th and 20th Centuries*. Copenhagen: Museum Tusculanum Press, 2003, 73-108.
Skagen, Kaare, "Otto Anderssen" in *Store Norske Leksikon* at http://snl.no/Otto_Anderssen, accessed November 2011.
Skeat, W.W., ed., *The Complete Works of Geoffrey Chaucer*, vol. 1-6. Oxford: Oxford University Press, 1894-7.
-, *The Chaucer Cannon*. Oxford: Oxford University Press, 1900.
Sonne, Jørgen, transl., Spang Olsen, Ib, ill.,"Geoffrey Chaucer, Forvalterens Fortælling" in *Cavalcade*, no. 4, 1947, 44-51. Revised editions in Knudsen, Mogens and Lundbo, Orla, eds., *Humor fra hele verden*. Copenhagen: Carit Andersens Forlag, 1952, 330-38, 2nd ed. 1967, 299-307. Sound recording by Ask, Jørgen, 1975, published by *Danmarks Blindebibliotek* as web file, 2004 at http://www.e17.dk/bog/DBB0022071, accessed May 2011.
-, "James Joyce, Mrs. Blooms monolog" in *Cavalcade*, no. 2, 1948, 78-80.
-, Spang Olsen, Ib, ill., "James Joyce, Kyklopen" in *Cavalcade*, no. 3, 1948, 37-9.
-, Spang Olsen, Ib, ill., "Geoffrey Chaucer, De sorte klipper" in *Cavalcade*, no. 6, 1948, 10-16.
-, "Geoffrey Chaucer, En ung piges hoved" in *Cavalcade*, no. 2, 1949 a, 46-8.
-, Spang Olsen, Ib, ill., "Geoffrey Chaucer, Den syngende hvide ravn og Føbus" in *Cavalcade*, no. 4, 1949 b, 77-80.
-, Christensen, Erik, woodcuts, *Geoffrey Chaucer: Canterbury Fortællinger*. Copenhagen: L. Ihrich, 1949-1950.

–, transl., Ezra Pound, *ABC for læsere*. Fredensborg: Arena, 1960.

–, *Lyrik*, vol. 40 in Nielsen, Erling, gen. ed., *Gyldendals Bibliotek: Verdenslitteratur*. Copenhagen: Gyldendal, 1967.

–, ed. and transl., *Europæisk lyrik fra 1100tallet til 1700 i England, Frankrig og Italien med biografier og essays*. Copenhagen, C.A. Reitzel, 2007.

Specht, Henrik, *Chaucer's Franklin in the Canterbury Tales: The Social and Literary Background of a Chaucerian Character*. Copenhagen: Akademisk Forlag, *Publications of the Department of English, University of Copenhagen*, 10, 1981.

Stangerup, Hakon, "Chaucer, Geoffrey" in Rosenberg, P.A., Schou, C.A. and Vogel-Jørgensen, T., eds., *Illustreret Dansk Konversationsleksikon*. Copenhagen: Berlingske Forlag, 1934. Revised in Jørgensen, Jørgen Budtz and Møller, Harald W., eds., *Vor Tids Konversationsleksikon*, vol. 2, Copenhagen: Aschehoug Dansk Forlag, 1942, 649-50, 2nd ed. 1950, 44-5.

–, "Jurister der blev forfattere." *Ledelse og Erhvervsøkonomi/Handelsvidenskabeligt Tidsskrift/Erhvervsøkonomisk Tidsskrift*, Vol. 34, 1970: 204-22.

Stein Pedersen, Jes, "Bibliopaten" in *Politiken*, 25 March 2005.

Stephenson Smith, S., *The Craft of the Critic*. New York: Thomas Y. Crowell Company, 1931.

Stigel, Jørgen, "Kampen om teatrets genrer" in *Dansk Litteraturhistorie,* vol. 4, 350-90, eds. Fjord Jensen, Johan, Møller, Morten, Nielsen, Toni, and Stigel, Jørgen. Copenhagen: Gyldendal, 1983.

Sørensen, Knud, *A Dictionary of Anglicisms in Danish*. Det Kongelige Danske Videnskabernes Selskab: *Historisk-filosofiske Skrifter, 18*. Copenhagen: Munksgaard, 1997.

Sørensen, Lene G., *Anvendelsen af konjunktiv i "The Parson's Tale" og "The Tale of Melibee"*. Copenhagen: University of Copenhagen, Unpublished MA thesis, 1975.

Sørensen, Søren, transl., *Petrarca, Francesco: Canzoniere eller Sangenes bog*. Copenhagen: Multivers, 2011.

Thing, Morten, *Portrætter af 10 kommunister*. Copenhagen: Tiderne skifter, 1995, also available as open access at http://www.historienu.dk/Forskningsportal/Portraetter.pdf.

Thodberg, Christian, "Grundtvig, Nikolai Frederik Severin" in Lund, Jørn, gen. ed., *Den Store Danske Encyklopædi*, vol. 7. Copenhagen: Gyldendal, 1997: 599-602.

Thorbjørnsen, Lis, transl., Spang Olsen, Ib, ill., Rubow, Paul V., introduction, *Geoffroy Chaucer, De tre drikkebrødre*. Copenhagen: Carit Andersens Forlag, 1946.

–, Ungermann, Arne, ill., "Geoffrey Chaucer, Maj og Januar" in *Cavalcade*, no. 1, 1947, 73-80.

–, "Geoffrey Chaucer, Konen fra Bath" in *Cavalcade*, no. 3, 1948, 32-5.

Thunbo, Margrethe, *Canterburyfortællinger af Geoffrey Chaucer. Glimt af Verdenslitteraturen*, No. 2. Copenhagen: Einar Harcks Forlag, 1929.

Togeby, Knud, "England: Langland, Wyclif og Chaucer" in Billeskov Jansen, F.J., Stangerup, Hakon and Traustedt, P.H., eds., "England: Langland, Wyclif og Chaucer" in *Verdenslitteraturhistorie*, vol. 2, "Middelalderen." Copenhagen: Politikens Forlag, 1971, 505-14.

Tveterås, Egil, transl., *Chaucer, Geoffrey: Canterbury fortellingene*. Oslo: Aschehoug, 1953.

Tyrrwhitt, Thomas, ed., *The Canterbury Tales of Chaucer*, 4th ed., London: William Pickering, 1830.

Utz, Richard. *Chaucer and the Discourse of German Philology: A History of Reception and an Annotated Bibliography of Studies, 1793-1948*. Turnhout: Brepols, 2002.

–, "Coming to Terms with Medievalism" in *European Journal of English Studies*, 15:2, 2011: 101-13.

Vammen, Hans, "Nationalliberale, de" in Lund, Jørn, gen. ed., *Den Store Danske Encyklopædi*, vol. 14. Copenhagen: Gyldendal, 1999: 269-70.

Varnhagen, H., "Die Erzählung von der Wiege" in *Englische Studien*, 1886, vol. ix, 240-66.

Venuti, Lawrence, *The Translators' Invisibility: A History of Translation*. London: Routledge, 1995, 2nd ed. 2008.

Voltaire, *Ce qui plait aux dames, conte*, 1764, at http://www.voltaire-integral.com/Html/10/02_Ce_qui.html, accessed January 2012.

Ward, A.W., *Chaucer*. New York: Harper & Brothers, 1880.

Warton, Thomas, *The History of English Poetry*. London: Dodsley, 1774-81.

Wessel, Johan Herman, transl., Schulz, J.A.P. and Thaarup, Thomas, rev., *Feen Ursel eller hvad der behager Damerne*. Copenhagen, 1792.

Westergaard, Charlotte Louise, *Veileder for de Besøgende i Thorvaldsens Museum*. Copenhagen: Louis Klein, 1851.

–, *Verdensmarkedet, eller Beskrivelse for Børn over den store Industriudstilling i London 1851. Tildeels efter det Engelske*. Copenhagen: Thiele Bogtrykkeri, 1852.

–, *Engelske Digtere*, 1-2., vol I: *Chaucer*. Copenhagen: Bing og Søns Forlag, 1853a.

–, *Den franske Tragedies national-poetiske Character og Grunden til den ringeagtede Bedømmelse, som den til en Tid har været underkastet*. Copenhagen: Chr. Steen & Søns Forlag, 1853b.

–, *Udvalg af engelske Forfattere: En Læsebog for Skolens Højere Classer.* Copenhagen: Louis Klein, 1867.

Winge, Vibeke "Rasmus Rask" in Lund, Jørn, ed., *Den Store Danske Encyklopædi.* Copenhagen: Gyldendal, 2000, vol. 16, 16-17.

Wright, Thomas, ed., *The Canterbury Tales of Geoffrey Chaucer: a new text with illustrative notes.* London: T. Richards, The Percy Society, 1847-1951.

Witting Lund, Maria, "The Marriage of Heaven and Hell: En analyse af to danske oversættelser af Blakes tekst" in *Danske afhandlinger om oversættelse*, 11. Copenhagen: Centre for Translation, University of Copenhagen, 2005, 30-49.

Wolf, Helmut, *Sir Francis Kynastons Übersetzung von Chaucers "Troilus and Criseyde": Interpretation, Edition und Kommentar.* Frankfurt am Main, New York: P. Lang, 1997.

Wollstonecraft, Mary, *Letters Written During a Short Residence in Sweden, Norway, and Denmark.* London: J. Johnson, 1796.

Wright, David *Geoffrey Chaucer: The Canterbury Tales.* Oxford: Oxford University Press, *World's Classics Series*, 1985.

Yager, Susan, "'I speke in prose': Lumiansky's translation of Chaucer." Unpublished paper delivered at the thirteenth New Chaucer Society congress at Boulder, Colorado, July 2002.

Zerlang, Martin and Holmgaard, Jørgen, "'Den liberale Classe' ved magten" in Busk-Jensen et al., ed., *Dansk litteraturhistorie.* Copenhagen: Gyldendal, 1985: 27-142.

Zibrandtsen, Marianne, "Paludan-Müller, Frederik" in Lund, Jørn, gen. ed., *Den Store Danske Encyklopædi*, vol. 14. Copenhagen: Gyldendal, 1999: 638.

Østerberg, J. V., transl., *Shakespeare, Dramatiske værker.* Copenhagen: Schultz, 1927-48 and 1958.

Østergaard Pedersen, B., *Litteraturleksikon.* Skørping: Skandinavisk Bogforlag, 1968, 62.

*Chaucer in Denmark: A Study of the Translation
and Reception History 1782-2012*

DANISH SUMMARY/DANSK RESUMÉ

Denne doktordisputats fortæller historien om den danske oversættelse og reception af den største engelske middelalderforfatter Geoffrey Chaucer (1340?-1400) fra 1782 til i dag. Som kontekst for undersøgelsen, der består af detaljerede oversættelsesanalyser og grundig diskussion af en større mængde kilder, behandles den overordnede historie om engelsk i Danmark fra oplysningstiden til i dag. Der er i denne forbindelse særlig fokus på det engelske sprogs status i forhold til tysk og fransk, både i uddannelsessystemet, i sprogets øvrige udbredelse og i den oversatte litteratur. Således er afhandlingen en eksemplarisk undersøgelse af en enkelt klassisk engelsk forfatter i et bredere dansk kulturhistorisk perspektiv.

Efter en introduktion til kilderne og metodiske og teoretiske overvejelser i de to første kapitler, behandles i kapitel 3 dramatikeren Johan Herman Wessels *Feen Ursel* og engelskprofessoren og forfatteren T.C. Bruuns *Slagelse-Madamen*, som er de tidligste kilder fra hhv. 1782 og 1823, der er baseret på en af Chaucers Canterburyfortællinger, nemlig hhv. *The Wife of Bath's Tale* og prologen til samme fortælling. Jeg viser i min sammenlignende analyse, at *Feen Ursel* efter adskillige transformationer gennem franske og tyske versioner ikke længere har ret meget at gøre med Chaucer, og at også Bruuns tekst, som er oversat fra Popes version af prologen, har mistet Chaucers bid og vid, men til gengæld givet sit daværende, overvejende engelsk-fjendtlige publikum en morsom dansk figur gennem en konsekvent såkaldt *domestication*-strategi, hvor Chaucers Wife of Bath bliver til en kone fra Slagelse, der spiser god dansk kost og tager til København på dagudflugt.

I kapitel 4 behandles den første grundige fremstilling om Chaucer i Danmark, skolebestyreren og kvindesagsforkæmperen Louise Westergaards *Engelske digtere: Chaucer* fra 1853, med baggrund i Westergaards rolle som engelsk-pionér i et ellers stærkt national-liberalistisk klima. Jeg viser hvordan Westergaards Chaucer-hæfte består af en særegen blanding af introduktion, redigeret originaltekst, oversættelse, referat og kommentar, og jeg har særlig fokus på en engageret præsentation af *The Clerk's Tale*. Mens Chaucers værker her nok bliver værdsat på fornem vis, så er den første akademiske diskussion to studier af Theodor Bierfreund i hhv. 1891 and 1892, som jeg i afhandlingens kapitel 5 tilbageviser som meget mangelfulde og direkte inkompetente. I samme kapitel behandler jeg som hovedkilde den store sprogforsker Otto Jespersens helt anderledes begavede fremstilling af Chaucers værk i monografien *Chaucer* fra 1893, et hidtil stort set overset ganske markant bidrag til Chaucer-forskningen, som bygger på Jespersens grundige orientering i den tyske filologiske tradition såvel som egne studier. Jeg viser her, at der går en lige linje fra denne tradition gennem Jespersen til dennes senere i Chaucer-forskningen berømte elev Aage Brusendorff, hvis epokegørende *The Chaucer Tradition* bygger bro mellem den tyske og den engelske Chaucer-forskning (kapitel 7).

I kapitlerne 5-7 behandles ud over de første leksikon- og lærebogsfremstillinger om Chaucer også Niels Møllers korte oversættelser fra 1880'erne og 1890'erne og Vilhelm Møllers oversættelse fra 1901 af dele af *The Summoner's Tale* samt hans temmelig bizarre introduktion til *The Canterbury Tales*. Efterfølgende analyseres de første mere autoritative oversættelser af hhv. *The General Prologue* og *The Nun's Priest's Tale* ved Uffe Birkedal fra 1911 og 1913. Jeg viser her, at Birkedal vælger et meget arkaisk dansk og desuden oversætter alt til danske forhold, inkl. Geoffrey Chaucers fornavn, som bliver til Gotfred. Kapitel 7 behandler også Margrethe Thunbos *Canterbury Tales*-genfortællinger for børn fra 1929, og her sammenligner jeg med Westergaards Chaucer-hæfte for samme aldersklasse, mens senere Chaucer-fortællinger for børn af hhv. Cecil Bødker og Aage Nørfelt, fra 1960'erne, behandles i kapitel 10. I kapitel 10 diskuteres endvidere en lang række kilder fra 1960 til i dag, der med meget svingende kvalitet omhandler den store middelalderdigter, og jeg analyserer en række mindre oversættelser, der ofte optræder i usædvanlige sammenhænge.

I kapitel 8 og 9 ligger en stor del af afhandlingens tyngde i nogle grundige oversættelsesanalyser. Jeg viser i kapitel 8 hvordan især maleren Flemming Bergsøe banede vej for seriøs Chaucer-oversættelse til dansk med sin *Konen fra Bath* fra 1943, men at også oversætteren Lis Thorbjørnsen og især digteren Jørgen Sonne bidrog med en række vigtige

Chaucer-oversættelser fra efterkrigsårene, som i det hele taget er rige på litterære oversættelser fra engelsk. Hovedkapitlet i afhandlingen er dog kapitel 9, hvor jeg analyserer og diskuterer de to komplette eller næsten komplette oversættelser af *The Canterbury Tales* fra 1950'erne, Mogens Boisens prosaoversættelse og Børge Johansens gendigtning. I kapitel 8 og 9 gives grundig oversættelseskritik, hvor jeg både analyserer revisioner, oversættelser og noteapparat. Desuden sammenlignes forskellige oversættelser, inklusive moderne engelske oversættelser. Herved afsløres blandt andet, at Boisen har plagieret ved ikke at oversætte direkte fra Chaucer, men fra Lumianskys amerikanske prosaoversættelse. Som jeg også viser, bør Boisens ofte mesterlige dansk dog respekteres højt, selv om Johansen uden tvivl er den hidtil vigtigste Chaucer-oversætter, bl.a. med en dygtig gengivelse af Sir Thopas, Chaucers bevidst mislykkede ridderromance. Jeg viser dog også, at Johansens sprog gennemgående er så gammeldags, at en ny dansk *Canterbury Tales*-oversættelse er tiltrængt.

I den overordnede konklusion opsummerer jeg afhandlingens kapitler og viser de væsentligste resultater. Jeg konkluderer blandt andet at klassikeroversættelser er en så krævende genre, at forlagene ikke blot bør stille gode redaktører og korrekturlæsere til rådighed for oversætteren, men også faglige konsulenter. Endvidere viser mine analyser af de mange leksikonfremstillinger og lignende forfatterpræsentationer, at fejl og mangler ofte overtages og gentages fra tidligere fremstillinger, og at et seriøst forlag derfor bør se sig grundigt om efter kompetente skribenter og redaktører.

Afslutningsvis argumenterer jeg for, at jeg har flyttet grænserne for litterære oversættelses- og receptionsstudier ved at insistere på en særdeles grundig emnebehandling, herunder udtømmende analyser, inkl. sammenlignende analyser på baggrund af kulturelle og historiske udviklinger. Jeg har benyttet den brede ramme "engelsk i Danmark" som afsæt for min fortælling om "Chaucer i Danmark", og jeg har samtidig vist, hvordan denne ramme udgør en kompleks kontekst med mange facetter. Afhandlingen er det første forsøg på at behandle hele historien om engelsk i Danmark både med et nuanceret breddeperspektiv og gennem et eksemplarisk dybdestudie af oversættelse og reception af en enkelt forfatter.